EXILE &
ECSTASY

EXILE & ECSTASY

GROWING UP WITH RAM DASS
AND COMING OF AGE IN THE
JEWISH PSYCHEDELIC UNDERGROUND

MADISON MARGOLIN

HAY HOUSE

Carlsbad, California • New York City
London • Sydney • New Delhi

Published in the United Kingdom by:
Hay House UK Ltd, The Sixth Floor, Watson House,
54 Baker Street, London W1U 7BU
Tel: +44 (0)20 3927 7290; Fax: +44 (0)20 3927 7291; www.hayhouse.co.uk

Published in the United States of America by:
Hay House Inc., PO Box 5100, Carlsbad, CA 92018-5100
Tel: (1) 760 431 7695 or (800) 654 5126
Fax: (1) 760 431 6948 or (800) 650 5115; www.hayhouse.com

Published in Australia by:
Hay House Australia Ltd, 18/36 Ralph St, Alexandria NSW 2015
Tel: (61) 2 9669 4299; Fax: (61) 2 9669 4144; www.hayhouse.com.au

Published in India by:
Hay House Publishers India, Muskaan Complex, Plot No.3, B-2,
Vasant Kunj, New Delhi 110 070
Tel: (91) 11 4176 1620; Fax: (91) 11 4176 1630; www.hayhouse.co.in

A catalogue record for this book is available from the British Library.

Tradepaper ISBN: 978-1-78817-960-7
E-book ISBN: 978-1-4019-7354-4
Audiobook ISBN: 978-1-4019-7355-1

This product uses papers sourced from responsibly managed forests. For more information, see www.hayhouse.co.uk.

Printed and bound by CPI Group (UK) Ltd, Croydon, CR0 4YY

TO THE HOLY REBELS AND
MY "FAMILY" OF ORIGIN,
SOUL, AND RAINBOW

CONTENTS

INTRODUCTION

"We tell ourselves stories in order to live."

— JOAN DIDION

This book is a lifetime in the making; it is collected from a few decades of handwritten journals, lived experience, and interviews with an uncountable number of artists, scientists, mystics, therapists, healers, activists, and fringe thought leaders engaging with paradigm-shifting encounters—mainly at the intersection of Judaism and psychedelia. In short, my heart—in all its fire and mess, and in my humble attempt to make sense of it all—spills out over the next couple hundred pages.

Almost a decade ago, when I set out to write about the intersection of Jewish and psychedelic experience, the topic was niche. It was rare to put the two explicitly in conversation with one another, despite how natural the pairing (more on that throughout this book). But in naming the Jewish psychedelic phenomena and giving it identity through media, the movement began to grow. We're seeing the birth of what feels like, in essence, a renewed Judaism, rooted in ancient ritual and expanded consciousness. Psychedelics are revolutionizing Jewish culture, reigniting our spiritual fire, helping us realize that even without added substance, Judaism itself is an expression of and a container for altered states.

In other words: *Judaism is psychedelic.*

This is the moral of the story, so to speak, which I deliver through the allegory of my own first-person narrative. In this book, I explore psychedelic Judaism and Jewish psychedelic experience; however, it's not just my own personal story, but a story that you, individually and collectively, may relate to, as well—whether you are Jewish or not. Your job, dear reader, is to glean from it what you will: whatever morals, practices, dos, don'ts, and learnings that you find most relevant and valuable, wherever you are in your life and in your relationship to psychedelics, religion, spirituality, medicine, healing, or simply getting high. Here is the story of my soul's own fractal path; I'm sharing it, hoping that it will ignite your soul, as well.

Through my own trials and tribulations, lessons, and lore, I aim to put forth what I've learned and absorbed along the way from my teachers and from the firsthand experience of living the story itself. Keep in mind, I am not a religious scholar; I have limited formal Jewish education, and so what I present in this book, as far as religious text, sourcing, and other fixed aspects of Judaism comes more from secondhand academics and observation.

Through memoir, I can provide in-depth insight into a character—myself—whose goal is to explore and test the practices and philosophies that I share throughout these pages. And through my research and reportage, experts may speak to the phenomena laid out in the story, and share just how and why these modalities work (or don't).

In truth, I never "came up with the idea" for this book, so much as that I've always had it in me and have been waiting for it to ripen so I could finally reach into the depths of my core and harvest it from my own being. Essentially, getting it out of my system has simply been a means of moving forward. In the rhetoric of ayahuasca, one might call this "purging" or "getting well," since the entheogenic South American brew has a tendency to invoke vomiting as part of the "healing process," but let's just say that I always take my "medicine" with a healthy dose of skepticism. I am a journalist after all, and this book is a collection of first- and third-person research—it's not a manifesto.

As such, "healing"—whatever this buzzword du jour actually means, and we'll investigate that later—is a prevalent theme throughout these pages, where I use myself as a guinea pig to explore whether any of this *stuff* actually works—the psychedelics (or "medicines," as they say); the religion; the spirituality; the rituals; the mindfulness, and the somatic practices. Are we all just bullshitting ourselves, crafting and extracting subjective meaning from our experiences, *telling ourselves stories*—as Joan Didion would say, about the things we do to feel whole, to feel better—*in order to live*? Or are we getting at a core truth, no matter the narrative or interpretation?

I have a specific allergy to New Age rhetoric and pseudo-spirituality that comes along with little rigor. I'm from LA, and there's a lot of that there, especially in the circles where most people are doing yoga, meditating, journeying with plant medicines—and wearing it all on their sleeve, which in some cases is where the *integration* begins and ends. Perhaps I sound bitter, maybe even jaded, but really where this comes from is a deep and sincere optimism that we all have access to our best selves that we can put to use in spirituality's highest form, which is *service*—if only we dig deep enough to not only find out *what* it takes but also to actually *do* it.

I'll take a moment to distinguish the difference between spirituality and religion, at least the way I see it. Spirituality speaks to our direct Divine connection. It's lofty, awe-invoking, and blissful. Religion—be it Judaism, Hinduism, or even something less rooted in ancient tradition—is the grounded, daily, sober practice that we do with our very own bodies, enabling us to harness that connection and infuse that magic into our mundane lives. Think yoga, *tefillin*, dancing, or eating certain foods (be they kosher, vegetarian, or even locally grown). In other words, embodied religious action that helps us cultivate the conditions for spiritual experience.

◆▼◆

Ever since I can remember, I've always strongly identified with my Jewishness and simultaneously, I've craved, throughout my life, authentic spiritual connection—through religion, psychedelics, movement, meditation, *practice*, and partying too. But perhaps I am, and have always been, most drawn to what guru

Neem Karoli Baba taught is the most basic form of spirituality, simply to be of service.

I grew up in the community surrounding Ram Dass—a nice Jewish boy and author of *Be Here Now*, formerly known as Dr. Richard Alpert, the Harvard psychologist who, along with colleague Dr. Timothy Leary, was expelled for experimenting too liberally with psychedelics. My father, Bruce—a prominent cannabis defense attorney, who later defended Leary in his trial for escaping from prison for a pot bust—met Ram Dass in India in the early 1970s, and through him was introduced to Neem Karoli Baba, otherwise known as Maharaj-ji. The religious and spiritual philosophy that my father, Ram Dass, and others learned from their Hindu guru defined my upbringing. And yet, my parents—flower children of the post-Holocaust generation—put me through Hebrew school and maintained Jewish traditions.

Experiencing the contrast between Hebrew school and my homelife, I wondered why my parents and all their friends were searching for spirituality outside the religion they grew up with. Wasn't there an authentic means to spiritually *connect* in Judaism in a way that honors our heritage without dwelling in the trauma associated with it—but perhaps, instead, even healing from it? Pondering these questions led me onto a path of both consciously and subconsciously interrogating the intersectionality between religion and rebellion, psychedelic states and emergent spiritual awareness.

◄▼►

When I went to journalism school ("j-school") almost a decade ago and moved to New York, by way of California and Israel, my reporting assignments led me into the underbelly of the Hasidic world, where I began to notice cultural overlaps with the "Hin-Jews" I grew up with. Among the fringe Hasidim and the *frum* hippies, I found that psychedelics and, more so, *psychedelic consciousness* (a concept we'll explore throughout this book) were at the foundational common ground between these seemingly disparate groups. And so, I began to interrogate the intersectionality between Jewish and psychedelic experience.

I'm far from the first person to take on this exploration; it began with our biblical forefathers, or even *members of the tribe* preceding them. In modern history, however, Rabbi Zalman Schachter-Shalomi is to be credited for integrating his experience with psychedelics into the consciousness of a new Judaism—what became Jewish Renewal (a movement, and ultimately a denomination). Reb Zalman hailed from a Hasidic family who fled Europe during the Holocaust. He received his rabbinic ordination through a Hasidic sect known as Chabad-Lubavitch, and came to rub shoulders—and drop acid—with countercultural icons like Tim Leary and Ram Dass (with whom he did acid under his *talit*, or prayer shawl).

Indeed, while Ram Dass represented the pull away from Judaism toward other traditions like Hinduism or Buddhism, Zalman, along with his contemporary Rabbi Shlomo Carlebach ("the singing rabbi"), drew them back in by presenting the mystical teachings of Chassidis and Kabbalah in a way that was both accessible and relatable to 1960s and '70s youth. The post-Holocaust era produced a generation of seekers, searching for meaning in the wake of inexplicable tragedy and the trauma of genocide, nuclear war, and nihilistic existentialism. A sampling of spiritualities came along with new music, new fashion, and new modes of consciousness that defined the psychedelic '60s. And so, Rebs Shlomo and Zalman took to the streets of Haight-Ashbury, meeting young Jews wherever they went in their journeys. Through his lively and soulful expression of traditional Jewish melodies, Shlomo lured many hippies back to observant, neo-Hasidic practice; Zalman, however, inspired by the spirit of Hasidism and his own psychedelic experiences, redefined Jewish practice altogether.

"When I can undergo the deepest cosmic experience via some minuscule quantity of organic alkaloids or LSD, then the whole validity of my ontological assertions is in doubt [such that] the psychedelic experience can be not only a challenge but a support of my faith," Reb Zalman once wrote. "After seeing what really happens at the point where all is One and G-d immanent surprises

G-d transcendent and They merge in cosmic laughter, I can also see Judaism in a new and amazing light."

The result of Rebs Shlomo and Zalman's experience with psychedelics (both observed and ingested) was a proliferation of colorful, yet Orthodox Carlebach shuls around the world, as well as colorful, non-Orthodox Renewal shuls. Both have Hasidic roots, both are musical, and both attract congregants with wayward, psychedelic backgrounds. And both were highly influential upon the crew of Jewish psychonauts I came to know and love, as well as global Jewish culture more generally.

But it wasn't so much that I wanted to simply interview rabbis, scientists, and underground ceremony leaders about *Jews on drugs* (bluntly put), but rather that I myself, as a Jew, wanted these experiences too. Those whom I initially met on the basis of my reportage during my one year of "j-school" and beyond turned out to be my soul family; they felt instantly familiar and reminded me of the far-out characters who colored my childhood. I didn't want to just get third-person quotes about combining Jewish ritual with psychedelics—I wanted to see it with my own eyes, feel what it was like in my own body.

Through these experiences—including an expanded outlook and a developed somaticism—I began to appreciate the roots of my own upbringing. It took growing up with hippies to find my way among Hasidim in order to ultimately come home to myself—in a full circle that enabled me to realize that it's all one, all the same thing, all part of one grand trip. Where I came from turned out to be close—in soul—to where I was going (although straddling California and New York, Israel and America, remains a challenging distance). In fact, the concept of G-d that I grew up with was strikingly similar to what I learned about through Hasidic texts and teachings. It was through psychedelic consciousness that I came to this realization. And so, as one friend—the late Shloime Freundlich—helped me phrase it for one of the many articles I wrote about this topic, I wanted to know, *can you serve G-d through psychedelics?*

Those who knew "Bundy," as he was called, might be surprised at such an apt articulation of this question—because his outer layer was more troll-like and crass than sensitive and contemplative. He was on the spectrum, would make off-color Holocaust jokes, and liked to introduce me to groups of Hasidic men by saying, "This is Madison, she's in *Playboy*," then wait a beat before explaining that I wrote for the magazine about topics he considered controversial, like cannabis. He loved to retell the story of how we met: "At 1:40 A.M., July 25, 2015, a girl in a short black skirt walked into my Shabbos meal. 'My name is Madison. I write for *The Forward*. I just came from a *Burner* party; give me challah.' We *farbrenged* till 4 A.M. about *Shabbos Chazon* and sang Shabbos songs."

In his way, Shloime's anecdote captures that zeitgeist for me, the summer I had graduated journalism school, working at a Jewish newspaper, using my off-hours to party my way through New York, maybe looking for some sort of transcendence—but ultimately finding it in Jewish spaces, flying and landing within the context of the religion itself. At which point I realized that Judaism has everything it takes to engender an altered experience, if only we knew how to activate its practices and engage with its perspectival frameworks in ways that were invigorating and soulful, rather than boring, traumatizing, or oppressive.

◂▾▸

With local decriminalization initiatives sweeping the country, while pharmaceutical interests aim to reschedule or develop psychedelic medicines in therapy, these substances are becoming increasingly mainstream. The size and quantity of psychedelic-inspired festivals like Burning Man, the popularity of Michael Pollan's *How to Change Your Mind*, and the fact that *DoubleBlind*—the psychedelic magazine and media start-up I co-founded—has garnered more than a million monthly page views, shows the extent to which the so-called "psychedelic renaissance" is in motion. What's more? Postmortem, Ram Dass is more popular than ever. The eye-rolling teenager in me would have her jaw dropped.

At the forefront of today's psychedelic movement is a focus on spirituality. Researchers at Johns Hopkins are investigating the nature of the "mystical experience" by giving psilocybin (the main compound in magic mushrooms) to religious professionals like priests, rabbis, and imams, while on the ground, as more laymen grow curious about these substances, there's an even larger need to integrate and make sense of those experiences in safe, grounded contexts. That's just one reason why people are turning to religion.

Exhibit A: In 2021, along with Rabbi Zac Kamenetz, founder of Shefa: Jewish Psychedelic Support, and Natalie Ginsberg, global impact coordinator at the Multidisciplinary Association for Psychedelic Studies (MAPS), I co-founded the Jewish Psychedelic Summit. In just one month of organic promotion for the Summit, we garnered more than 5,000 global community members. Since then, dozens of Jewish and psychedelic events have sprouted up throughout the world, from panel discussions at shuls and universities to psychedelic conferences and therapy trainings that include Jewish programming (like Shabbat). Israeli psychedelic activist and social worker Pinni Baumol even put out literature about "kosher playlists" and musical considerations when administering psychedelics to Orthodox Jews. But it's more than that. The special attention paid to treating PTSD in psychedelic therapy trials is making it easier to identify and talk about trauma. And for Jews, that's massive progress—to acknowledge this wound, this attribute so central to our religion and peoplehood, so that we may heal from it.

But it's not all rainbows and rugelach. Stumbling into the Jewish psychedelic subculture has been rife with equal parts beauty and contradiction. There's the stuff that gets you "well" and then the stuff that simply makes you purge. And yet, it's walking that line between shadow and light that renders this dialectic into a dance. It's learning to move with grace—as your heart and mind are blown open, and all your assumptions challenged—that makes this dance of moving through modes of constricted and expanded consciousness both challenging and redemptive. And it's the integration of those lessons that lands within our waking reality like a kiss of magic upon the mundane.

That's what this story is about.

◂▾▸

After having taken the first stab at this manuscript in New York before rewriting it all in Tzfat, I drafted this introduction from Nachlaot—a cluster of microneighborhoods in central Jerusalem, where sandy stone apartment buildings piled one on top of the other surround public courtyards; flowers, weeds, and vines poke out from stairwells; feral cats lurk about; and the walls of the cozy, narrow alleyways carry spiritual messages scrawled into graffiti and murals lit up at night by the orange luster of old street lamps. Just south of the bustling *shuk* Machane Yehuda, it's impossible to go anywhere without seeing familiar faces—holy rebels, curious seekers, religious hippies, friends from California or New York, coming and going, everyone on their journey.

On a wall near a shul, someone's tagged "LSDMT" underneath a series of red, yellow, and green stamps that read נ נח נחמ נחמן מאומן (*Na Nach Nachma Nachman Meuman*)—a mantra, of sorts, associated with Na Nach, an eclectic subsect of Chassidim following the 18th–19th-century Rebbe Nachman, father of the Hasidic sect known as Breslov, whose overarching spiritual philosophy to *be happy always*, not just in spite of but because of hardship, is woven throughout this book—alongside the teachings of Ram Dass. The juxtaposition of the psychedelic graffiti with the Na Nach stamp is fitting because, after all, many of Reb Nachman's lessons are, to quote my editor Eden Pearlstein, "trippy as fuck," while many of his followers today have found his teachings and a connection to Judaism through wayward paths—through sorrow, psychedelics, and a search for meaning and transcendent, grounded joy. Inside a Nachlaot rooftop guesthouse where a rabbi friend *holds space* for those journeying with psychedelics, he's adorned a tiny bookshelf with just two books: *Be Here Now* and Nachman's seminal work

Likutei Moharan. There is a nuanced, natural relationship between the philosophies of Ram Dass and Reb Nachman, but to grasp it, you'll have to read to the end of this book.

And yet, it's also palpable in daily life here in Jerusalem, on the streets, and in nature. Everyone here is talking about psychedelics—whether because they're seeking to try them, have trauma they're aiming to treat, or because they've already had life-changing experiences with them at festivals, prayer circles, in therapy, or rogue. I'm walking through the shuk when someone stops me—a local musician I know from Brooklyn—and wants to tell me about his most recent experience with Bufo, or 5-MeO-DMT, a powerful dissociative psychedelic extracted from the venom of the Sonoran Desert toad. A few days later, I'm at a party inside a sukkah (for the weeklong holiday of Sukkot), where friends swap stories of plant medicine ceremonies in the forests outside Jerusalem, the latest in ketamine clinical therapy, raving with MDMA back in the day, or trying mushrooms at a couple's retreat.

In a tiny bookstore behind the shuk, I notice on display a recent reprint of my friend Yoseph Needelman's book, the OG psychedelic Jewish memoir, *Cannabis Chassidis: The Ancient and Emerging Torah of Drugs* (2012), for which I wrote an introduction. Yoseph played a pivotal role in the events that will unfold throughout this book. And so, as he and I sit down to coffee nearby, I relay to one of my greatest inspirations what's in the pages of this story now here in your hands.

What I'm getting at is that psychedelic consciousness is increasingly pervasive in our culture, including secular and progressive Jewish communities, but now it's also experiencing a pointed upsurge in the traditional (Orthodox/Hasidic) Jewish world. In describing today's Hasidic fringe, as one friend put it—Hershy Lefkowitz, who initiated me into Brooklyn's Hasidic underground back in 2014—"It's like the '60s, man, but for the Jews."

PART 1

EXILE

*"If you think you're enlightened, go spend
a week with your family."*

— RAM DASS

Chapter 1

THE REBELLION OF *NOT* BEING HERE NOW

"1-800-420-LAWS, Bruce Margolin's down for the cause." That was the radio jingle that SoCal stoner punk band the Kottonmouth Kings rapped for my dad's 2003 gubernatorial campaign when he ran in California's recall election against Arnold Schwarzenegger and more than 100 other candidates on the platform to legalize weed. That jingle earned my dad enough attention to not only land him in 11th place, but also to pique the interest of my middle school teachers and our wholesome, lurking D.A.R.E. officer, who would take a seat next to me in the cafeteria to ask a quiet, straight-A student "how things were at home."

In truth, my homelife was a *balagan*—beautiful chaos—interwoven among six kids, three baby mamas, and a notable criminal defense attorney as the patriarchal hub of it all. But contrary to whatever the cop was looking to sniff out, my parents' cannabis use wasn't *the problem*, if there ever was one. If anything, the haze of pot smoke that drifted through my father's home on any Saturday night—as New Age hippies would meander in and out of our Spanish-style casa on the south side of Beverly Hills, wearing their flowing garments and bindis for the occasion of sitting on pillows in our living room to chant the "Hanuman Chalisa" at a *kirtan*—was a welcome indicator that at least everyone would be in high spirits (rather than arguing), including and especially my mother. High-strung and neurotic, yet loving and earnest, even after my parents' divorce and my father's subsequent remarriage (followed by another divorce), she'd graciously do what she could to uphold a unified sense of family.

That, of course, was no easy feat in a family that looked like *The Brady Bunch* meets *Jerry Springer*—but Jewish, vegetarian, and drug-friendly, with affectations like Nag Champa incense and an unspoken microwave ban. But rather than move us back home with her to New York when my father left her (she wouldn't have been allowed to anyway), my mother maintained a home within a few blocks of his house. She'd bring her signature sweet potato-pineapple-marshmallow dish to large Pesach seders attended by other HinJews, coordinate with him for the rest of the holidays, plan our bar and bat mitzvahs, and in periods of peace, she'd even still come to kirtan.

When my father remarried, my stepmother would order gourmet Indian food and make a large pot of chai, while Shiva, my father's best friend's son, might step in as the chai wallah and tend to the milky cardamom brew. In the living room, drums and a harmonium would be set up by the *puja* table, a low, wooden cabinet adorned with precious tchotchkes, photos, crystals, small statues of Hindu deities, and candles, all underneath a large photo of the Hindu guru Neem Karoli Baba, in a frame adorned with a dangling, fresh flower *mala*. A menorah and Shabbos candlesticks, alongside hundreds of spiritual volumes and novels, were on a shelf nearby.

You could always tell when my father was hosting one of his kirtans before you even walked into the house. Our quaint, treelined block would become uncharacteristically crowded with Priuses or beat-up hippie mobiles covered in a few common bumper stickers: "Love Serve Remember" or "Love Everyone." That's how you could tell Maharaj-ji's *satsang* had trekked into town—east from the breezy shores of Venice Beach and Santa Monica, inland from the rustic hills of Topanga Canyon, or if it was a truly special occasion, west from farther off, like the arid desert of Joshua Tree or even Taos, New Mexico, where family friends maintained a stateside Hanuman Temple and Neem Karoli Baba ashram.

My father and his community, or satsang, are devotees of Neem Karoli Baba (1900–1973), endearingly known as Maharaj-ji (Sanskrit for "great king"). Perhaps his most notable devotee was Ram Dass, né Richard Alpert, who had worked as a psychologist at Harvard in the early 1960s, alongside colleague Dr. Timothy Leary. Before President Richard Nixon launched the Drug War in 1971, psychedelics like LSD or psilocybin were still legal. And as such, Alpert, Leary, and other academics conducted extensive research investigating their profound healing potential in conjunction with therapy. But when Leary and Alpert gave psychedelics to undergrads and tripped alongside their subjects, the Harvard administration deemed that their research had gone too far and expelled the duo in 1963.

Leary went on to become a countercultural icon, LSD evangelist, and, according to Nixon, the "most dangerous man in America." He espoused the slogan "Turn On, Tune In, Drop Out" to flower children across the country rebelling from society in a peace movement that peaked during the late 1960s Summer of Love. My father, who has represented more cannabis clients than anyone else in the country, would later defend Leary when he escaped from prison, where he was serving a ten-year sentence for a pot bust.

Alpert, on the other hand, disillusioned by the cycle of getting high and coming down, was looking for a psychedelic trip that would last. In other words, prolonged spiritual sustenance that wasn't contingent on acid. After Harvard, he traveled to India, where he became a disciple of Maharaj-ji—and, based on the guru's teachings, wrote *Be Here Now* in 1971. Born into a well-to-do Jewish family from Boston, Alpert took on the name Ram Dass, bestowed upon him by Maharaj-ji, and went on to become a spiritual teacher in his own right, authoring many other titles, giving lectures back home in the States, and hosting retreats in his later years in Maui, where he lived.

Maharaj-ji's central teaching was "Love everyone, serve every-one, remember G-d"—hence the bumper stickers. And yet, I was skeptical. Ask my father or his peers about their relationships with their ex-wives or their kids, and see if you get a rigorously evolved answer from a place of integrity along the lines of "love everyone." With everyone so quick to wear their spirituality on their sleeve—to wrap *shmatas* around their heads, appropriate a bindi, or go by a Hindu name (think Grammy-nominated kirtan artist and family friend Krishna Das, a.k.a. Jeffrey Kagel, from Long Island; or my father, Bruce, a.k.a. Badri, short for Badrinath, among the satsang, or Baruch Meir, should he be asked by anyone wearing a yarmulke)—there I was scratching my head, rolling my eyes, hiding in my room, poring over my studies, joyriding around LA, running away on six-mile jogs, starving myself, dissociating—*davka* not *being here now*. Because how else could I rebel in a family where Ram Dass was a household name—not in a celebrity kind of way, but more as a fixture mentioned in passing?: "Ram Dass is coming to town"; "Ram Dass is coming over for dinner"; "Daddy's going to see Ram Dass in Hawaii."

I like to say that G-d put me into a family where the spiritual tools that were a given, that I took for granted from birth (yoga, meditation, Ram Dass, psychedelic consciousness), were also tools I would immediately need throughout my upbringing—but I wouldn't immediately know how to use them, and might even reject them at first. When the people (read: your parents) who make it most difficult for you to *be here now* tell you to *be here now*, then you may find yourself in a spiritual conundrum. I was an escapist and would eventually need to leave home, only so that I could return to it—to whatever *home* means—on my terms, through a process of rediscovering and learning to embody the most basic teaching of mindfulness: *be here now*.

Chapter 2

THE NYC FLOWER CHILD AND THE LA HINJEW

I was born late in the morning on Father's Day to a then-unmarried couple who had known each other for a little over a year. My grandmother—and sole living grandparent—flew out from New York to greet her second grandchild and her daughter's firstborn. My father, meanwhile, found himself straddling St. John's Hospital in Santa Monica, and celebrating the holiday with his 13-year-old daughter from a previous two-year marriage to a notoriously fierce divorce attorney raised by Holocaust survivors. My older sister and my mother never got along, at least until my parents got divorced a decade later.

My mother, a beautiful Jewess and champion bodybuilder from Queens, was in California on her own, having followed an ex-boyfriend out West, where she got caught in a turnstile with my father at a gym by Venice Beach on the Ides of March. He looked familiar to her. "Do I know you?" she asked, determining that if he wasn't from New York, then they hadn't met before. And so she went along her way, and he trailed after her. An Angeleno through and through, my father was a valley boy, but in his dating prospects, had been looking for a Jewish girl from New York. My parents ended up in Hawaii together a month later, and pregnant with me after half a year, on a trip back east to visit family. Shamelessly, my mother likes to boast that I was conceived in Queens.

She was in her late 30s and looking to settle down, become a housewife; he was a single dad pushing 50, but with the spirit of a teenager, a nice Jewish playboy from the San Fernando Valley with a successful criminal defense practice, specializing in marijuana law. They were terribly matched—he a commitment-phobic free spirit, she overly excitable. The relationship "was challenged early on," my mom told me. "It was a shit show." Gorgeous and with the purest of hearts, my mother has the mouth of Fran Drescher (from *The Nanny*) on a good day and Susie Greene (from *Curb Your Enthusiasm*) on a bad one; over the course of their decade-long relationship, there would be enough drama to turn my father off to Jewish women altogether. (His current partner, half his age, is a Buddhist "tantrapreneur" from Thailand whom he met at yoga.)

A month after I was born, my parents took me to the Oregon Country Fair, something of the Rainbow Gathering afterparty, where hippies from across the country came together in a festival geared toward peace and love, health food, and folk music. At six months, they took me to the ashram in Taos, New Mexico, for *bhandara*—a feast, in this case for something of a *yahrzeit* event, commemorating the *mahasamadhi* of Maharaj-ji, who "left his body," as they say, on my father's 32nd birthday, September 11, 1973. The day before my second birthday, my parents finally got married in the morning; later that day, they got into a screaming match. I wore a white dress with an embroidered fruit motif to their "wedding" at the courthouse—the same courthouse where almost 20 years later, my father, without telling any of us, legally married my (now, technically, former) stepmother almost a decade after Ram Dass performed their "spiritual wedding" ceremony at the casa (because what JAP from LA worth the title doesn't have at least one ex-stepmother?).

Despite the fact that both my parents came from traditional Jewish households, they were both rebels—she a flower child, he a "HinJew."

My mother—a black sheep turned off by the dry "conserv-adox" Judaism that defined religion for many boomers—as a teenager would perform séances in her bedroom, where during one of these occult rituals she created a spontaneous stain on the green carpet at my grandparents' two-story Tudor on a quiet, middle-class block in the placid, unassuming neighborhood of Hollis Hills. On weekends throughout her early adulthood, she and her ex-husband or best friend would head into the countryside of upstate New York or into the city, dropping acid or mescaline, listening to the Grateful Dead or the Allman Brothers, and taking quaaludes after a night of disco. As a child, I remember my mother telling me stories about how she almost walked off a cliff during an acid trip, or about that time she "died" on angel dust, a.k.a. PCP (a chemical cousin of the now-trendy ketamine).

Her psychedelic tales did little to turn me off to drugs—which I doubt was her point anyway—but did make me wonder if my mother was a little bit crazy. Would her psyche be different if she hadn't done all those psychedelics during her formative years? Would she be more stable, or would her mental health be in better shape if she'd actually integrated her psychedelic trips—growing from them, rather than simply growing out of them? Only now in her 60s has she begun to dabble again.

My mother's family back East are fairly conventional, if not a little quirky in their own right. My maternal grandparents were both raised by widowed single mothers—Galitzianers from the Alte Land of Eastern Europe—in Brooklyn's now Hasidic neighborhood of South Williamsburg during the Great Depression and Second World War. Their descendants are now mostly in New Jersey, or south Florida (for all intents and purposes, a beachside southern outpost of New York). Their greatest source of entertainment is keeping up with the Margolins out West. "Absurd" would be how my uncle—a Scrabble tournament champion, former obituary writer for his north Jersey town paper, and a freelance reporter for *The New York Times* real estate section—describes the *mishigas* my mother married into, and never quite divorced from.

On the other hand, my father barely has any living family left, who we're in touch with at least; although a long-lost cousin—a rabbi from Ohio—once wrote to us saying we're descendants of the 11th-century Talmudic commentator Rashi. But he makes up for his lack of blood relatives in his satsang of chosen family.

My father grew up in North Hollywood, where my grandfather—a Belarussian immigrant and dedicated patriot who joined the U.S. Marines when World War II broke out—moved the family from Cleveland when my father was four. Yiddish-speaking "New Yawkers," as he calls them, my grandparents were hardworking, blue-collar people; and my father, the youngest of three boys, was a "latchkey kid" who flunked third grade. (To this day he remains a terrible speller; he even misspelled the initial three words of his first paper in law school, but nevertheless got the highest grade in the class. "When you become a lawyer," the professor told him, "you'll have a secretary to prepare your correspondences.")

Growing up in the '50s, and coming of age in the '60s, my father was a greaser, then a hippie. His father founded two shuls in the Valley. When my uncle Ralph—a Torah scholar, prodigy, suspected gay man, and the oldest boy in the family—lost his life to leukemia shortly after my father's bar mitzvah, my father joined my grandfather in shul to say the mourner's kaddish. Six years later when my grandfather passed away unexpectedly during an operation, my father, 19, and supporting himself and later helping support his mother, found himself alone in shul for a year, saying kaddish again. He received no warm embrace from the other congregants; no one even said hello or asked what he was doing there. That experience of spiritual indifference turned him off to Judaism.

"I remember going to the mortuary with the rabbi, in the back of the limousine, and I called him every filthy, disgusting name in the world, asking him to give me some answers," my dad told me during our "interview" for a profile *Tablet Magazine* asked me to write in honor of 4/20. "I was angry at him because he represented that lack of communication that I needed so badly, and I believed [religion] was the place I could get it from. This man wasn't able to communicate any solace to me, and I realized in my anger, that was one of the reasons I wanted to rebel against the world and the establishment that the rabbi represented and which, in part, failed me. Only recently did I figure out that my anger wasn't at society, it was at G-d—and those whom I felt represented him in my life, these (nerdy) Jews."

My father, as with many of his peers, suffers from a degree of internalized anti-Semitism, although I'm not sure they'd call it that. But there was something "uncool" about being Jewish, at least where he grew up: a mostly Mexican neighborhood, where the other kids would pick on him for being Jewish, calling him a Christ killer. On Shabbos or holidays, my father says he was scared that the neighbors would hear the family singing too loudly. He was embarrassed to be Jewish, wondering as a young child in the wake of the Holocaust, *"What's wrong with us that they want to kill us?"*

Like many Jews of his generation—most notably Ram Dass— my father found spirituality in Hinduism, Buddhism, cannabis, psychedelics, the Rainbow Gathering, everywhere and anywhere except Judaism. While certainly not the sole reason, it's possible that the internalized trauma of the post-Holocaust era encouraged, among some, dissociative tendencies rather than an embrace of religious and cultural identity.

And yet as a child, my intuition made me wonder if what my parents were searching for in all these far-out places was actually available in Judaism. It's not that there was anything wrong with exploring other traditions, but even as a kid, I was never quite able to take on Hindu customs the way my parents did. My parents had given me a Hebrew name—Margalit Rachel—but not a Hindu name (I never felt called to take one on anyway), and even though I eventually dropped out of Hebrew school, I nevertheless strongly identified with my Judaism. I never questioned my belief in the Jew*ish* concept of G-d that my parents taught me, but I was genuinely curious whether that sense of mysticism, spirituality, or mindfulness that they sought out in Far Eastern traditions was actually accessible within our own backyard. After all, Judaism felt like home in a way that Hinduism didn't, even if I did grow up with certain elements of it that had been appropriated into our own blended tradition. Besides, as a kid, I found it entertaining that all these Jews who couldn't connect to Hebrew were somehow better able to connect with Sanskrit—yet another language most of us could barely understand.

Or maybe it was all just a case of what Groucho Marx speaks to in his classic quote: "I don't want to belong to any club that would accept me as one of its members." (Obviously, Marx was Jewish.)

Chapter 3

WHERE COCAINE
COMES IN

Out of "necessity for a Jewish education," my parents sent me to a conservative Jewish preschool in the LA shtetl of Pico-Robertson—before it became too obvious how little the Margolin family freakshow fit in with the nice Persian, Israeli, and otherwise square Ashkenazi families who comprised the congregation; and within a matter of a few short years—which at the time defined the majority of my life—we left the shul.

My younger brother was a baby, and my parents were breaking up. They separated, and the majority of what I can remember was me hiding under the bed when they'd be out in front of the house screaming at each other. The tender outings with both my parents before my brother was born, and while they were still together—father-daughter dates to the carousel at Santa Monica Pier, or "Mommy-and-me" at the park—faded into fleeting snippets of time spent between two homes. Their separation lasted a few years, almost as long as the time they spent back together, until they split up *again*—and permanently divorced—when I was 10.

I dissociated from the situation, bottled up my feelings and channeled them into my schoolwork. I was a hardworking student, although academics always came easy to me, and I found solace in reading, and relating to my favorite heroines—Anne Frank (whom I impersonated in a "living biography" book report) and Jackie

Kennedy (whose parents also got divorced). I had friends at school, but I was quiet, and too shy or embarrassed to let most people in on how sad and dysfunctional things were at home. I didn't want to be pitied.

I would also craft stories of my own, specifically related to my characters in *The Sims*. I spent a lot of time on that computer game to create nuclear families, then have the parents cheat on each other, remarry other characters in different households, split up, and create a virtual neighborhood of motley, intertwined Brady Bunches, with emotional backstories that I'd make up to justify the whole thing—which of course was based loosely on my life. On occasion, I was more malicious toward my soulless simulated characters, playing G-d by trapping them in a pool, then deleting the staircase used to get out of it, and letting them drown. Other times, I'd put them in a room and delete the door, allowing them to starve to death.

Killing a character, forcing a single parent to remarry—as was the case for my soon-to-be stepmother—and having all the children of Sim City be connected through the types of incestuous webs that would come to define my own reality made me feel a little more *in control*, or maybe it was just a way for me to express my anger through a computer game, or find consolation in relatable situations, albeit ones that I'd contrived.

Meanwhile, my mother was wrecked, threatening that we'd end up homeless on the street while my father took on another family—a single mom and her two daughters.

The three of us—as my mother, brother, and I had become one dysfunctional unit—hadn't any idea it was coming. That morning was as mundane as ever. We ate breakfast and got to school, while Dad went to work. When I came home in the afternoon, a moving truck had already come to collect my father's belongings. My mother relayed the news as I ate my afterschool snack at our round, wooden kitchen table (which she would later use her alimony or child support to replace with a chic Moroccan mosaic—one that 18 years later would end up in the kitchen of my own studio apartment, which I'd then sublet to my stepsister after I moved back to New York—oh, how healing works).

Angry and catatonic, I took a pencil and drew a straight harsh line on the white wall behind me, underneath an antique bulletin board tacked full of family photos. My brother, meanwhile, had run to the master bedroom, fact-checking that Daddy's closet was indeed empty, before unraveling into a tantrum, as my exasperated mother—the neat freak that she is—took Windex and a sponge to the wall that I'd vandalized. She was so anal, we weren't so much as allowed to put our grimy little palms on the walls, lest we leave a mark.

My mother is brilliant in her way, but she had abandoned whatever career aspirations she might have had over the duration of her ever-ailing marriage. Always stunning, her looks took her only so far. With no money of her own, no job, no self-esteem, no family closer than 3,000 miles away, I watched her crumble, and swore to myself to never end up like her.

In the aftermath of the divorce, I watched my mother struggle with money while cycling through different career paths, starting law school and dropping out, launching a home organization business with another single mom, becoming a yoga teacher, and finally taking on a job she hated, working as a near-minimum-wage teacher's assistant in the special ed classes at my high school, until she retired. A beautiful writer, her only real professional goal was to draft a memoir, or compile her lifelong collection of poetry into a book.

Disillusioned, I stopped believing in marriage, and while once I too wanted to be a writer, I set my sights on becoming a lawyer. I was in fifth grade and claimed to be inspired by my older sister, who had just graduated from Harvard Law, following her undergrad at Columbia. I thought I would join the family business, and before even hitting my teens, I began to take an academic interest in drugs and drug policy. Later in high school, I would read drug-inspired literature like Aldous Huxley's *The Doors of Perception* and Danny Sugerman's *Wonderland Avenue* (a sex, drugs, and rock 'n' roll memoir set in Hollywood, under the influence of heroin).

Meanwhile, around that time, my older sister struggled with her own addiction, a cocaine habit that I only became privy to when she got divorced, as her ex-husband—a doctor with a trust fund—entered into rehab, just five years after their Prince-themed, half-million-dollar wedding at the Beverly Hills Hotel. I was 16, as I grew hip to the R-rated details of my sister's life; still, I looked up to her. She was smart, pretty, and controversial, staking out a name for herself in cannabis and drug law as "LA's Dopest Attorney." Within a year of her divorce, she was pregnant with a daughter whose father was a friend of hers, another lawyer she dated briefly (although he's since ingratiated himself as a member of our family and a brother to me). With my sister as an example of sorts, her rejection of a "normal" family structure only fueled my teenage jadedness with anything conventional.

Cocaine had collateral, if indirect, effects on our family, although it only played an ancillary role in my own life. (To this day, I've only tried as much as a line, and more typically key bumps, a handful of times—all mainly out of curiosity to better understand the experience of it.) Before my father met the woman who became his fourth wife*, my stepsisters' father had died of a "heart attack," leaving their mother alone to survive with two daughters under the age of five. My stepmother, just a dozen years older than my sister, blonde, and taller than my dad, who's "5'6" with two pairs of socks on," came from Orange County, by way of Utah, from where she'd left the Mormon fold. Before settling down with my father, she lived the life of Nancy, the main character from *Weeds*—a show which she claims is based on her life (because, yes, she knew the filmmakers). Somehow, she had to support her own unit of three.

To her credit—and although, I initially hated her for it—my stepmother was resourceful. She met my father because she had a legal question; they connected over Ram Dass, and eventually, he left his miserable marriage for a fresh start in creating a new, blended family.

◂▾▸

---

* His first marriage lasted only a few months; his second was with my older sister's mother; his third was with my mother and my brother's; his fourth was with my now ex-stepmother and younger sister's mother.

My dad's law office in West Hollywood was a freestanding bunga-low, a quaint house with a gravel backyard underneath a terrace, with a hot tub and a tree that I liked to climb. He'd come out here on his lunch break and smoke a joint, before afternoon meetings with his clients, who'd be waiting in a cozy living room decorat-ed with shelves of legal volumes and leather couches around a fireplace and coffee table, where my dad laid out copies of "The Guide" (i.e., his annual publication *The Margolin Guide to Marijua-na Laws*) and put mints into a crystal goblet he received as "Crim-inal Defense Attorney of the Year" in 1999. The bedrooms of the house had all been repurposed as offices for partner or associate attorneys—including briefly, my older sister, who, in true *Legal-ly Blonde* (er, brunette) fashion, had hers painted pink when she graduated Harvard Law and started working at "the office." The phones were always ringing there. When I was really young, the hold music was jazz; later on, it was "Get Up, Stand Up," courtesy of my stepmother, who came to manage the place and loved Bob Marley so much, she had even named my step-sister after him.

As director of the LA chapter of the National Organization for the Reform of Marijuana Laws (NORML), my dad held an annual party at "the office," on Holloway Drive, right off the Sunset Strip, and just a few blocks from the now defunct Hippocampus—a headshop, psychedelic boutique, and general store known to sell drug paraphernalia. It wasn't really a "thing" to bring your kid to a nighttime NORML party, but the Margolin kids were an exception. I remember getting all "dressed up" in whatever funky bell-bottom jeans my mother had bought me from the Gap, and worming my way through crowds of hippies, activists, and my dad's clients, all in a cloud of cannabis smoke, schmoozing, laughing, dancing to live jazz. My dad had defended some notable clients—Linda Lovelace (famous for her appearance in *Deep Throat*), members of Guns N' Roses, Marlon's son Christian Brando, San Francisco civil rights attorney and tax resister Tony Serra, and, of course, Tim-othy Leary—and his parties reeked not only of that legacy, but also of the zeitgeist itself. "The office" was a landmark and hot spot during what was no doubt a historical moment in California cannabis culture.

In 1996, California became the first state in the country to legalize medical marijuana—and West Hollywood, with its gay clubs on Santa Monica Boulevard and its rock clubs on Sunset, once frequented by those like Jim Morrison, was one of the first cities to offer licensing to medical cannabis dispensaries. In great thanks to those like Dennis Peron, cannabis activist and AIDS patient, the gay community became a hotbed for cannabis activism, given the dire need among AIDS patients for relief.

Since the '60s, my dad has been involved with the marijuana legalization movement—and as such, his life has always been filled with a colorful cast of characters: gem collectors and Rainbow Gathering "family"; hippies from Venice Beach, Topanga, Laurel Canyon, or San Francisco; other activists, politicians, and even countercultural icons like Leonard Cohen, Hunter S. Thompson, Allen Ginsberg, Hugh Heffner, and (former governor) Jerry Brown.

He opened his law practice in 1967 and struck gold, so to speak, defending cannabis "crimes" at the onset of the War on Drugs. He became the lawyer to the hippies. In one of his earlier cases, my dad represented about 10 kids living communally in Hollywood who all got busted for weed. In his own memoir, *Down for the Cause*, my dad writes, "They were all arrested and had been locked up in jail with robbers, murderers, and rapists. I was shocked that these kids were being treated as if they were the real criminals and facing years in prison as punishment for something that seemed so innocent and harmless as being involved with this G-d-given plant." More and more he took on cases like this and was able to get felony charges for marijuana offenses dismissed based on unlawful police searches and the suppression of evidence. His practice boomed.

In one case, my dad argued with the judge against taking the case to trial because he felt the client didn't belong in jail in the first place. "Your honor, my understanding of the law is that under the American Bar Association standards regarding punishment, the court should consider the intended wrong in order to punish.

In my mind, there is no intended wrong with people involved with marijuana," he told the judge. "They didn't intend to hurt anybody, didn't try to coerce anyone or take advantage of anybody. There is no basis to punish them, your honor, so how can you justify punishing this young man?" The judge hesitated and responded: "Counsel, he broke the law." At that point, my father says, "I realized we had to do more than just be in the courtroom fighting these cases; we had to go outside the courtroom and change the law."

And so he got involved in the marijuana legalization movement. Inspired by the success of other organizations at the time like the NAACP, my dad founded the Campaign to Abolish the Marijuana Prohibition (CAMP), and publicized it in local news like *The LA Free Press*, the most widely distributed and one of the first underground weekly newspapers at the time. Later he would join the national movement to work with NORML and promote the cause through political campaigns, running not just for governor in 2003, but also for California State Assembly in 1970 and 1992 and for U.S. Congress in 2012. I don't think my dad ever ran for office with the expectation that he would win, but his repeated, single-issue efforts over time normalized the idea of marijuana legalization for many ordinary voters. In 1996, he served as an adviser for California's Proposition 215, the first bill in the country to legalize medical marijuana. With the legal cannabis industry hitting $24 billion in value by 2021 and spanning more than half the states in the country, it obviously only snowballed from there.

In many ways, through his efforts to legalize marijuana, my dad partially put himself out of business. But that was ultimately the point. When California legalized weed for "adult use" in 2016, a judge asked my dad what he would do now. "Your honor," he responded, "I'm gonna try the stuff."

Chapter 4

THINKING YIDDISHLY

All my parents were avid pot smokers, but its effect on my mother was the most noticeable because it gave her a sense of chill in the way my dad and stepmom had more naturally, at least on the outside. While my dad could only sometimes mask his generalized Jewish anxiety, my stepmother especially was the refined counterpoint to my mother's hysteria. She was also much younger, born a few years after my mother was picked up early from fifth grade the day Kennedy was assassinated. But they also kind of looked similar in that they were both blonde—she a natural, whereas my mother had taken a blow dryer and hair dye to colonize the same brunette curls she'd passed on to me, fitting the LA stereotype along with two nose jobs. I remember a Chanukah, during college, where my stepmother offered to get me a Brazilian blowout to permanently straighten my disorderly locks. I declined, but to this day, I have a complex about my hair—like many other curly-haired Jewish girls in the diaspora.

Not only do I look Jewish, however, but I also sound Jewish in the way I communicate with family. In college, I pursued an interdisciplinary major in Rhetoric & Cognitive Linguistics. I wrote my senior thesis on the theory of linguistic relativity: how the language a person speaks (and the dialect or other ways in which they speak it) influences their perception of the world, their culture, and their outlook on life. And so, I focused on the languages that I studied at Berkeley—French, Russian, and Yiddish (which I knew bits and pieces of from home).

The title of the book *Born to Kvetch*, by Michael Wex, says it all: that the attitude inherent in Yiddish—not only as a language, but as a culture—fosters complaint. For instance, *"vey iz mir* (woe is me)" is a staple in my mother's daily vocabulary. "Like so much of Jewish culture, kvetching has its roots in the Bible, which devotes a great deal of time to the nonstop grumblings of the Israelites . . ." writes Wex. From our slavery in Egypt to wandering through the desert, there is always something to kvetch about. The trauma of the Jewish experience is baked into our foundational narratives— its lamentations a cultural norm—and yet, it's also provided us an opportunity to practice resilience.

The summer after I graduated from journalism school, I worked at the *The Forward*, a Jewish newspaper where I wrote an opinion piece on thinking "Yiddishly" and how the tone of the language, and the culture that it spawns, even influences the way we communicate in English. The article began with an anecdote from college about what I thought was a regular conversation with my mother, until the boyfriend du jour asked me why "that argument really needed to happen" in front of him. "What argument?" I asked him, perplexed. "The one that you had five minutes ago with your mother, about the curtains in your room." (That was the instant I knew the relationship would never work.) He maintained that we were yelling at each other, but I assured him that's just how we talk. The boy had clearly never witnessed an actual argument—at least of the nature that was common in our household (although not in that moment); this, however, was simply the cultural inflection of our mother-daughter rapport.

My mother always resented the word "pleasant," which my father would often use during the time they were still married, in reference to the way he wanted things to be—because, mostly, they weren't. Whereas shrill is in my mother's quotidian range of tone, my father rarely raises his voice—only when he's very angry. You see, my father is from California, where people are surface-level "nice," despite the quality of their character and whether their actions back up their pleasantries; my mother, on the other hand, is from New York, where my dad jokes, the best way to ask for directions is, "Can you tell me where 34th Street is, or should I go fuck myself?" But what I've experienced on the East Coast is a warmth and *heimishness* unrivaled anywhere else in America.

Yiddish for "homey," the term *heimish* (pronounced "haymish" among most Ashkenazim, and "hi-mish"—or for the purposes of this book, "high-mish"—among Chassidim) connotes a community-driven way of life, replete with all the cultural hallmarks (food, language, rituals) of black-hat Jewry. "A sense of heimishness entails looking out for one's fellow Jew"—a "with us or against us" mentality, left over from the Holocaust, European pogroms, and other instances of anti-Semitic persecution, as a native Yiddish-speaking friend from South Williamsburg, Hershy Lefkowitz, once explained to me for a story I wrote on the "Chassidish Summer of Love." And so, in New York, where, as the joking adage goes, even the goyim are more Jewish than a Jew in Nebraska, that sense of heimishness permeates the culture at large.

My family are heimish HinJews. Part of this heimishness is treating your community like family—which could mean opening up your home to them for a few nights, weeks, or even months. I always laugh when people fancy Ram Dass and his peers as gurus because, in my case, I saw them all as uncles and aunts, with the familiar air and thick accents as my mother's family back East. Take, for instance, my father's best friend, once called Steve Baum, who came from Long Island and sold high-end hot tubs, now Mohan, who lives in Goa, India, and spends most of his days shirtless, with a lungi wrapped around his tummy and a beard that almost reaches his belly button. He's among the many hippies who'd come through the revolving door of my father's house for an extended stay.

Growing up, I was used to guys like Mohan frequenting the kirtan scene, so it was especially weird for me when I began to notice the crowd getting younger and younger as I got older. Why were "my parents' friends" closer in age to me than to my parents, and why were they drawn to the stuff that I thought (in the context of my conventional classmates at Beverly Hills High School) was so embarrassing? Rather than fade into a thing of the past, *Be Here Now* and Maharaj-ji's spiritual guidance, I noticed, only increased in popularity, even becoming trendy. And at first, I resented it. As a teenager, I'd roll my eyes every time I'd come out from my room to grab a snack during a kirtan and someone would ask me my name, or how I'd "arrived" at such a function. To me, Ram Dass was just another one of the guys, and the concept of all these New Age pseudo-hippies traveling to Maui for a retreat to go kiss his feet was just too weird; and why he allowed for it was another question altogether. Ram Dass wasn't a guru; he was simply a messenger for *the* guru. He said so himself!

"What you see in me is just a reflection of Maharaj-ji," he told my father, when they first met in Delhi, in 1971, before swiftly sending him off to go find the real guru at his ashram in the holy (and hectic) city of Vrindavan—the kind of place with the same religious fervor as Jerusalem.

Speaking of sounding Jewish, you see, if you ever listen to Ram Dass's lectures, you'll hear that he too has that soft, familiar wit sprinkled with Yiddish. That's part of what made Ram Dass so accessible; his message was so easy to grasp—especially for his audience, a majority of whom were Jewish. On a visit to Jerusalem while writing this book, I interviewed Jonah Gelfand, a Jewish scholar around my age who had become a Maharaj-ji devotee in high school before going on to become a *baal teshuva*. "When Ram Dass comes back from India, he has this joke which really encapsulates his relationship to Judaism," Jonah pointed out. "He'll use a Yiddishism, like referring to chutzpah as an ancient Sanskrit word, making the assumption that his audience knows not just what he's talking about, but will also find it funny."

Chapter 5

THAT TIME RAM DASS
—MY TROLL—
FLIPPED ME OFF

I always wondered if Ram Dass was in on his own bit. Did he see beyond the fanfare surrounding him, or was he just as full of it as those who'd dress up in robes to pay their respects when he passed through town, or to visit him in Hawaii when he settled down there?

He officiated the "spiritual marriage" between my father and stepmother when I was 11, which meant at the time that he was automatically on my tweenage shit list. I remember they bought us girls saris to wear at the wedding held at the casa; I didn't even unpack mine from its plastic covering and showed up in black sweats, taking a corner seat in one of the rented white folding chairs that filled up the courtyard, facing an outdoor staircase leading up to a balcony where the ceremony took place. I was loyal to my mother, and within just a year of my parents' split, I wasn't ready to digest the new reality. I don't think I stayed so much as half an hour before I ghosted the wedding in tears, meeting my mother outside the house to get picked up. From my hurt, childish, and dramatic perspective, I didn't think Ram Dass appreciated all angles of the situation he was party to. Or maybe he was just being a pal to my dad.

I was in middle school and becoming quite skilled at bottling my feelings. But as they say, the body keeps the score. The following year, I was in seventh grade when I lined up inside the girls' locker room, until it was my turn to bend down and touch my toes as an admin traced the path of my spine. Wearing my green mesh P.E. shorts and one of those sparkly pink training bras my father bought me from the Gap, attempting to fill out the drawers for my bedroom at his house (where I kept only very little of my actual stuff), it was easy enough to see, by the hunch on the upper right side of my back, that my spine was curved. They sent me home with a slip, saying that I needed to see an orthopedist, and lo and behold, I was diagnosed with moderate to severe scoliosis.

I would be forced to wear a brace until I was done growing, which luckily was only a year or so later, but unluckily meant I'd have to wear it to school. When all the other girls were donning skintight tops and low-rise jeans, I tried to hide "the brace" underneath baggy sweatshirts. I avoided surgery by the skin of my teeth, although no doctor would have denied it to me. My parents, however, being the hippies they are, explored alternative treatments, eventually forcing me into a yoga practice at the age of 12—and which has stayed with me ever since.

The yoga mat became my safe space, and suddenly I was doing "grown-up" things with my parents, accompanying my mom to level 2–3 *vinyasa* classes at YogaWorks, where she herself was trained as a yoga teacher, or going with my dad on weekend mornings to Dancing Shiva on Beverly Boulevard or Bhakti Yoga Shala in Santa Monica. For my father, yoga is a religious practice—one he's devoted to as much as any Orthodox Jew is devoted to daily davening. Yoga was sacred in my family, and I never questioned that. How could I when it was our saving grace, and the only thing that would come to save me from myself as my mental health spiraled during my teenage years?

I fell in love with the open space of the studios, the hardwood floors, the exposed brick walls, the wafting fragrance of incense or essential oils filling the room. As a kid, I'd never stuck to anything athletic, even though I'd cycled through everything from soccer to ballet to tap dance to gymnastics. Although in high school, I did run on the cross-country and track teams. Still, yoga was different. I'd pride myself in arching from *tadasana* into wheel, getting my hands flat on the ground in *uttanasana,* balancing into the "perfect" tree pose. But the point of yoga, my parents and teachers taught me from the get-go, was that there was no perfect, no competition, no pride. It taught me to be humble, while simultaneously motivating me to be strong and flexible. When I was younger, I would walk down the hallway, attempting to balance a stack of books on my head, in order to hone my posture. Yoga gave me the tools to refine the way I held myself, and the awareness to articulate my body and, ultimately, the way I felt in it.

There was also a rigor to yoga—spiritual and embodied—that felt genuine, in a way that weirdly paralleled the authenticity I picked up on in more traditional Jewish contexts. Yoga was like Chassidis for the body, although at that time, I wouldn't have had the vocabulary, let alone the exposure to articulate it. But I knew that *bhakti,* the devotional aspect of yoga (which in Hinduism parallels the concept of Chassidis), felt like a direct, unmediated connection to G-d, while yoga felt like a prayer made with the body.

I was always curious about Hasidism, but there was little opportunity for exploration. Though, on occasion, when walking through the neighborhood, my father might wander into an Orthodox shul to soak up the singing. "At least they actually know what's going on, or what they're talking about," he would joke, referencing how little "Reform" Jews tend to grasp about the religion. With all my family's *mishigas,* Judaism always felt like home, a common ground we shared, where the lack of authentic religious depth I suspected in New Age circles was less of an issue, at least as much as the lack of substantive education I experienced in Hebrew school. Generally, though, in my family, "Be here now" was the catchall for spiritual sustenance. Be *here* now? Be here *now*? Really? It felt like trolling. For much of my childhood and teenage years, the here and now were not places I wanted to *just be*—and yet, telling me to "be" was the best my parents could offer.

I grew angsty, dissociative, and escapist. Yet, there I was secretly listening to Krishna Das in my headphones to fall asleep at night. The irony of my upbringing is that the foundation upon which I was brought into the world and in which I would come of age would be the ultimate test to see if the spiritual teachings and tools that I was raised with actually work. It's as if G-d said to my soul, upon bringing me down to earth, *I'm going to give you the whole package—the very tools you'll need to get through the situation I'm going to throw you into. Let's see what you do with them.* There's a Talmudic adage: From the forest itself comes the handle of the ax that fells it. In other words, the source of your injury is also the source of your healing. My family life contained both the source of my pain and the lessons to help me get through it.

I was 16 or 17 on a trip to Hawaii one summer when my mother took my brother and me to visit Ram Dass. She and I had gotten into an argument that day, and in the throes of teenage nastiness, I'd flipped her off in the not-so-sly way of scratching my cheek with my middle finger. When we arrived at RD's house, what did she do but of course use him as the shrink that he is, and lay our problems on the poor guy. Granted, I was ashamed of myself when she "told on me" to Ram Dass, but he simply sat there calm, taking nothing about our mother-daughter spat too seriously. As we parted ways, Ram Dass waved good-bye to me, scratching his own cheek with his middle finger. In one small gesture, he belittled the whole thing in the most loving way, my damaged ego left with nothing to grasp onto.

Chapter 6

HOW MUCH DOES MY ANXIETY WEIGH?

"Sixteen years old, 4.8 GPA, 100 pounds," running myself into the ground toward that six-minute mile. That's taken from the first line of the essay that got me into college. Midway through high school, I'd spiraled into an eating disorder that took over my life. On the outside, it all looked perfect: I was vegan (though I hadn't gotten my period in almost a year); my hair was long enough to reach my lower back (though it came out in disturbing chunks that clogged the shower drain when I combed it); and my grades were flawless (because I would do whatever it took to escape LA, and college was my ticket out). Internally, I was completely obsessed with my weight, the one thing in my life I had any control over, or so I thought. I'd check the scale every morning to find out whether I could love myself that day.

On bad days, I'd check after I pooped, after I ate, before I ate, before I went to sleep, with my clothes on, with my clothes off, before and after I drank mugs and mugs of tea, and on either side of a jog. I was on the cross-country and track teams, but whatever benefit running did for my sanity went past the point of diminishing returns. I'd hit the pavement through the West Hollywood Hills, a few miles northeast of my mother's duplex, logging my mileage, running away, running toward myself, as if my life depended on it. But I abused whatever spiritual practice running was for me and used it to justify eating; on days that I couldn't jog, I'd drink "Smooth Move" senna tea to ensure that I'd rid myself of the calories I'd guiltily indulged in. All 1,200 of them. I knew, because I counted.

On the worst of days, I'd weigh myself more than a dozen times. That part I wasn't counting, but my mother secretly was. Because my parents loved me, they conspired to hide the scales in each of their houses. A rare moment of co-parenting.

Today, I can accept the fact that I may never have a completely "normal" relationship with food or body image, but my goal nowadays, rather than perpetually losing weight, is to perpetually return home to the physical residence of my soul. As my mother has tried to impart to me, "Your body is a temple." But we didn't even go to "temple," which my little brother called "G-d's house" (except on the High Holidays, or for Hebrew school, which I hated). What was the significance of a temple anyway? I'd certainly abused my body, my temple, so much so that I couldn't even feel it.

I know that this, as any therapist would put it, is my "core wound," baked into my psyche, like the center of an onion that I've attempted to peel back over the years. How I've used metaphysical shovels full of ayahuasca, LSD, mushrooms, and MDMA to dig it out—never mind that consciously doing so had rarely been my primary intention during these entheogenic trips—and still, at times, I've only been able to dig up psychedelically inspired questions like, *How much does my anxiety weigh?*

I was a perfectionist. I was obsessed with lightness. With light, *b'chlal*. It wasn't only that I wanted to be light—as in, the opposite of heavy—but I craved to feel the light of authentic spiritual connection, that *ruach* that would infuse my veins inside my pale, bruising skin, and light up the potential I had inside to fulfill everything I knew deep down I was capable of. I felt, somewhere in the memory of my *neshama*, despite whether I'd articulated it, that such a thing was possible, that such a light was within reach. I oscillated between self-love and self-loathing, a confidence in my abilities and my own literal gut punch to the stomach when

I (believed that I) was fat—bloated with food or anxiety, with the pain of my childhood, with emotions I was never able to express or healthily process.

Love in my family was rarely about emotional safety. In fact, it was often about the opposite. As much as my parents clothed me and fed me and put a roof over my head, meeting my emotional needs was beside the point. Love came in the form of what any and every therapist I've spoken to would label as some form of abuse, but which was pretty standard nonetheless. Family was defined by loving dysfunction.

To sustain my participation in this type of loving paradigm, the only thing I could do was dissociate, starve myself out of my feelings, divorce myself from my gut—both physically and metaphorically. Sometimes it was too hard to study when inside I was crying, and not even *I* wanted to hear it from *myself.* And neither did my dad, who was just living his life; and neither could my mother, who was struggling to live hers. I just had to deal. *Just be*, sit with it. I'd sooner jump out of my own skin. I thought that tending to my feelings, letting myself cry, spending time on emotional processing would only be a waste of my time, keeping me from doing my schoolwork, getting in the way of studying my way out of Los Angeles on the ticket to enrolling in schools far enough away for me to live my life in peace.

Chapter 7

BREATH, SOUL, AND MAKING LOVE TO G-D

Only in the process of my escape did I actually begin to find myself. The college admissions process was a practice in self-discovery, as I took pen to paper on no less than a dozen drafts of a personal statement that would land me a rejection from Columbia (my top choice, because it was in New York), and accepted to the cheaper, and arguably just as "prestigious" option (since both attributes mattered to my father), UC Berkeley.

The thing is, I wanted to get as far away from LA as possible, and despite having crushed on the hippie boys towing a slackline in the shade of the Campanile bell tower while touring Berkeley's campus, I had my heart set on New York. Although, it wouldn't be until grad school that I'd have an "excuse" to move there; for now, my father made it clear that a fancy private school like Barnard (Columbia's "sister school," which accepted me) wasn't an option when I'd gotten into all the affordable California state schools I'd applied to. At first I was heartbroken—but it was for the best.

Writing my college admissions essay was in fact a kind of spiritual process, one that would help me reconcile not only my eating disorder, but also my upbringing altogether. As a (white-passing) Jew coming out of Beverly Hills High School, I knew there was little going for me in the perceived adversity and diversity departments. And yet, my privilege wasn't to discount whatever struggles I did have, nor the uniqueness of where I was coming from. Whereas the beginning of my college essay began with the numbers that I used to define my self-worth, I ended it with insight on how I'd breathe my way into something more personal, that didn't reduce me to the value of the digits I thought described me. Yoga and jogging—for the joy of the movement itself—offered me a certain attention to breath, I wrote, which kindled my spirit and helped me access my soul.

In that essay, I drew from Latin to show the obvious relationship between the word for breath—*spiritus*—and spirit. Hebrew draws a similar correspondence in a common *shoresh* or root between the words for soul—neshama—and for breath—*neshima*.

"In this way, the breath is the appropriate vessel through which a person can uncover the root of his soul," the Baal Shem Tov (the 18th-century rabbi who began the Hasidic movement in Eastern Europe) wrote in *Amud HaTefila*. Breath was also an important theme for Rebbe Nachman, who taught that with each breath and every new moment, we have the opportunity to connect to our soul and to the source of all life: *HaShem*.

No one ever taught me this in Hebrew school; and despite that yoga mandates conscious breath, I always grew bored or resentful in the hippie scenes where someone might assume the role of performative mindfulness and offer unsolicited breathwork instruction. On the flip side, in the mainstream Jewish world such a thing was rare. And so, it was like uncovering a long-lost secret when I began many years later to learn just how much Jewish thought centers on breath. And because no one was imposing it on me, it became easier to accept and lean into.

In the years since, I've meditated on this relationship between breath and soul. In Hebrew, there are many names for G-d: *HaShem, Elohim,* YHVH; the list goes on. This play between Divine names and attributes is not altogether dissimilar from the hippie Hinduism I grew up with, in which the names of the various deities all refer back to different character traits of a unified, singular Source. Of these many names for the Divine, the letters of the tetragrammaton—YHVH (יהוה)—signify the sound of a breath. "Its brilliance as a Name of G-d is that It alone, Breathing alone, is 'spoken' in every human tongue," Rabbi Dr. Arthur Waskow wrote for *The Forward*. As Rabbi Aryeh Kaplan explains in *Jewish Meditation*, the human *neshama* (soul), is the *neshima* (Breath) of G-d.

Ironically, Hanuman, the Hindu deity of which Maharaj-ji is considered an incarnation, is also known as the "breath of Ram" or the "breath of G-d." He is depicted as a flying monkey, defined as a messenger—which in Jewish terms would be represented as an angel (the Hebrew word *malach* means both messenger and angel).

As Rebbe Nachman put it, through just a simple sigh, you can "release yourself from . . . the old and impure and open yourself to the pure air [in order to receive new vitality]. This is *teshuva*, returning from impurity to pure, from old to new, in order to gain new life." In the simplest of terms, breathing is making love to G-d, through this giving and receiving relationship or ruach. Breath reproduces the moment, creating life itself.

Breath is what carries us through a jog, or from one yoga posture to another. It's what got me, time and again, to actually *be here now*. The thing is, although I had this realization as early as high school, the rebel in me couldn't admit that to my parents; not even to my mother, alongside whom I taught yoga to the boy's baseball team during lunchtime meetings of the BHHS Yoga Club that I founded. The yoga mat remained the only place I felt safe from the judgment of the digits that weighed on me. In yoga, there was no track coach, timer in hand, encouraging a team full of anorexics to judge their worth by numbers; some days were easier than others to get my heels to the ground in downward dog, but there was nothing official I could really use to measure myself in yoga—and that was a good thing.

Because yoga was baked into our family's religion, because I respected it as sacred, because I knew how good it made me feel, because I knew there was a tradition behind it that was as holy and ancient as Torah, I therefore knew it was one of the few real-world places I'd been exposed to where the phrase *"be here now"* didn't feel like bullshit. Because when you're dripping in sweat, trying to root your right foot into the ground, keeping your leg straight, while taking your left foot into your left hand, arching your back as much as possible, and stretching your right hand forward and up, there's little else to do *but* be here now, and breathe into a deeper expression of the "dancing Shiva" posture. (Fun fact: the blue-skinned Hindu deity, Shiva, is known as the father of both yoga and of mind-altering substances.)

His devotees have a particular affinity for the sacrament of cannabis—in the form of ganja (flower); bhang (potion); or charas (hashish). In India, you might recognize them by the ash on their faces, heads full of floor-length dreadlocks, and in some cases, a three-pronged *trishul* in hand, representing various trinities like creation, maintenance, destruction; past, present, future; body, mind, atman; and so forth.

Atman—the soul, the breath, the self as distinct from the ego—was something I always strived to access, but in high school, I had little opportunity to explore how. Despite all the experienced meditators and psychonauts surrounding me, there was the rebellious side of me that didn't want to admit or give my parents the satisfaction of knowing that I was actually curious about some of the things that they were into, like breathing techniques. And so, *b'davka* I'd have to *leave* home to discover the same stuff that drew some of my parents' friends *into* our home.

Chapter 8

PB&J WITH A SIDE
OF SHROOMS

In college, I dove headfirst into the quintessential Berkeley experience. Whereas at Beverly, I felt socially stifled, unable to relate to the majority of my classmates—future frat bros and sorority girls, straight-edge honors students and the "Persian mafia," druggie freaks, and emo skaters—when I got to Berkeley, I found myself going a bit wild, partying at the student housing co-ops among free and kindred spirits.

In the fall semester of my freshman year, I wrote about psychedelics for my very first research paper. It's as if I was reading guidebooks to Paris before visiting, and by the time I was ready to trip for the first time, I would have as much information as I could gather about what I'd be getting myself into. Intellectually, I knew I might see patterned trails or experience a sense of timelessness. And still, I had no idea what was coming for me, what kind of mind-blowing event was about to change the course of my life forever.

After completing that research paper for my intro class to the Rhetoric Department, I had come home for winter break and found myself at a New Year's party at a student apartment near the UCLA campus, where some grungy dude named Kyle with long blond hair offered to sell me magic mushrooms. I bought about half an ounce, and made a plan to shroom with an old friend from high school and a new friend from college. Two gals and a queer guy, the holy trinity. My older sister offered to tripsit us, and made the right call to team up with the family medical marijuana doctor, who was a seasoned psychonaut and former Orthodox Jew, holding a Ph.D., according to Facebook, in "bs, bioengineering, and partying" from Columbia.

The January sun was beating down through the open windows of my older sister's Porsche SUV as we cruised down Pico Boulevard toward the beach, bumper to bumper with other cars in the westward traffic of a warm Sunday afternoon.

"That smells good," she hollered to the guys in the next car over, pot smoke billowing between lanes. They motioned to pass a joint through the open windows, my two friends and me giggling in the back seat. I was 18 and by this point familiar with the terrain of a cannabis high, but I wanted to keep my head clear for later—for what my sister described as "weed plus."

Unlike acid (which back then I still hadn't tried yet), mushrooms felt like they would be the next level up from cannabis. The psychedelic experience, or "trip," would be longer than a regular weed high, but shorter than 12 hours of LSD. After that first time tripping, I soon learned that, for me, mushrooms and cannabis edibles bring on similar visuals of swirling floral patterns and paisleys in a pink technicolor palette.

When we arrived at the hippie doctor's ground-floor apartment in one of those alleyways off the Venice Beach Boardwalk, my friends and I each squished an eighth of shrooms in between peanut butter and jelly sandwiches, which we washed down with orange juice (since we had heard it would make the psilocybin—the active compound in the shrooms—more potent). And then we waited. Periodically, I'd wave my hand in front of my face to see if I'd start to see trails. I journaled a little bit, and eventually I noticed that the cover to MGMT's *Time to Pretend* EP, which I'd been playing on my iPod, began to swirl.

I tiptoed, maybe even danced, around the apartment, peeking out the shades toward the street, sitting down at the piano, pondering the magic of simply being alive, lost in wonder. I was completely outside myself, but not in a way that was scary, just in a way where the regular me didn't exist, and I felt I was pure spirit emanating from the core of my neshama. I lost all sense of time as my ego faded away, leaving me to wonder after I'd come down, if without my regular degree of self-consciousness, I'd said anything I'd regret. For lack of a better description—and because the experience was truly beyond words—I was tripping balls.

When our crew decided it was time to go outside to check out the drum circle on the sand, I wrapped a violet prayer shawl around my shoulders, bare from the flowy, spaghetti-strap Free People dress I wore for the occasion. "I'm shivering, but it's not me," I said through chattering teeth. We walked toward the ocean, and into one of those pink cotton-candy sunsets that only happen in the wintertime when the sun sets right in front of you, rather than in the summer months, when its descent happens farther north, behind the mountains extending out from Malibu. In the winter, it's easiest to blow out the sun, as my father taught me to: wait for just the right moment when the sun's about to dissolve, and begin to blow, pushing out air as that burning ball of light gets smaller and smaller, until it's extinguished by dipping below the horizon.

As I sat there watching the sun set, completely at peace, held by the universe, in touch with myself, with nature, with G-d, with my friends and sister, I likely would have checked off the criteria for what psychedelic scientists have dubbed the "mystical experience."

The Mystical Experience Questionnaire (MEQ) was originally developed by Dr. Walter Pahnke, a minister and psychiatrist at Harvard, who conducted the famous Good Friday Experiment at Boston's Marsh Chapel under the auspices of Richard Alpert and Timothy Leary in 1962. In the experiment, Pahnke gave psilocybin or a placebo to 20 divinity school students during a Good Friday service. In years to come, those who were actually dosed claimed it was one of the most meaningful days of their life. An evolved form of the MEQ continues to be in use today, including at institutions like Johns Hopkins, where scientists are conducting an ongoing study in which they give psilocybin to religious professionals like rabbis, priests, and imams. The big joke with the rabbis is that one must be psychedelic-naive in order to qualify for the experiment; and hence, a handful of rabbis who applied to be subjects have been rejected on the basis of already having had psychedelic experiences.

Measured up against the accounts of mystics from varying religions, scientists are still qualifying mysticism through metrics like Hood's Mysticism Scale, or today's States of Consciousness Questionnaire, which consists of 100 questions, rated on a scale of 1–5, and categorized into seven domains, which I'll paraphrase: I. internal unity (loss of usual identity; fusion of personal self into the whole; experience of pure Being); II. external unity (experience of oneness with surroundings; "All is One"; "oceanic boundlessness"); III. transcendence of time and space (loss of usual sense of time and space; sense of being beyond time or sense that time doesn't exist); IV. ineffability and paradoxicality (inability to do the experience justice by describing it with words; needing to use contradictory words to describe it); V. sense of sacredness (amazement; awe; humility; or reverence before the majesty of that which is felt to be holy), VI. noetic quality (sense that the experience is more real than mundane reality; ultimate reality; insightful knowledge at intuitive level); VII. deeply felt positive mood (overflowing energy; joy; universal love; tenderness; ecstasy).

Like the subjects in the Good Friday experiment, my first time taking mushrooms was easily one of the most significant days of my life: playful, exploratory, spiritual. I felt like I was reborn, discovering the world and its wonders for the first time. The shrooms turned down the volume on the anxiety that defined my day-to-day experience and turned up the brightness on my appreciation for simply being, of life itself and living it outright.

With my feet dug into the sand, giddily smiling at the universe, with the orange light of the sun warming my face by the breezy shore, I looked over at my childhood best friend, Rachael, before bursting out into giggles. On an embodied level, I had finally tuned in. "Ohhhh," I giggled. "'Be here now.' I get it."

Chapter 9

"CLOYNE IS SUCK"

From before I could remember, I always wanted to be in New York. I didn't know how I was getting there, but I knew that's where I was going, no matter what.

But Berkeley, and then Israel, were necessary pit stops before diving into the *promised land* of my ancestors: Brooklyn. Before that return—intuiting that I'd probably never settle back down in LA—I knew I needed to make peace with where, and more specifically whom, I came from.

On my first acid trip at the age of 20, a friend and I ran out of Berkeley's glittering pink Saturn Cafe, where we'd come for a Coca-Cola, and escaped a crying baby that was freaking her out—only for me to freak out at her student co-op on the north side of campus, where I looked in the mirror, and as the baby of my own parents, saw both their faces in my own.

For better and for worse, I've always been an obvious consummate product of Bruce and Sherri, Badri and Durga, Baruch Meir and Sima Yachad. My father and I share a tendency to wake up in the morning with anxiety (though on Shabbos, thank G-d, this isn't a thing for me), while my mother's fears belonging to a deep-seated Jewish trauma live within my gut. And yet, I always say, if you want to understand me better, meet my parents. My mother taught me to love New York, and my father taught me to fight the Drug War.

As a freshman, I joined UC Berkeley's chapter of the national organization Students for Sensible Drug Policy (SSDP), and soon found myself attending SSDP conferences with speakers like Ethan Nadelmann, founder of the nonprofit organization Drug Policy Alliance (DPA), where at 18, at a DPA conference afterparty in San Francisco, I did MDMA for the first time. It was one of those magical nights spent dancing, then wandering through the city's tunnels and past bodegas into the wee hours of the morning, until piling into a hotel room with a dozen other hippies, and attempting to hotbox the space without setting off the smoke alarm.

On Thursday nights, after I'd finish my homework, I'd venture over to a friend's apartment on the south side of campus and smoke weed out of a hookah until we were both too baked to do anything but laugh over anything that caught our attention. Matt and I were fast friends and still are to this day: We were both from LA, loved Judaism, and were curious to explore the highs Berkeley's drug culture had to offer. Two years above me, he was a queer theater kid and brilliant polyglot who became religious in high school following his recovery from suicidality and an "electrifying, transcendent experience" during his first time at the Kotel. We christened our friendship by sharing a first mushroom trip. The same way I was perpetually on my way to New York, Matt was on his way to *the other Jewish homeland* from before the time I met him. And of course, not long after he graduated, he made aliyah—but not before first living with me in Berkeley's student co-op system, a federation of independent houses known for their wild parties and affordable rent. The kids who lived in the co-ops were brilliant academics, free spirits who'd run naked through the library during finals week, and simultaneous activists, shutting down campus buildings during tuition fee-hike protests, or camping out at Occupy Oakland in 2011. I met some of my best friends through the co-ops, kindred spirits who'd go on to integrate the cooperative and psychedelic ethos into their adult lives, like Daniel who later founded a housing co-op for artists in LA, or Angelica, who went on to work at MAPS.

With the exception of a summer and semester where I lived at a vegetarian, clothing-optional co-op called Lothlorien, or Loth for short (known for its "naked pizza Fridays"), I spent three and a half years living in an even more feral fun house called Cloyne. A converted hotel home to 150 students, Cloyne was covered in psychedelic murals in every corner of the C-shaped structure that surrounded a massive courtyard and garden, where I'd teach myself to do tricks with my Hula-Hoop during raves. Cloyne was beautiful chaos, spirited anarchy. Its cheeky tagline, inspired by an international exchange student who ran for the hills? "Cloyne is suck." Most residents burned out on Cloyne after a year; the only way I was able to live there as long as I did was that I was (and remain) always moderate with my drug use.

Every drug under the sun floated through the trippy hallways of all three stories of the house. Acid, shrooms, molly, ketamine, 2C-b, 2C-i, uppers, downers, poppy flowers, pills, and powders . . .

During my freshman year, I crushed on a boy from French class who lived at Cloyne. John was a talented DJ and a notorious drug enthusiast. On one fateful evening, Matt and I were shrooming and were led by a dreadlocked friend of mine from SSDP to the boy's room, on the second floor of the central wing. Because I was tripping, it looked like the most beautiful room I'd ever seen: colorful *shmatas* were draped from the ceiling, embroidered cushions on the floor, massive bags full of shrooms on the coffee table, and a glimpse of John's naked, muscular ass as he changed right there in front of us. Everything glittered, and I was having the time of my life.

But that all flipped in a second when I realized that not only did Matt and John know each other, but also they had fallen out of friendship over, of all things, conflicting views on Israel–Palestine (a controversy and hot topic at Berkeley I still didn't understand at that point). At Berkeley, students would throw insults at Matt like "Zionist clown"—ironic since he's now an ardent leftist living in Tel Aviv, working in human rights with refugees, and marching against the occupation. But back then, he was part of the Hasbara, and John belonged to Students for Justice in Palestine.

I sensed the tension, and our trip went south. John's roommate tried to lead me in a meditation, but I was too far gone and couldn't focus. "So this must be what a 'bad trip' is like," Matt seethed, before going home. Left there alone, I wandered downstairs, where I met a dapper upperclassman who went by "Huxley" (one of my favorite authors), and two sympathetic girls who gave me a ride back to my dorm in their Merry Prankster–style Burning Man bus.

A few weeks later, John went missing from French class for a few days, then a week, then forever. News came out that he had overdosed and suffered an anoxic heart attack, leaving him in a coma until he passed away from an infection seven years later. Cloyne was hit with a lawsuit. And then I moved in.

John's story would forever change the co-op world in the coming years, but in the immediate aftermath it sobered me up real fast, and I instantly became much more careful about drugs. Set and setting—one's internal state going into a trip, and its external environment—was key. From then on, I rarely took anything willy-nilly, or without some premeditation.

The thing is, I could never go *that* crazy in Berkeley, in part because I also went to Shabbat dinner every week—where I was subject to the watchful, caring eyes of young, relatable rabbis who knew the deal with the co-op kids.

And although the co-ops were known for their top-notch, local, organic hippie food, there was something grounding and familiar about stumbling into Hillel (or on occasion, Chabad) for challah and soup. When things got too hectic at Cloyne, I'd sometimes crash at the Bayit, an independent co-op with a kosher kitchen, neighboring Loth. The kids there were on the nerdier side (one of them even became a Republican, in reaction to Berkeley's unbridled liberalism), and would poke fun at the shenanigans and militant hippie politics next door.

The thing is, the co-ops were full of Jewish kids. And the rabbis knew it. So as part of a fellowship where I learned *Pirkei Avot* with a hipstery 30-something rabbi, they gave me a job whereby I'd put on a "Co-op Shabbat" every semester. On Hillel's dime,

I'd buy enough Two-Buck Chuck from Trader Joe's that everyone could have a bottle each, get homemade challah donated from the Challah for Hunger student group, and solicit my friends' jam band—a trio of Jewish boys from LA, led by a Bob Dylan doppelganger—to play klezmer. The band's Yiddish alter ego was named *Ziseh Tukhus* (Sweet Ass).

Matt would lead kiddush, then hide from any Jew who tried to take his photo (as it's *muktzeh*; never mind the live music). The Shabbos parties were wild, drawing co-op Jews out of the woodwork, and the gentiles too. We held Co-op Shabbat at Loth, where Naked Pizza Friday happened in another part of the house, and sometimes the nudists would make an appearance. Even the frum kids from the Bayit or the Chabad scene would roll through, greeted with (and trolled by) a Palestinian flag hanging from someone's bedroom door off the living room entrance. Despite the severity of Berkeley's politics around Israel–Palestine, at Co-op Shabbat, it was all in good fun.

Berkeley was the needed counterpoint to Beverly. My eating issues quickly resolved, or at least were demoted from front of mind, because I was too busy *living*. I felt free. As my older sister once described, referring to her own time in college, in New York, "[it] takes you out of yourself"—and I found that to be true. During summer break, I would travel to New York as I had done since childhood, wander the Village, hole up in cafes studying for the LSAT (thinking I'd go to law school), or run around Brooklyn, catching shows or taking street photography with my then-new SLR camera. My uncle had a thing for visiting cultural neighborhoods, such as the Arabs in Paterson, New Jersey, or the Italians by Arthur Avenue in the Bronx, and would sometimes take us to South Williamsburg to see the house where my grandmother grew up, and the house where her *bubbe* and *zayde* lived, now inhabited by Chassidim. Around the corner, we might stop by Sander's Kosher Bakery, still standing all these years later.

The summer before my senior year at Berkeley, I lived on the Lower East Side, in a tiny, windowless apartment that smelled like garbage and Chinese food, interning for a criminal defense attorney. My roommate was a friend of a friend—a party girl in the fashion scene who'd take me under her wing and show me the "good" Brooklyn warehouse raves. Still, I had as much fun going out with Sarah as I did sticking my head out a cab window at 5 A.M. on my way home, or grabbing a slice of dollar pizza, drunk after a night of dancing. There was something to those in-between moments that are possible in New York City, of reading the graffiti on the walls while walking to my destination, or crying on the subway, that made life feel vibrant.

Chapter 10

FLEEING FAMILY COURT, LANDING IN TEL AVIV, FLYING IN TZFAT

I graduated Berkeley into a big question mark: I thought I'd be going to law school, but I was disgusted with the profession. My father and stepmother were getting divorced, and as such the entire *mishpacha* gathered in court downtown—not far from where a few years earlier my stepmom had set up a tent, decked out with pillows from Anthropologie, during Occupy LA when she'd also placed a handwritten sign in front of our casa in South Beverly Hills reading "We are the 99%." Now, old traumas resurfaced in what felt like a war that had undone years of progress and healing, especially since the birth of my younger sister. Ironically, now my father's attorney in the divorce was my older sister's mother, and if it weren't all such a heartbreaking, expensive mess, the image of his three ex-wives together in family court was actually kind of funny.

At the time, I was working at my father's law office, answering phones, greeting clients (some of whom were kids my own age, busted for drugs), and editing his annual publication *The Margolin Guide to Marijuana Laws*. In my off time, I applied to every alternative graduate program that seemed relevant, from public policy to linguistics, looking for an excuse to stay in school and move to New York. On a whim, I opened an application to Columbia Journalism School, but didn't complete it.

Meanwhile, I found solace in my first love—an aspiring screenwriter living in Hollywood, with a degree from Yale, born into a well-to-do family from the northern suburbs of Chicago. He had my attention at first text: "Gemini, Jewish, walking contradiction, existential thinker to the point where I drive myself crazy." I couldn't tell if he was talking about me (from what he'd picked up on from my online profile) or himself; in the end, it was both of us. Our first date was at a strip mall bar off Sunset Boulevard, where—despite him being sober from alcohol at the time—we spent hours until close, talking about our psychedelic trips, books we loved, our hopes and dreams. We spent our second date joyriding into the hills, making out over lookout spots, listening to M83's album *Hurry Up, We're Dreaming*. We'd spend our relationship oscillating between fighting and professing our love, though the best moments were spent going out, dancing at the hipster ratchet techno club Low End Theory in Lincoln Heights or at the glittering gay A Club Called Rhonda, in Silverlake, or canoodling in the corner of a local bar in Franklin Village or at my favorite spot in Los Feliz, the now-defunct vintage Chinese-themed dive bar Good Luck, where we'd nestle into a velvet booth, sipping the coconut cream-based Potent Potion.

He played golf, introduced me to films like *A Serious Man* and *A Clockwork Orange*, and taught me about beer. I loved being in love, and having an ally amid the shitstorm I'd returned home to—but I didn't actually want to be in LA, and as much as I enjoyed the relationship, deep down I was too afraid to admit that it wasn't *matim*. If anything, our differences highlighted the life I actually wanted. On Saturdays, he'd hit the bars with his buddies and watch the game; in my heart of hearts, I wanted to spend my Shabbosim on some mountaintop in Tzfat, singing *niggunim* with a cast of holy freaks (despite that it was all a subconscious calling at the time, since I'd yet to have such an experience). Once and only once, I got him to come with me to the drum circle at Venice Beach.

Six months after my graduation, I went *home* to visit New York, where I'd find myself late one night at Waverly Diner in the West Village, writing down options for my "life plan" on a napkin, with a Coke and cookie (the same meal my dad had in India, before he met Maharaj-ji, who psychically guessed what he'd eaten for "dinner" the previous night). On a frosty weeknight during that trip, I got a random call from the dean of admissions at Columbia Journalism School; she noticed that I'd abandoned my open application (I assumed I wasn't qualified, so why bother?), and encouraged me to finish it.

I did, then made a plan to spend the next six months in Israel, as I'd come to see other friends do when they were feeling existential or when life went on hiatus. My sister had just had a baby—this time with a cannabis grower she'd married while eight months pregnant, at Temple Emanuel—who was born on Jim Morrison's birthday. Dad's divorce was clearing up, and I needed something to do, some spiritual kindling, and was desperate to get the fuck out of LA—before ending up in whatever grad school would accept me.

I signed up for a program in Tel Aviv, where I'd take Hebrew classes, volunteer with an organization teaching English to Eritrean refugees, and ultimately get acquainted with a piece of myself I'd yet to really meet.

I didn't go to Israel because I had any sort of religious or Zionist urge to be in the "Holy Land" or the "Jewish state" (neither appellation I particularly identified with). It was simply calling me. I'd only been once before, on a Birthright trip and bonus week in Tel Aviv that left me feeling confused about the politics of a place I fell in love with. I didn't grow up with Israel as a conversation piece; my family wasn't anti-Zionist per se, and certainly not antireligious, but we just didn't talk about Israel. We were diaspora Jews, and New York was the motherland—literally and figuratively.

But whenever I've lived in Eretz Yisroel (10 years later, from my apartment in Tzfat, I still struggle with what to call it), I've realized, on an embodied level, the inherent, undeniable holiness of "the Land." But not in the obvious ways; at times when I'd visit religious hot spots, like the Kotel, I might even feel unmoored, anxious to get back to Tel Aviv, where I could breathe easy and escape the tension that felt so palpable in certain parts of Jerusalem. I wasn't on a mission, at least not the kind of mission that brought frum girls to seminary, or postcollege Zionists to their NGO jobs. I wasn't looking for a husband, and I wasn't (at that point, at least) trying to make aliyah. I actually just wanted to party. And to me, there was something holy about that, especially in that place and at that time of my life. Simultaneously, I was seeking something—myself, transcendence, connection—in what might have appeared to be a shallow escape from real life, as I found myself allowed to have a moment, finally taking a breath, my life suspended between the past and what was about to be a chapter launching me into the rest of my future. Living in Israel during that liminal time, I experienced a kind of joy I'd never known before; I relished in the present, *being here now* on a day-to-day level, in a way that would have previously been unfathomable, and to this day still feels somewhat impossible.

By day, I'd take classes in Hebrew or on Jewish ethics vis-à-vis the Israeli–Palestinian conflict, scour the best hole-in-the-wall *sabich* in between café-hopping, where I'd do some journaling, intern at an African refugee organization, or volunteer at an after-school program in the south Tel Aviv neighborhood of Shapira with children whose parents emigrated from Eritrea, Sudan, or the Philippines. By night I'd go clubbing till 3 A.M., wander home drunk on Tubi and on the freedom of being so far away from home, and so at home—in myself, in this place—all at the same time.

I lived with five other girls and a one-eyed neighborhood cat next door to a Bukharin family and their rooster, in the shadows of Tel Aviv's central bus station—Tachana Merkazit—a monstrosity of a structure that doubles as a bomb shelter and a mall, where trance music blasts from boom boxes for sale, flies hover over *burekas* and green-olive pizza, and merchants hustle, or shoot the shit, in Hebrew, Arabic, Tagalog, Russian, and Tigrinya. You can get anything and everything there, from lingerie to Hula-Hoops, SIM cards to HIV testing, and sad-looking pets at the pet store. On the outside of the cement monolith, a homeless woman used to sit on the sidewalk perpetually picking a scab on her leg; and on weekends, hipsters would line up around the block, waiting to get into the city's hottest underground club with a Berlin vibe, nestled in an expansive corner of the station, luring techno DJs from around the world.

I made friends easily, and even joined a camp for the first-ever Israeli Burning Man (called Midburn), where I'd be rolling face on "MD" in the expansive Negev Desert, dancing with my Hula-Hoop, under the stars, falling in love, over and over again, with each twirl of my hoop, with life itself. I was invigorated, and inspired—despite sobering calls with my mother, for whom the ever-present threat of conflict in a bloodstained, war-torn region never left her front of mind, serving as a reminder that life is precious. Her neuroses run deep, and so it didn't take much for me to pick up on the trauma that also permeated society in Israel–Palestine—but I didn't have the ability back then to name it. I just knew there was a vigor and a rigor with which people lived, partied, and prayed.

Toward the end of that chapter, however, I was beginning to burn out on the *Chiloni* life. Living in Tel Aviv—an aggressively secular city—was the least religious experience I'd ever had. I was spiritually kindled by life itself, but I was beginning to miss ritual.

I sought out the Hare Krishnas on the beach and found myself at a kirtan, feeling a bit homesick, before I stumbled upon a community of frum-ish hippies holding beachside Kabbalat Shabbat services and potluck dinners. Although I was excited to come upon a community that I felt at home in, I already had one foot out the door. I'd just been accepted to Columbia Journalism School and would be moving to New York by the end of the summer—but not before connecting with a family friend—a musician and another HinJew, so to speak, who was studying at a yeshiva in Tzfat.

I had instantly fallen in love with Tzfat when I first visited on my 20th birthday during a Birthright trip, where I took a photo in front of a building that would come to be the apartment I would rent 11 years later to write this book. My dad had primed me to love Tzfat, telling me about the blue doors that awaited in the mystical city, the birthplace of Kabbalah. You can lose yourself and find yourself all at the same time, meandering through Tzfat's narrow alleyways and staircases made from smooth, tan Jerusalem stone, underneath a canopy of vines and with a view of the mountains ahead. At night, if you know what you're looking at, you can see the twinkling lights of Mount Meron, at the *kever* of Rabbi Shimon bar Yochai, the fabled author or protagonist of *The Zohar.* The streets are populated by women in beautiful flowing skirts and oversized colorful *tichels*; men in white linens, long thick *peyos*, and beanie-like yarmulkes; unattended children running about. Life is simple in Tzfat; the rat race isn't *a thing* like it is elsewhere. At the top of the mountain, where else is there to strive toward? People have *emunah* and they live like it, name their kids after it. Breslov Chassidim are prolific in these parts, and it's not uncommon to see tiny hatchbacks decked out in tie-dyed Na Nach stickers the size of the car door.

The Na Nachs are a sect of Breslover Chassidim—followers of Rebbe Nachman (who they endearingly call Rabbeinu; similar to how my family's satsang calls Neem Karoli Baba *Maharaj-ji*). Their mantra, of sorts—נ נח נחמ נחמן מאומן—can be seen all over Israel, from the graffiti tagged upon stone walls, to bumper stickers, to white crocheted yarmulkes.

According to Na Nach lore, Breslover Rabbi Yisroel ber Odesser, a.k.a. Saba (Hebrew for "grandfather"), received a note—the Petek—in 1922 from the long-deceased Rebbe Nachman, bearing his signature in the form of נ נח נחמ נחמן מאומן (a total of 10 letters spelling out Na Nach Nachma Nachman), (MeUman—from Uman). Saba encouraged his followers to take vehicles and go around dancing, to put up Na Nach signs everywhere, to go house-to-house distributing Breslov literature, to disseminate Rabbeinu's teachings, and to spread joy. Saba inspired a very particular offshoot of Breslov Chassidim—Na Nach—which, like the psytrance they often play, is both loved and reviled by many.

Rebbe Nachman said the greatest mitzvah is to be happy. To that end, the Na Nachs go around Israel in colored, Merry Prankster–style vans, blasting trance music, and getting out at stoplights to dance in the streets or park in heavily trafficked areas to hand out Breslov literature and Na Nach stickers.

Many are baal teshuva, having returned to Orthodox Judaism through storied paths, which often have included (and in some cases, continue to include) psychedelics. It's no surprise then, that they're drawn to the region of Tzfat.

Tzfat is known as the City of Air (whereas Jerusalem is fire, Tiberias is water, and Hebron is earth). Originally it was populated as a city of refugees—fuckups who accidentally killed someone and were exiled to Tzfat to escape their own demise. To me, perched on a balcony in the Old City as I complete this book, it's *mamash* psychedelic; being here is a trip unto itself. Words don't do it justice; you have to feel it.

. You see, there's something more real than real in Tzfat, on this mountaintop; disconnected from the rest of reality, it's almost as if Tzfat is more connected to a noetic reality, a mystical channel that is more transcendent than the mundane.

There's a certain magic in the ground—maybe from all the *tzadikim* who are buried in the cemetery at the base of the Old City. Some of the *kivrei* tzadikim lead into caves, musky and dark, sometimes cozy with a few tea light candles and old *sfarim* or half-moldy *Tikkun HaKlali* pamphlets. In the decade-plus since I first spent significant time here, I've kept coming back, and I discover a new layer to it each time. If you spend some time in these caves, as I have, daven, do *hisbodedus*, you come out feeling a certain way. Maybe it's the sensory deprivation, especially if the cave is dark—as there's a tradition of tzadikim and sadhus all over Israel and India spending time in caves—or maybe it's the energy of the prayer itself. In Yiddish, the term is *ozgelatet*—purified—the way you might also feel at the end of a psychedelic trip, a spiritual cleanse, tender and open. Despite my familiarity and comfort with easy, breezy Tel Aviv, Tzfat has always felt like the true home to my neshama. My experience in Tzfat gave me a taste of a certain kind of consciousness—and I wanted to experience more of it in my life.

PART 2

ECSTASY

נ נח נחמ נחמן מאומן

Chapter 11

CAN YOU HAVE A JEWISH EXPERIENCE WITH PSYCHEDELICS?

By the time I moved to New York, I was lit with a fire that would blaze a trail ahead of me, lined with serendipitous events that would kindle my soul and define the course of my life. I was ripe and curious.

Columbia's "j-school," as we called it, was a bit of a culture shock. I felt like I was in a cohort of the global elite, 20- through 40-somethings getting second and third degrees, who had ties to media conglomerates in Paris, London, or Beirut, whose parents were ambassadors to places like Pakistan—in other words, wealthy hipsters. My dad helped me a bit for a limited period of time, but I'd taken out loans (which I'm still paying back a decade later) to cover the cost of the program and living expenses. So when, early on in the program, my "career counselor" told me I'd probably be among that small percentage of the graduating class who wouldn't end up getting a job in journalism because I didn't have prior experience in the field, I asked myself, and her in kinder terms, "WTF did I just pay $60,000 for then?" I missed the rootsy, public school bootstrappers at Berkeley.

I'd left Tel Aviv in the summer of 2014, just as the government launched "Operation Protective Edge." "The worse the better," was a motto among some of the j-schoolers, always on the lookout for tension in a story. The latest episode of the Israeli–Palestinian conflict was great fodder for *New York Times* aspirants. I was happy enough to take the train downtown, hit a cafe for hours on end to do my schoolwork, and finish my day at Yoga to the People, on St. Marks. What I can only appreciate now was that the extent to which I was aloof at j-school also gave me the time and social flexibility to make lasting friendships through my journalism itself.

That first semester, I was one of two Jews in my Reporting 101 class, where every student was assigned to an "ethnic beat," like the Dominicans in Washington Heights or the Bangladeshis in Queens. Because I studied Russian at Berkeley, I hoped I'd be assigned to the Russians in Brighton Beach, plus I thought I wanted something that felt less familiar than the Jewish beat. But *someone* had to do the Chassidim, and it was deemed that I'd have "easier access" (to the world's most insular religious community) than my gentile classmates. In the end, it was *b'shert* and I wasn't mad about it.

I can't tell you how many rugelach I bought up and down Lee Avenue in South Williamsburg until I found someone who would speak to me. I'd spent days in the sticky heat of mid-August, donning the most *tzniusdig* outfit I knew how to put together at the time (long black skirt, blue floral cardigan, and tights) zipping in and out of kosher bakeries, grocery stores, and take-out spots, hoping to snag someone's ear—the guy behind the counter, or maybe someone in line for checkout. Of course, my outfit only got me so far, as I'd failed to scrub my nail polish or remove four of the six total earrings I wear daily.

It wasn't until I stumbled upon a kosher pizza shop nestled in a corner of the BQE overpass that I met someone who would talk to me. Benzi must have been 19 or 20, with a partially grown beard, and a thick Yiddish accent. He lived at home with his parents, but was somewhere on the spectrum of OTD—off the *derech*—a (debatably pejorative) term used for those who've deviated from the straight and narrow religious path. I joined him outside the stout brick building during his cigarette break, and we agreed to meet up a few days later. Then he flaked.

It couldn't have been more fortuitous. When we finally linked up for an evening walk along the East River at Domino Park, in the shadows of the Williamsburg Bridge, he apologized for rescheduling. "I was at a psytrance festival upstate," Benzi told me, naming off the psychedelics he and his friends liked to party with: acid, ketamine, mushrooms, molly, the list went on. I noticed how easy it felt talking with Benzi, that this buttoned-up "interview" felt more like "a chill" (as they say in the heimish—or Yiddish-speaking—world), and I wondered if it was okay and professional to feel this way. As the evening grew dark, I didn't realize that Benzi had arranged for his friend Hershy Lefkowitz to come by in a black SUV with tinted windows to bring over some weed. Together they rolled a joint, caught up in Yiddish, and offered me a hit.

In j-school, our old-school professors taught us "no free lunches," and so I was reluctant to take anything from a "source," let alone get high with them. I'd later realize, as I became a weed journalist, that this approach would only get me so far in relating to my sources, and I'd eventually drop the pretense—and in some cases, go gonzo. Accepting a joint—or whatever else—wasn't going to sway me toward a bias (as if bias doesn't occur naturally anyway). If anything, in the event that someone did offer me something, the interaction often made me more discerning.

As Benzi told me about these psytrance festivals upstate, I tried to wrap my head around it. I'd been to my fair share of festivals, but never had I come across Chassidim there—how did these kids, coming out of a community known for its Internet bans, even find out about these things, let alone get into the musical genre altogether? I knew I needed to see it with my own eyes. But the psychedelic piece was even more fascinating: Because Hershy and Benzi came from such a religiously observant background, I wondered if Judaism ever factored into their psychedelic trips. I distilled my curiosity into a question, one that's motivated my life's work ever since: can you have a Jewish experience with psychedelics?

Chapter 12

THE MAGIC JEWS

A few months after I met Hershy and Benzi, I came across an article from 2008—drug journalist Hamilton Morris's first ever story for *VICE* magazine—titled "The Magic Jews." He detailed what it was like hanging out and doing drugs with heimish renegades. I later learned that he even got the magazine to expense a sheet of acid that he'd do with his "sources."

The son of Oscar-winning documentarian Errol Morris, Hamilton pioneered early 21st-century gonzo journalism, and would come to be one of the most respected drug journalists of our generation. My old-school j-school professors would probably have frowned upon his less-than-sober approach (even though he skillfully has maintained a simultaneous air of distance), but it's precisely that approach that landed the staid and lanky, bohemian drug nerd-cum-researcher the star role in his own Viceland docuseries, *Hamilton's Pharmacopeia*, something of an Anthony Bourdain-style, international deep dive into the world of esoteric mind-altering substances.

I read the Magic Jews article with curiosity. Reporting on the phenomenon was one thing, but there was something else that kindled me—a desire to experience it altogether.

I had never felt at home in any Jewish denomination. Certainly not the bland Reform congregation my parents switched to after we dropped out of the conservative shul. And the SJW ("social justice warrior") granola Jews headquartered in the Bay Area didn't really hit the spot for me either. To the hardcore Chassidim, I was probably as good as goy, and I never took to being *mkareved* by Chabad (religiously curious, I've always been the perfect bait). You couldn't pay me to attend a Young Jewish Professionals function, and I couldn't help but roll my eyes at the self-proclaimed "cultural Jews," who related to Judaism mainly through bagel memes. Plus, despite growing up in the satsang, I myself didn't really identify as "HinJew," never went by a Hindu name, never really chanted kirtan, and never claimed to be a devotee, myself, of a Hindu deity or guru. If anything, the closest I'd so far come to relevant was the Judaism I experienced with the Na Nachs in Tzfat or the hippies on the beach in Tel Aviv (who also had roots in places like the bohemian Jerusalem neighborhoods of Nachlaot and Ein Kerem, the area surrounding Pardes Chana, or the Moshav).

I wanted something holy and heimish, frum-informed yet free, psychedelic and somatically embodied. I remember once the rabbis at Berkeley Hillel asked us to write on a poster board when we felt "spiritual." The obvious answer to me was my first psychedelic trip spent shrooming at Venice Beach, but I was too shy in that context to write it down. Still, I held in my heart a yearning for a Judaism that not only honored that experience but also gave me the tools, language, ritual, and framework with which to integrate it. I wanted to understand and relate to my psychedelic experience through a form of religion that on a daily basis gave me daily soulful nourishment and *chizzuk*. Because, as Ram Dass learned, you can come up and come down countless times—but only through sober (religious) *practice* can you harness and sustain a sense of expanded awareness and elevation. I remember being sad at the end of my first shroom trip because I wanted to experience that quality of presence and mysticism on my own, not with outside assistance. Maybe Judaism, the language of my soul, was the place to look?

Without consciously realizing or articulating it, I began to query what it meant to be a Magic Jew. Perhaps "magic" was the denomination that could offer me a new Jewish paradigm, rooted in healing and authentic, accessible spiritual connection?

The heimish essence runs thick as an undercurrent through the realm of the Magic Jews. Heimish is a way of life, and a mentality, rooted in the word for "home."

It's heimish to invite a stranger in for Shabbos dinner; it's heimish to take the bus from Williamsburg to Monsey, where a *mechitza* separates men and women and the bus driver speaks Yiddish. It's heimish to eat the traditional stew called *cholent*—a culinary mix and metaphor of everything in one. The psychedelic experience itself has elements of heimishness to it too, in that it may connect your soul back to its home in the body, and sheds light on that sense of cosmic oneness and connection to community—especially if you're tripping in a Jewish setting or on a holiday.

It's this psychedelic notion of oneness—the concept that's so central to the "mystical experience," to the entheogenic experience, and to Jewish theology (there is one G-d; *Adonai Echad*)—that connects us back into an integrated unitive whole, comprised of ourselves, our community, and ultimately the Divine. How could so many disparate things in the world actually be One? Rather than pose the question, attempting to intellectualize it, maybe we're better off just experiencing it through the body. The daily practices that remind us who we are enable us to use our bodies to harness spiritual insights, providing us with rituals to consistently ground our highs, and giving us opportunities to incorporate community ethos. I'm not talking about far-out stuff, but rather the most accessible embodiment of prayer: *shuckling*, yoga, wrapping *tefillin*, washing your hands before you break bread, or using your lips to say *Sh'ma* and *Modeh Ani* every night and morning—*brachot* and religious practices that hold the magic in mundane activities like eating, going to sleep, waking up, and everything in between. That's what encompasses the kaleidoscope of the Jewish and psychedelic experience.

Chapter 13

MEETING SOUL FAMILY I'D KNOWN FOREVER

By serendipity, I would come to meet the Magic Jews themselves, the very characters featured in Hamilton's article. In a class called "Journalism of Ideas," my professor—an award-winning author and contributor to magazines like *The New Yorker*—encouraged me (and gave me honors on account of it) to pursue whatever far-out ideas sparked my interest—and so I returned to the questions that first came to me when I met Benzi and Hershy, but which in my first semester I thought would raise too many eyebrows.

I queried Facebook, seeking anyone who knew anything about the intersection of Judaism and psychedelic experience. Two people—Lex Pelger, a drug researcher/writer whom I met through Brooklyn's psychedelic scene, and Marissa Nuckels, who hosted Tel Aviv's Kabbalat Shabbat potlucks—both tagged a fellow named Yoseph Needelman.

Yoseph grew up in South Williamsburg not among, but adjacent to the Chassidim. Now he lived on a moshav near Jerusalem. Known among his friends as "Crazy Yoseph," publicly he was best known for his book *Cannabis Chassidis: The Ancient and Emerging Torah of Drugs*. The book's tagline asks and answers in Yoseph's signature style: "Is marijuana kosher? Yes, of course it is. But the better question is: If I am going to get higher than high, isn't there some useful, traditional guidance about how to best do so? And if not, then what good is the Torah?"

One of my greatest inspirations and a dear friend, Yoseph is my spirit animal—part hippie-part intellectual, brilliant, funny, and lighthearted, last seen in a reggae-style knit hat/beanie/yarmulke, known for his mishmashed stews made of any and all leftovers, and adored by those who can appreciate his winding, Aquarian, philosophical discourse. Psychedelic Judaism incarnate, he's an ecstatic dancer, famed among his *chevra* for doing a naked rooftop Shabbos in his 20s with an old school crew known as Gefilte or "Jahfilte."

It's like that Dali quote, "I don't do drugs, I am drugs." That's Yoseph; you need to be on a level to get him, then to love him, but once you're there it's almost like a litmus test as to how much you've actually tuned in to the Jewish psychedelic vibration.

When I had my first video call with Yoseph one afternoon from an East Village cafe, we discussed *all the things*, but he was in Israel, and I needed to connect with locals in New York. Reaching into his Jahfilte rolodex, he told me I had to meet Aaron Genuth.

◄▼►

From the first moment I met Aaron and Yitzchak, I was enchanted. April 17, 2015. Upon first sight of the duo, what Aaron—donning his Mets cap, plain T-shirt, and skinny jeans—lacked in aesthetic weirdness (at least for someone I was supposed to interview about Judaism and psychedelics), Yitzchak made up for in his long curly hair and outstretched arms, as they walked toward me on Columbus Avenue, as if greeting an old friend they hadn't seen in a while.

Upon those first hugs, I knew I'd met my soul family—people, neshamas I'd already known for a very long time, especially Aaron.

Seven years later, as I write this, cross-legged on the couch of an upstate bookstore cafe (shout out to Rough Draft), I text Aaron:

MM: "Hey, this goes without saying, but as I am writing my book, I'm realizing you might be making some appearances. There's obviously no way to describe certain experiences, or my entrypoint into certain things, without including you as a character . . ."

AG: "Hey thanks, I sure hope I'd be mentioned lol, I think you've also said you intended to."

MM: "Yes, I totally intend to. I mean, it's a reported journalistic piece, and it's also a memoir, with sections about my family and other stuff. I guess there's a weird, heimish, dysfunctional love story in there too. But I'll try to make us look as not-crazy as possible."

AG: "Why, it's a completely crazy heimedelic love story, and at least one of us was crazy for at least part of it."

That initial meeting with Aaron had been a few weeks in the making as coordinating a time to meet up took its own twists and turns. I thought I'd simply sit down with him for an hour and do an interview, but one thing led to another and our first meeting was on a Friday afternoon, settling into Shabbos. I didn't know anyone else would be there, let alone people who'd come to be fixtures in my life from that day forward. And I didn't realize that I'd end up staying through the entire Shabbos dinner until midnight—and then could have hopped the train downtown with Aaron to a party in SoHo with his friends from the fashion scene.

As fate had it, Aaron and Yitzchak—the duo behind that first night's Shabbos meal, and former business partners in a few downtown event spaces and vintage stores, circa 2008, when Yitzchak worked as a runway fashion designer—were also the two main characters in Hamilton Morris's story about the Magic Jews.

While I sat there at the kitchen counter of a messy Upper West Side penthouse (and feral Chassidish crash pad) that I'd arrived at—belonging to an often-absent, in-and-out-of-town businessman, academic, and author of a memoir about his own travels in the "Hasidic underground"—it didn't take long to realize that my relationship to these people wouldn't be, uh, strictly professional. I didn't want to simply report on the scene from a distance. I felt like I was one of them, and knew instantly that these were birds of the same feather I'd grown up with, of my father's ilk. As it turned out, I'd come to learn that Ram Dass himself was friends with Rebs Shlomo Carlebach and Zalman Schacter-Shalomi—major influences in this scene.

Besides, I'd already broken rule number one (don't get high with your sources) when I took a hit of the freshly rolled spliff Aaron had just sparked to keep himself occupied as he dutifully began rolling another spliff for everyone else. I spent the rest of the night slightly cross-faded, hanging out with old friends for the first time.

Remembering I had an assignment for school, I took in the scene. A balding, gap-toothed fellow paced anxiously around the apartment, while another guy in an oversized, white-collared shirt and messy ponytail lounged on the couch, and someone else fuddled with the TV remote, opting to play some Bob Marley from a music channel.

I exchanged an empty glance with the guy on the couch. He and I were the only ones not really *doing anything*, or at least pretending to. "I feel useless," I said. "Can I help somehow?" Yitzchak had begun to mix salmon with kale and sweet potatoes in a pot. He turned to me. "It's okay, you're in Shabbos mode now." It wasn't until Rishe arrived on the scene that things really got going, as she brought with her some fixings for the meal, and a sense of order to the place, giving direction in her thick Australian accent.

I'd been there since around 5, and now it was 9 P.M., and still we hadn't eaten. Yitzchak had finished his cooking duties and disappeared for a while. Dinner was prepared and waiting on the kitchen island, with an assortment of challah. Finally Yitzchak reappeared carrying a small vial of what looked like olive oil.

Aaron switched the music channel to traditional Shabbos niggunim, and a video of a Chassidish rabbi superimposed upon a yellow heaven-like background played from the television. The commotion that had permeated the space for the past few hours settled into a stillness, everyone captivated. Even the constant puffing on joints went on hiatus. Yitzchak stood over the make-shift Shabbos candles (i.e., reappropriated birthday candles) with his eyes closed, eyebrows furrowed, rocking back and forth, lead-ing the prayers in song. I'd seen this type of trancelike state in the HinJew scene, but growing up I had never seen it authentically in Jewish spaces. When it came time to bless the wine, Yitzchak rolled a joint, as well. And following the blessing for challah, he opened the vial of what wasn't olive oil, but cannabis oil to use as a dip. By the time everyone began eating, Aaron switched the music channel, which had been turned off during the ritual, to Simon & Garfunkel.

Despite the fact that no one here was expected to be "keep-ing Shabbos," at least halachically speaking, there was no way I could whip out my computer, which I'd been carrying with me in a worn-out black zippered designer bag, to match my knee-length flowy black dress, black tights, and chunky, black, heeled boots. I was tempted to try for a brief interview with someone there, take notes, holding out whatever hope was left, if it ever existed, for me to play the role of objective reporter, but it just wasn't the vibe; that ship had sailed farther and farther away with each sip of wine. It was Shabbos after all. Work is prohibited on Shabbos. I was fully participating in the ritual, in the sacred container of time, as a Jew, as much as anyone else there.

Still, as I was meeting people who'd arrived for dinner and asked who I was, I explained that I was a journalism student curi-ous about the use of intoxicants in Judaism. "We call them plant medicines," a middle-aged woman with glittery eyeshadow softly corrected me. "The medicine" indeed was running through the veins of the community.

Chapter 14

HEIMEDELIC
LOVE STORY

My heart was so full when I returned home that night; something special had occurred, and we all knew it. I sent Yoseph a message in gratitude for the introduction.

> YN: "Oh good. No one parties and unparties like Aaron Genuth."
>
> MM: "Ha-ha yeah, I'm beginning to see that."

Then he somehow figured it out. I hadn't even figured it out yet.

> YN: ". . . you didn't fall in love, did you? We all make that mistake (sigh). He's like a prince in that way . . ."

In the coming months, I found myself smoking spliffs at Mets games, even though I didn't even follow baseball; accepting invites to Shabbos dinners in Brooklyn or downtown city hangs; barhopping on sticky summer weeknights after I graduated j-school with Aaron and friends he introduced me to.

There was one time Aaron and I switched phone chargers by accident, so I went to meet up with him in Bed-Stuy to make the exchange. He was coming down from an acid trip with a friend, and by the time I had gotten to his friend's house, a light rain had cleared. The charger was at his apartment, a short bike ride away, so in the sweet, crisp air, the reflection of street lamps glistening on the wet, empty pavement, Aaron gave me the seat of the bicycle so I could wrap my arms around him as he pedaled standing up in front of me. *This would be cute if I actually liked him*, I thought to myself.

And yet, there I was falling in love.

Aaron had eight years on me. He was skinny and scruffy, handsome and heimish, charismatic and compelling. He smoked spliffs on almost an hourly basis, tripped on what seemed like, back then, an almost weekly basis, and had a reputation for dating models and fashionistas. From the limited perspective of my fresh and curious 23-year-old self, Aaron bore the wear and tear of his dedication to partying and to anti-capitalism. I admired his values and was greatly influenced by his perspectives—but his lifestyle to me was as nerve-racking as it was fun. He had a soft spot for tequila and what seemed like a commitment to financial struggle, which occasionally manifested in housing insecurity. He came from a traditionally Orthodox family, originally from LA, but moved to the ultra-Orthodox suburb of Monsey after his bar mitzvah. Like the handful of Jewish bad boys I'd come to fall for, he got into psychedelics, along with other mind-altering compounds, and was kicked out of multiple yeshivas—despite being the smartest person in the room. He took a practice LSAT once, and got an almost perfect score on the first shot. In the process of me writing this book some seven years later, he got arrested for every psychedelic under the sun; and classic to his *mazal*, had the case dismissed.

On paper, I didn't think he was a practical option, at least at first. He lived on the edge—too much edge to handle for my own nervous system (and all the trauma I had from my mother threatening us with homelessness). And yet, I was deeply drawn to him anyway. He had a heart of gold, and was one of the most principled people I knew. He was a true feminist, an activist, and obviously we shared the belief that all drugs should be decriminalized. We also both loved being Jewish—and shared a similar sense of religiosity, despite coming from disparate levels of observance.

He taught me a lot about Jewish practice and thought, claiming that because he recognized my potential and where I was coming from, he intentionally guided me into situations that he thought would advance me professionally and personally, hoping that together we could effect positive social change. He was often by my side as I gained exposure to the type of ecstatic Judaism—all of us up till the wee hours of the morning, singing, dancing, clapping our hands, *farbrenging*—that made me wonder if my parents, especially my father, had experienced Judaism like this, would they have gotten more into Chassidis and less into Hinduism?

There are so many tales, so many moments of ritualistic rhapsody that have colored the past decade for me, especially in New York and Israel. One in particular was Baruch's birthday at what became a notorious three-story Park Slope brownstone on Lincoln Place, rented by an often-absent friend of the chevra who let everyone live, party, and hold prayer there. A student of Reb Zalman who had grown up with the Lubavitcher Rebbe, Baruch had just gotten back into town from a "biodynamic" farm in Northern California. Everyone went wild at his birthday Shabbos party, linking arms in a circle to dance ecstatically, singing niggunim together, nearly out of breath from bouncing up and down so much.

In the middle of the party, Aaron led me upstairs for a breather. Dappled light from a streetlamp outside poured through the window into the dark room, our backs on the bed, legs dangling over its ledge as he explained to me a theory of how the shape of a baseball diamond is based on Kabbalah. (Like the men on my mother's side of the family, he was a diehard Mets fan, always rooting for the underdog.) It all felt especially ecstatic, maybe also because earlier that night, Aaron offered for me to dip my fingertip into a plate of molly powder that was going around to a select few. But it wasn't really the molly; this was the vibe around that time in general, even in moments of calm.

There was something so open and nonjudgmental about this chevra, simultaneously both familiar and familial: the way people related to each other, quibbled, laughed, coexisted, came together over Shabbos and the *chagim*, and even became romantically entangled amid a web of incest that was like a dysfunctional family. It felt like the satsang.

One thing led to another, and Aaron and I had an on-and-off fling over the course of almost two years that led to us dating for several more. But because we had a personal relationship, I felt, according to my journalistic ethics, that I couldn't, shouldn't, feature him as a source in any article I might write about Judaism and psychedelics. Plus, I thought there was something sacred about the underground—and wanted to keep it that way. Not until we broke up did I feel I could mention him and his community organizing work, when relevant, in a few first-person articles. Still, this dynamic remains a central tension in our ongoing friendship, and one I hope acknowledgment in this book might resolve. He is, and always will be, after all, one of the best friends I'll ever have.

To his credit, Aaron understood the NYC media scene very well—as well as he grasped the heimish underground. His dynamic sensibilities and multifaceted Gemini nature were part of why we got along so well.

The Jewish counterculture lit me up. Aaron had shepherded me into his world, giving me a strong foundation from which to understand the ideas and experiences I'd come to navigate as I sought to more deeply understand the essence of what it is to be a "Magic Jew."

Chapter 15

REPORTING ON "JEWS AND DRUGS"

Contrary to the bleak predictions of my career counselor, I graduated j-school into a brief unpaid internship with the trendy *PAPER Magazine* (the one where Kim Kardashian broke the Internet), under the tutelage of an editor I'd later come to work with at *Playboy*, before I quickly accepted a paying summer fellowship with *The Forward*, a 100-year-old English-Yiddish newspaper. I used my press cred as an opportunity to interview Jewish "celebrities" (in my eyes), like the then-up-and-coming Yemenite–Israeli sister trio A-WA, or the "Kirtan Rabbi" Andrew Hahn, who leads Hebrew prayer in kirtan style of call-and-response.

At the same time, I was seeking a home for a story I had written in my Magazine Feature Writing class about New York State's budding medical marijuana industry. Having grown up in California's weed scene, I was curious about what cannabis policy looked like across the country. Reporting on weed in New York presented both a comfortable familiarity with the subject matter, as well as a fresh challenge, as I worked my ass off to connect with every relevant source I could find on the topic. Despite the fact that a few of the cannabis industry folk I interviewed recognized the last name Margolin, the connections I made came from my own hustle.

I pitched the story to a *Village Voice* editor I had met at a career fair and who had taken a liking to me. He not only accepted the article—which eventually ran as a cover story several months later—but offered me a summer gig (which became full time after I completed my *Forward* fellowship) reporting on cannabis for the paper. New York was on the cusp of a legal medical industry. It had taken Assemblyman Richard Gottfried 20 years to get the policy through the state legislature, and it was due to take effect in 2016.

And so I spent the summer reporting on "Jews and drugs" for my two jobs, and exploring their intersection in my personal life, doing "drugs" with Jews. I couldn't tell if I was living for the story, or if the story was simply my life. Nevertheless, it wasn't something to waste time getting confused about. I was laser-focused on making it in journalism. Plus I had loans to start paying back.

Reporting mainly on cannabis, I would say that writing about weed was a means to write about everything else: policy, culture, science, industry, agriculture, and so on. Meanwhile, on the side, I also wrote Jewish culture stories for publications like *Tablet*, *The Times of Israel*, even *The Voice*. I especially loved to cover music—profiles on the all-girls Orthodox punk band Bulletproof Stockings, the Israeli expat jazz musician Yonatan Gat, the Na Nach punk band Moshiah Oi!, or a music festival headlining bands like Zusha or G-Nome Project (and low-lining "medicated" kugel), which my editor dubbed the "Jewish Woodstock."

More and more, I began to notice a lot of overlap between my two beats. My visits back to Israel started to become work trips. Most notably, I got to meet the beloved chemist Raphael Mechoulam (1930–2023), famous for being the first person to isolate THC, in 1964, from a confiscated batch of hashish given to him by the Israeli police force. This was a year *after* he first isolated the non-intoxicating compound cannabidiol, or CBD. Israel, in fact, was leading the world in cannabis science—and still is—with the added bonus that medical marijuana is federally legal (unlike in the States).

Though, it wasn't just Israel. I'd go to a cannabis science and policy conference in New York and notice a plurality of Jewish last names on the panel lineup, or on attendees' name tags. Even

Richard Nixon, father of the Drug War, remarked on this pattern in a 1971 Oval Office conversation with his right-hand man Bob Haldeman: "You know it's a funny thing, every one of the bastards that are out for legalizing marijuana is Jewish. What the Christ is the matter with the Jews, Bob? What is the matter with them? I suppose it's because most of them are psychiatrists."

Contrary to Nixon's assumptions, these conferences and legal or underground weed parties weren't necessarily *all* full of psychiatrists, but the new industry folk weren't the old-school activists I grew up with either: people like my father, one of his best friends Gene Schoenfeld (okay, yes, a psychiatrist, but also a Bay Area advice columnist called Dr. Hip); or hemp activist Jack Herer (the namesake for the popular sativa strain). Instead, some of them were Wall Street types, others young college or business school grads looking to get into legal weed, fashionable influencers from LA or San Francisco posing with bud or pot plants. Still there were also the policy wonks like Amanda Reiman, the growers and extractors who doubled as DJs like Nikka T, or old-school chevra I met through Aaron, like "Sticky" Green, the namesake behind the Berkeley-based cannabis company Doc Green's, along with Zev, who ran a successful greenhouse company with national reach out of his spot in Berkeley. Sticky and Zev, who both became friends of mine, had known each other since they were teenagers, frum rebels from Flatbush who'd since traversed both Israel and California.

I grew curious about the phenomenon of why so many Members of the Tribe are, as my dad would say, "jokers, smokers, and midnight tokers." So when I queried the "weed kikes" (as alt-right newspaper *The Daily Stormer* once called them in an article about their opposition to Jeff Sessions as attorney general) many told me the same thing: *tikkun olam*, and trauma.

In a political atmosphere that marginalizes the underdog— Muslims, Mexicans, other minorities, drug users, and the economically disadvantaged—"Jews are acutely sensitive to being scapegoated, and drugs are a scapegoat for all sorts of problems," Rick Doblin, the founder of MAPS, told me once in an interview. In the words of Nixon's domestic policy chief John Ehrlichman,

"We knew we couldn't make it illegal to be either against the war or black, but by getting the public to associate the hippies with marijuana and the blacks with heroin, and then criminalizing both heavily, we could disrupt those communities. . . . Did we know we were lying about the drugs? Of course we did."

As for the trauma piece, maybe it's obvious that Jews are self-medicating generations of inherited and lived trauma—which is why stats indicate at least 30 percent of Israelis—a population of military vets and a "nation of Stoners" according to *Haaretz*—have tried weed within any given year.

But Dartmouth Jewish studies professor Shaul Magid sees it a bit differently. One of my favorite people to interview, Magid always sees the bigger picture: "Things like smoking marijuana, not so much today, but in its time, was considered to be deviant behavior," he once told me in an interview. And the Jewish tendency to deviate, the Jewish role among the counterculture, he said, grew out of a broader tradition of Jewish involvement in the left—in European socialism, Marxism, and anarchism.

Chapter 16

A TASTE OF BUBBE'S KOOL-AID

On my own in NYC, I found myself on two simultaneous tracks of seeking and escape, partying and prayer. In the months following that fateful Shabbos dinner on the Upper West Side—the night that changed everything—I was totally enchanted, while feeling existential about where life was going. Jewishly, I was lit up; professionally, I didn't have a "plan" for how I'd "make it" in journalism. On both fronts, I was simply going where a combination of intuition, serendipity, and the hidden hand of G-d led me.

During this era, there was also a certain magic in the air that was palpable to all of us. It was high times, and I was energetically open to experiences that would speak directly to my neshama, carving out a *derech* I didn't even fully realize I was on. "You know that thing, that twinkle in the eye, that spark that everyone has?" Rishe once probed me. "It's the medicine." Everyone was drinking the Kool-Aid, and I wanted a taste.

My first invitation to do ayahuasca came not long before the ceremony was scheduled to happen. As much as I craved the experience, I was scared shitless. I hadn't done a classical psychedelic, like LSD or shrooms, in three years, following one particularly traumatizing trip—the first time I did acid—in Berkeley, August 2012. During the trip, I got into an anxious loop of fearing I'd "never come back," which was only exacerbated when a friend's boyfriend told me that after his first trip, he dropped out of school and moved to Santa Cruz.

And so, returning to "the medicine," I wished I'd had more time to "mentally" prepare. It wasn't until a few years later that a friend and Indigenous-trained medicine man—a formerly Orthodox Jew from Flatbush serving plant medicine out of his Bushwick apartment—put it to me frankly in his thick Brooklyn accent: "You don't need to 'mentally' prepare." The head isn't where it's at, but rather in the heart.

Besides, once I'd received the invitation to ceremony, the consciousness of the medicine had already begun to permeate my psyche, seeping into the heartspace upward from my gut. By now, I truly believe that the moment you start to explore the possibility of taking a psychedelic is when the experience actually starts. You take a keener look at your life, you start to ask yourself different questions, searching more deeply for answers, and (hopefully) you evaluate your set and setting.

I spent the next two days in emotional anguish, that cleansing kind of brokenheartedness, sobbing, journaling, investigating *why* I was still so called to do this. *But seriously?* I wasn't going to miss the opportunity; it was the psychedelic Jewish experience I'd been after this whole time. It felt like fate was pulling me to ceremony, so much so that I didn't have much choice in the matter.

Ayahuasca is often personified as "Grandmother," but as Aaron—who's mostly abstained from the ceremony scene—joked, with this crew, it would be more accurate to call it "Bubbe." The ceremony took place in the basement-level salon of Lincoln Place. Shiva, our "shaman"—of half-Hindu, half-Indigenous South American descent—had been described as a "cowboy," a man of few, yet wise words, which were wont to spill out in a gruff monotone. He was seated opposite the fireplace, and beside him was Yitzchak, wearing a *kittel* and native beaded *gartel*. Pillows, blankets, and backjacks were set up in a circle around a Persian carpet, at the center of which was adorned with feathers, rattles, a *rapé* applicator, candles, flowers, other precious religious tchotchkes, and of course a pitcher of thick, brown brew and a few shot glasses.

Rishe, who was sitting near me, offered a few guidelines for the ceremony: Don't talk to other people; try to sit up straight the entire time, since the medicine could wash over you if you lie down; drink the brew when it's your turn, but no, you don't have to keep up with everyone as they keep drinking throughout the night; do contribute, lend your voice, lend your song; unlike tripping on shrooms or acid, there would be no opportunity for journaling *during* the ceremony; just sit, "just pray."

The common wisdom around here seemed to be, when in doubt, "just pray." Or as Shiva often said, "It's not about the quantity of the medicine, but the quality of the prayer."

At the time, I hardly knew what that meant. To praise G-d, to have faith in him? To repeat a scripted line in Hebrew from a siddur? I couldn't even understand half of what the words meant (not that there isn't merit to the meditation of reading and pronouncing the sounds anyway).

Now I appreciate that it can be simpler than any of that. In fact, my lack of quality Jewish education might even make it easier for me to do as Rebbe Nachman prescribes: *hisbodedus*—speaking freely to G-d from the heart, as if talking to a best friend. And still, it's taken me years to attempt this, let alone practice it, daily no less, in earnest. But ayahuasca in particular has helped because, in essence, I've found it to be a lubricant for prayer: Feeling stuck? In a loop? Scared? Happy? Nauseated? Feeling like the medicine has backed you into a corner facing your own mortality? Just pray. In situations like that, it feels like there's nothing else to do anyway. Ask G-d (for) what you want. That's the point of an entheogen anyway—a substance evoking a spiritual experience: it puts you in touch with G-d and with your core self—your neshama—such that you realize those two things aren't actually so disconnected.

Sensing my nerves, Rishe handed me one of the several books she had brought with her (*why did she bring books she wouldn't be able to read?* I wondered, considering that maybe she merely wanted their energy nearby). She handed me a six-inch navy-blue hardcover, with etched silver lettering—עֲנֵנִי—*Aneni: Special Prayers for Special Occasions*. I hardly opened the book, but clutched onto it throughout the night as if holding on to dear life, as if it were the only stable grounding I had as the rest of me was floating up into the unknown psychonautic ethers. The words, the *tehillim*, contained within the book were ancient, rooted in tradition. And I found Judaism—in this blue book, in the context of the ceremony—to be grounding.

Aneni—G-d, answer me.

When I was called up to drink my first cup, there was no taking a microsip of the brew and handing the rest back to Shiva. I had to finish what he'd given me; the custom amount he intuited would be the right dose.

"You don't trust the medicine," he told me. *Correct, why should I?* I responded internally. How could I be confident that I wouldn't freak out, or that my perspective wouldn't change so radically that I'd be forever alienated from the life I held dear? And yet, so what if I didn't trust the medicine? Was it that the medicine had to earn my trust, or was the onus of blind faith in it on me?

Once I'd swallowed "the medicine," there was no going back. I felt like the rest was in G-d's hands. I tried to console myself: G-d wouldn't lead me here, compel me to drink ayahuasca, if it weren't ultimately for the good—because G-d's intentions are for the best. *Bitachon*. It really did feel like a leap of faith, a spiritual experience just by virtue of putting myself in this position. "What's happening to me right now is the best possible thing that could be happening to me," I told myself, echoing the mantra that my father had scribbled onto a Post-it, and taped to his bathroom mirror. I convinced myself that G-d wouldn't let me fuck up my life. Bitachon, bitachon, bitachon.

The first few times I did ayahuasca, once a year over the course of three summers (until I changed my rhythm), are all somewhat blended together in my memory.

I remember a Conservative-ordained rabbi was present for at least one of the ceremonies—someone with a real job and a young family to feed, or in other words a functional adult who'd been drinking the Kool-Aid and hadn't lost his mind yet. He was a safe space for me, and became a good friend in the years to come.

I remember we sat once in ceremony on Shabbos, Friday night, which also felt safe—tuning in to this container of sacred *time out of time*, wrapped in the nurturing blanket of the *Shechina* (the Divine Feminine expression of G-d, because after all, Judaism personifies Shabbos as both a bride and a queen).

As I've come to understand it through the writings of Rabbi Abraham Joshua Heschel—who describes the Jewish Sabbath as a "palace in time"—over Shabbos we are meant to divert our attention from quotidian matters of space—materialism, consumerism, possession, dominion over property—in favor of dipping into the eternal wellspring of time. He refers to Rabbi Hayim of Krasne, who calls Shabbos the *ma'ayan*, or fountainhead of eternity, "the well from which . . . the world to come takes its source."

The *real* reality is the infinite, the eternal, the intangible matter of the universe, everything and nothing all at once, the all-expansive Divine. Or in more secular terms, as the poet William Blake put it, which writer Aldous Huxley made psychedelically famous, "If *the doors of perception* were cleansed, everything would appear to man as it is, Infinite." As such, on Shabbos, Heschel writes, we're called to engage with the eternal spirit, "to turn from the results of creation to the mystery of creation; from the world of creation to the creation of the world. . . . [The Sabbath] is not a date, but an atmosphere. . . . Spirit in the form of time."

What really gets me is that on Shabbos, it's a sin to be sad—and so, if I'm doing a psychedelic within this container, it automatically informs my set and setting. In fact, Shabbos becomes the set and setting—the setting being obvious as a surrounding atmosphere, but the set being more important and resonant as not just a state of mind, but as Heschel put it, the climate of *being* altogether. Shabbos is the ultimate "be here now"—because being here now is the ultimate timeless transcendence, rooting us into the infinite depth of the moment.

And so doing ayahuasca on Shabbos, for the first time in my life, I was able to feel the energy of this holy day in a way I never had before. Literally. The brew puts you in your body like other medicines don't, maybe because for at least half the journey, you're reckoning with a fluttering heart, *shpilkes*, thirst, or nausea—which might culminate various times throughout the night in purging or "getting well," before all of that lifts, the jolt to the nervous system settling into bliss, bringing you home to yourself, only to realize you actually never left, you just didn't *feel* it before.

Often, the purge might be related to something deeper, some trauma stored somatically in the body; and it comes out in the physical form of vomit. It's this relationship between body, psyche, and soul that psychedelics put so well into relief, and on Shabbos no less, which, as Heschel writes, is "a day that ennobles the soul and makes the body wise."

After my first cup of the brew, I remember going back to my seat and trying to meditate, gripping onto *Aneni* (which I've brought with me to almost every ceremony and psychedelic trip since). In my head, I repeated the words, *"here and now, boys, here and now,"* borrowed from Aldous Huxley's *Island* and which I used in the late Professor Americ Azevedo's meditation class at Berkeley. Another time, I used the mantra *Na Nach Nachma Nachman Meuman* to channel the wisdom of Rebbe Nachman, who encourages us to harvest joy from the hard work of shifting our perspective to see everything as for the good. Thanks to my associations and experiences with it, there's no way I could think of Na Nach and not feel a sense of happiness.

It was all so *matim*, after all, sitting in ceremony those first few times with a Hindu shaman, singing a combination of (mostly) niggunim, chants I knew from kirtan, and some Indigenous South American *icaros*. But it was the Jewish music especially, even if I didn't learn all the words in childhood, that I *knew*, and ultimately which helped me, in conjunction with the medicine, connect most deeply back to myself. I was flying and rooting all at the same time. I saw my life, my family, as if in a snow globe. Precious, peaceful, and beautiful all at once.

Chapter 17

CHASSIDISH
SUMMER OF LOVE

I was glowing in the weeks, even months, following each of those first few times doing ayahuasca, about once a year apart. As one returns to the same prayers every day, or the same holidays as the seasons roll around, it's the thing that stays the same—the tradition and the ritual—that serves as the control, helping us to measure how *we've* changed in the interim, and who we are each time we cyclically *return*.

Over four years of living in New York since I'd initially come for grad school, I had found a home within the friendships that I'd forged along the way, including a handful of women I had met through Aaron who became like sisters to me.

By 2018, I had cycled through four apartments, written for no less than a dozen news outlets, and had grown immeasurably into the life that *hashgacha pratis* had in store for me. In winter months, I'd spend Shabbos at cozy get-togethers, dozens piling into a Brooklyn apartment to sing, feast, and schmooze. And over the summer, the weekends became busy with music festivals and Shabbos camping trips upstate into the Catskills. It was a formative period in which I was introduced to people and ideas that would help me evolve in my relationship to religion, love, and other drugs (as the saying goes).

But mostly, I was learning about myself, using journalism as a method to engage in situations I was curious about but had no official "excuse" to explore, to talk to people I'd have been too shy to otherwise approach, and to start conversations that might have been deemed too provocative, were they not for the sake of an interview. At the same time, through a journalistic lens, I was always able to maintain a position of one foot out, one foot in; curious and amused from an objective perspective; soulfully nourished on a personal level. I always knew I would write a book; and in collecting quotes for articles I had written over the past 10 years, I was simultaneously collecting experiences that would shape the narrative of this story and my life. And each time I tripped, I only gained more insight into and conviction about the path that I was on. As one psychonaut who goes by "Mincha" once put it, "Psychedelics make you more you."

Coming from a guy like Mincha, it had to be true; he looks like an old-school rebbe (belly, beard, *bekeshe*, *shtreimel*, and all), speaks Yiddish, and is totally frum—but he's a rapper and a baal teshuva from the South, who has the sensibilities of and sounds more like a regular American than any of his heimish peers with their Yiddish accents and limited experience of the world outside New York. A rolling stone, blitzed out on acid the majority of the times I've run into him, Mincha and I first met at one of these heimish psytrance festivals in the Catskills that happen almost every weekend of every summer—the ones that Benzi had told me about during my first week of j-school.

Under the moonlight, I saw him dealing acid out of a siddur, while I observed other partygoers blend rituals like wearing tefillin while dancing to techno, or preserving pounds of gefilte fish inside beer kegs.

I'd often arrive to these festivals just before *shkia*, squeezed into the back seat of a car filled with camping supplies, hotboxed with weed smoke, Hershy and crew shooting the shit in Yiddish, competing with the blasting volume of psytrance as we'd cruise along Route 17, passing green open fields dotted with yellow goldenrods, abandoned farmhouses, and Yiddish billboards, speaking to the droves of Chassidim who make the summer exodus from Brooklyn to the Borscht Belt (as the region was once called), populating bungalow colonies and filling out otherwise empty towns like Woodbourne.

I didn't go camping so much as a kid, and often sat out the camping trips my Berkeley friends would invite me to because I wasn't so enthusiastic about the outdoorsy component back then. So it came as a surprise, even to me, when my favorite part of living in New York became leaving the city, heading upstate to nature.

But it wasn't only the nature I was after; in the woods, under the twinkling stars—easier to see up there than back home in Brooklyn—Shabbos just hit differently.

Letting my phone die or stashing it away in my tent for the whole weekend, away from the distractions of a Friday night in NYC, a little wine tipsy, and hearing the yearning cries of the davening, everyone singing together (in a way where they actually understood the words) completely transformed my sense of Shabbos—on an embodied level. Plus, unlike the city that beckons you to be here, there, and everywhere—for this meal, or that chill—in nature there's no temptation to be anywhere but right here and now. Spending the duration of the whole 25 hours or longer at the same campsite, outdoors, tracking the movements of the sun, and counting the stars to signal the bookends of Shabbos gave me a different insight into the way Shabbos could *feel*.

Everyone around me was often *on something* at these festivals, but I was usually pretty moderate with my drug use—high from simply being there, high from dancing, high *on Shabbos*. In later years, I'd go with a crew of close friends and we'd trip together, but in the beginning of my time on this scene, I was mostly just interested in taking it all in.

Sometimes the kids would put on a whole festival at a camping site with a big barn house where forested hills surrounded a lake; other times, they'd rent the grounds at Bethel Woods, the site of the original Woodstock; and still on other occasions, they'd simply take over a big property and crash wherever there was room—on mattresses in a house halfway through renovations; in hammocks; in tents nestled in the thickets behind the house or in the open, grassy yard often muddy from dew or summer rain. I usually brought my own tent, but once a couple girlfriends and I crashed in sleeping bags on top of mattress pads in the wooden attic of a barn house, quaint with the smell of musk and dimly lit with rainbow-colored fairy lights. For most people, however, sleeping wasn't a primary concern at these things anyway; mostly they were up partying the entire weekend.

One time I remember sitting in the corner of a barn house with Hershy and Aaron, observing a skinny musician with long hair call out, "Who has medicine?" *Interesting word choice,* I thought to myself, noticing that even here the kids might be using drugs not only to get fucked up, but maybe to get a little fixed up too— because, in my experience, partying in community, supporting each other in what might come up during a trip—especially when everyone comes from such a specific background that they can relate to each other's struggles—has been just as healing (or even more so) than "medicine ceremonies." *On the other hand,* I thought to myself, *maybe the term "medicine" has just become a mainstream euphemism, and is being thrown around way too much, bypassing the nonchalant or abusive ways people can use drugs.*

Either way, the request made its way over the raucous Shabbos dinner table, scattered with plastic plates of half-eaten gefilte fish, hummus, and ripped up loaves of challah. A guy with long hair, a long beard, and a white Na Nach yarmulke that fit like a beanie said he had ketamine, but the medicine-seeker was looking for shrooms. It took only a second for someone else to make an offer.

"It's like the sixties, but for the Jews," Hershy whispered into my ear. *Say what?* He has a thick Yiddish accent, and I could hardly hear him over the garage band belching out niggunim. "You know," he reiterated, "it's like the Summer of Love, but by the Chassidim."

In the decade since I began hanging out with these holy rebels, the heimish psychedelic fringe has only blossomed and become more crystalized. What's happening today is like a reincarnation of what happened with the followers of Rebs Zalman and Shlomo Carlebach during the '60s and '70s, but here, rather than psychedelics turning once-secular people on to religion, seekers coming from religious backgrounds are using psychedelics to arrive at a more peaceful and reconciled relationship to G-d and to Judaism—vis-à-vis themselves. They're not using psychedelics to become less religious per se (although some of them had already made that leap before they found "the medicine"), but they're returning to the original essence of what they say Chassidis is all about.

As one friend, Yitzy Schwartz, described to me, echoing many others with a similar sentiment, psychedelics helped him better understand what the founder of the Hasidic movement was getting at: "What the Baal Shem Tov meant to teach was for people to understand what I saw, but without the technology of LSD."

With Yiddish as a first language, he described his younger self as "very frum," attending yeshiva 14 hours a day, following all the rules, and studying Torah—but when he entered adulthood, he began to question what actually gave meaning to the Hasidic rituals that for him were so routine, not to mention mandated. And so, he drifted off the *derech*, so to speak, and into atheism—that is, until he got into acid and mushrooms at these upstate festivals. "It went from 'This has to be something requiring faith' to 'I saw it and there's no question,'" he told me in an interview for an article I wrote about this heimish festival scene. Psychedelics affirmed Yitzy's belief in "G-d as spirit, [not] as the almighty with rules about things that he doesn't want you to do, [but rather that] G-d is in everything and there's G-d within all of us."

This concept of G-d that Yitzy described reminded me of the way I was raised to believe in G-d too. As a young child, my father, especially, taught me to see G-d in everything—in the sky, in the trees, even in inanimate objects, all manifestations of G-d and Divine will. Yet at the same time, in Hebrew school, through tales of the Torah, I was simultaneously taught to believe in the old man in the sky, watching over and judging us. He knew everything we did and thought, and as my mother liked to guilt us, was especially observant of our actions in advance of Yom Kippur, the Day of Atonement.

Still, as much as I believed that G-d was always looking out for my best interest, I didn't come away unscathed—albeit far less religiously traumatized than some of my Hasidic-raised counterparts. "What if G-d won't watch over me because I hate Hebrew school?" I wrote in my journal at the age of 12. "Am I a good person?"

I largely connected to G-d through fear—fear of the world from which I sought out his protection, and fear of G-d himself. I knew G-d was always present, and in everything I saw and experienced, but the Judaism it seemed that I and my Hasidic friends alike were raised with didn't necessarily emphasize a connection to G-d through, well, fun—even though, in some ways, that was part of the Baal Shem Tov's point.

When I learned about the roots of the Hasidic movement, founded by the 18th-century Rabbi Yisrael ben Eliezer, a.k.a the Baal Shem Tov or the "Besht" for short (literally meaning "master of the good name"), I was immediately inspired by the way the core of Chassidis encouraged finding magic within the mundane, infusing everyday activities of the body—eating, singing, making love, hanging out, being in the moment—with a sense of something sacred. "This chill let a Jewish world stay as pious as ever, if not more so, all the while having a great time," Yoseph Needelman writes in *Cannabis Chassidis*. Drinking, smoking, dancing, clapping, straight-up breathing became avenues for *yichudim*—unifications (with the Divine).

Partying became a prayer in and of itself. Getting high was holy. Regular people had the opportunity for righteousness. Laymen were now *leibedik*. As Yoseph so aptly put it, central to the Chassidish mentality—most expressed in the holiday of Purim—was the idea that "sometimes it might be better to get fucked up than to be fucked up."

In reaction to the bookish, academic, dry form of Litvish Judaism that was popular at the time, for the original Chassidim, serving G-d was a primary matter of the heart, rather than just the mind. Through joyful embodiment, rather than just cerebral study, everything became an opportunity for holiness, for elevation, sometimes even trancelike states.

The Besht made it his job to spend time with simple working people *in* villages throughout the region that is now Ukraine, learning how they connected to G-d. A movement grew around him, based on the idea that one need not be a rabbi, a prestigious, learned Torah scholar, or an advanced Kabbalist to mediate a person's connection to the Divine. The prayers of a simple person could be just as powerful.

The job of Chassidis was to undo what Joseph Campbell warned about when he said that "religion often gets in the way of religious experience." Nowadays, Yitzy said, in the heimish psychedelic festival scene, "people are looking at religion and making it work for them, not the other way around. They realize religion is meant to make your life happier."

And just maybe that's what I stumbled into upstate on these camping trips, or even among the "Magic Jews" in Brooklyn. Back in that barn house, on one of countless such occasions, the energy was wild and ecstatic. One guy was doing ketamine on a blow-up couch, another guy with spots of wine on his white collared shirt was offering to pour for everyone else, and a third guy—a mid-20s musician and low-key mystic from Williamsburg, dressed in white jeans and a crisp white sweatshirt, was telling me how he likes to take ketamine, hit the dance floor, and talk to G-d, or to run into the forest and scream out the Sh'ma.

There was often little order to the Shabbos meals themselves, as everyone would swarm toward the potato kugel and meats; fold-up tables covered in plastic would become bedecked with loaves of challah that no less than a dozen people each had stuck their hands into, not to mention the spillage of dips—tomato, onion, olive, garlic, dill—all delicious, all made from canola oil or mayonnaise, often with a splash of sugar. This cuisine would be cringe to anyone who's into "clean eating," especially because greens are mostly absent; but if you were looking for heimish soul food, you'd need to look no further.

I once observed one girl with long blonde curls, a soft angelic face, and a floor-length blue tie-dyed dress with a *shell* underneath sing out to the crowd, never mind *kol isha*. It was revolutionary in a way.

Everyone here had such a specific and unique look, like the blending of North Williamsburg fashion sense with South Williamsburg tradition. Some guys had skinny *peyos* pushed behind their ears; thick, rimmed hipster glasses; tight jeans; subtle tzitzis hanging out beneath patterned collared shirts. Others looked like they'd been shipped in from Tzfat, wrapped in blankets, white tzitzis on top of all white clothes, or otherwise tie-dyed tzitzis or DIY made from a colorful rewoven blanket or pashmina scarf.

In the middle of a meal, it wouldn't be uncommon for one of the guys from the Breslov crew—bearded, with long hair, beanie, skinny jeans, hemp amulet necklaces, with something of a hip-hop feel—to scream out suddenly and randomly over the chatter of the room: "Na Naaaaaaaacchhhhhhhhhh!!!!" Everyone would stop what they were doing and join in, screaming in unison, "Na Naaaaaaaaaaachhhhhhhhhh!!!!!" Then, as if nothing happened, the room would erupt back into a fervent frenzy.

At these weekend events, some people would keep Shabbos (according to halacha, or Jewish law), while others would be playing psytrance by their tents all night. The *chiddush*, or novelty, was that everyone was doing their own thing, doing Judaism in their own way, but still doing it together. On one Shabbos morning, I saw someone unravel a Torah scroll underneath a camping tarp, while psytrance music blasted from a parked car in muddy grass nearby. One guy in full Chassidish garb even shuckled to the beat. The intention all around, it seemed, was a collective one: connection, no matter the method—to self, to community, to nature, to Source.

It's with a full cup that I would return home every weekend, grimy with the scent of smoke in my hair, Birkenstock-clad feet covered in dirt, exhausted yet invigorated from staying up all night singing niggunim around a campfire, watching the sparks ascend toward the moon, or dancing for hours with my Hula-Hoop as psychedelic beats echoed into the dark of the forest.

This is the stuff I live for.

And to be honest, I've found such weekends just as cathartic and soul-cleansing as these premeditated, intentional ceremonies. Maybe, in some cases, even more so.

Because, let's get one thing straight: there's no "right way" to have a psychedelic experience (or for that matter, a religious one, either). If your intention is to feel a sense of "healing" or "spirituality," as is often the case for ceremony goers, partying might offer these aspects too, especially when the *set and setting* is Shabbos, another holiday, or another situation otherwise curated with care and purpose. That doesn't mean partygoers have to keep Shabbos or practice it in an agreed-upon way—but the appreciation for what Shabbos is (for the collective and the individual) gives the recreational atmosphere a degree of meaning.

Or, even more simply put, having fun can be healing, and the healing "work" that one does in a psychedelic ceremony or clinical or therapeutic setting (such as lying down with headphones and an eye mask) can also have elements of fun. I've even considered that calling it "work," and subsequently acting like it can't be fun on account of it, is a capitalist notion, feeding into antiquated, industrialist, even corporate paradigms of "work culture." If we are truly to decolonize our minds, and our culture—using psychedelics, and, not to mention, Chassidis—then it needs to start with the nature of the psychedelic work, or undertaking, itself. In Hebrew, *avodah*, which also means "work," refers to the dedicated worship, ritual, and spiritual efforts we put in to connect with G-d, and which I'd argue have helped me personally deconstruct the square concept of "work" in favor of something more joyful, playful, and ecstatic—within the context of personal purpose.

In the "medicine" world, I've noticed the culture may teeter on pretension if everyone takes things too seriously; not that the medicine shouldn't be treated as sacred, in a reverent way—but let's not forget, we're dealing with matters of the soul. Not even Yom Kippur, the most "serious" of all Jewish holidays, is meant to be so solemn. So my question to those I've observed taking "the medicine" so frequently and so seriously that it borders on *avodah zarah*—idolizing the substance, saying things like "Grandmother told me this," and treating it as the be-all and end-all, rather than as simply what it is: a *door* to a path that's outside our habitual ways of thought and feeling—is, why not just *lighten* up a little?

Light is what we're going for anyway, no? If we're truly going to honor the medicine, and our intentions in taking it, then it's our responsibility to walk that path in our sober, mundane life. If Grandmother told you to do something, it's not Grandmother, but that realization you came to on your own (with her nudging) that is the medicine. The consciousness *is* the real medicine. So once we apply that consciousness to our everyday lives, make those changes that Grandmother "told" us about, try that for a while, and we *still* have questions, *then* we can return to ceremony for more "medicine."

And still, despite all this talk of healing and medicine, it is possible to receive *too* much light at once, and shatter one's vessel, and I've seen it happen in the context of all these festivals and ceremonies. Where there's light, there's darkness; but even then, it's important to remember that darkness too comes from G-d.

Chapter 18

GOOD DRUGS, "BAD DRUGS," AND WHEN THE TRIP GOES SOUTH

Weirfield Avenue, Brooklyn. From the outside, the two-story paneled apartment building was rather unassuming, amid the muraled, graffitied Bushwick neighborhood of Dominican families and single hipsters, hanging out on stoops, smoking cigarettes, strutting down the street to the local bar.

The first time I ended up at Weirfield was just a month or so after I'd met Aaron. He was having a barbeque, and in the spirit of his brilliant social engineering, curated an eclectic crowd of old friends—creatives, fashion models, cannabis growers, and goofy Jewish socialites like Daniella, who over the years grew into one of my closest friends.

Aaron didn't live in this apartment alone. It was owned by a Chassidish family who also maintained a dilapidated property upstate that functioned as an unofficial heimish halfway house/ nature refuge, on the basis of not evicting Jews. "The Teyveh," as this notorious Catskills property is known, draws out the under-belly of the fringe Chassidim, its 100 acres having seen everything from forest psytrance parties to all-night jams around a firepit to the highest highs and lowest lows known to this world. At the Teyveh, I've camped out under the stars, frolicked through its field of high weeds and golden rods, jumped into its murky mikveh, helped build a sukkah with "family" from the Rainbow Gathering, smoked CBD out of a crack pipe, listened to the midnight cries of Shabbos davening from throughout the neighborhood, and attempted to befriend its miserable, resident peacock, coocooing at everyone in its way.

In this case, here in Brooklyn, they knew the tenants and let them live there, run an "office" out of there, party there, do drugs there, and G-d knows what else, all for reasonably cheap rent. And lo and behold, who did I run into but none other than Benzi, who lived there with a crew of Chassidish black sheep who'd left their parents' homes in Williamsburg, just a few stops away off the J train.

While there was some intermingling between Aaron's friends and the native Yiddish speakers, the crowds were fairly distinct, and not only because there was at least a 10-year age difference between them (with me somewhere in the middle). While almost everyone here was raised, but no longer practicing, Orthodox, and had some relationship to Chassidis—whether because they grew up with it or they had a hippie exploration moment of going Breslov in Israel during their early 20s—the native English speakers had an advantage that their counterparts didn't—mainly that, due to their education and mainstream sensibilities, they had a shot at making it (or at least more fully participating) in the secular world. There was some solid crossover, sure, but we're talking about different brands of trauma, different kinds of neuroses, different drug cultures, different present-day relationships to Judaism, and—*stam*—different tastes. Aaron loved the Grateful Dead; his roommates loved psytrance.

(I, for one, loved both.)

I'd venture upstairs to say hi to Benzi, and hang out with the other 20-somethings when the old school crew started reminiscing about stuff before my time. The place felt like a dingy dorm for wayward seekers zonked out on ketamine or whatever they could get their hands on, watching videos of Burning Man or Goa Gil psytrance festivals from beanbags on a grimy floor in a dark room. The windows were shut behind blackout curtains, obscuring any light that was still left at the end of a spring day after daylight savings. Still, there was something sweet about it: a total lack of pretension, maybe. The kids were now out in the world—unendingly curious and open to whatever—raising each other along the way and learning how to party. The heimish culture and mentality spilled over the borders of Williamsburg, to wherever those from the heimish *velt* would congregate.

The most telling part, though, was a yellowed wall where the kids scrawled out every drug they could think of in a vertical list, marking the ones they'd done—including compounds like 2C-i or roxies, in addition to "basics" like LSD or magic mushrooms.

Intrigued as I was, I also saw the shadow side of this world. It was nothing I hadn't seen before, though, given the delinquency that graced the halls of Cloyne. I was no stranger to the nerds of Erowid (a '90s-era online drug education encyclopedia), psychonauts with a soft spot for uppers and downers, or the experience-junkies seeking highs to fill the lows of a bottomless existential pit. The "shadow" of either scene wasn't so much about the presence of "hard drugs," but rather about the absence of any discriminating manner when it came to taking any "drug."

I never had a tolerance for psychedelic exceptionalists anyways—people who acted like shrooms, weed, and acid were "good drugs" and coke was a "bad drug." It's one thing to destigmatize psychedelics amid working toward legal reform; it's another to do so at the expense of further stigmatizing other drugs and communities who use them. Worse were the plant medicine exceptionalists, those who only do mushrooms or in some cases, essentially abused ayahuasca—always doing it, never integrating—but frowned upon synthetics like MDMA, acid, or even Adderall. To each their own, I say, as long as you're healthy, functional, and not hurting anyone.

Indeed, any plant, drug, substance, or medicine can be life changing—for better and for worse—depending on how you use

it. From heroin to LSD, people have enjoyed pain relief and transcendence, suffered from dependency and "bad trips." To reiter-
ate the words of my UC Berkeley "Drugs and the Brain" Professor
David Presti, the difference between a medicine and a poison is
simply the dose. He credits Swiss physician and alchemist Paracel-
sus with this adage, writing in his book *Foundational Concepts in
Neuroscience: A Brain-Mind Odyssey* that even substances essential to
human life, like water and oxygen, can be poisonous if taken in
"sufficiently large amounts." Of course, set and setting (i.e., your
state of mind and surroundings when doing a substance) make a
difference too, whether you're talking about meth, mescaline, or
anything in between.

As one of my heroes, Columbia University psychology professor and neuroscientist Carl Hart, once put it: "We're all seeking
to alter our consciousness." Never mind the drug; what matters
is whether a person uses it safely, and that their use doesn't cause
them to hurt others or infringe on meeting their responsibilities,
he told me in an interview.

Often, when drug use is seen as a problem, that perception
(or reality) in part has to do with class: the more disadvantaged
the community, the greater "risk" that "drugs" seem to pose. And
for the heimish fringe, sometimes drugs are indeed a problem—
especially among a demographic with no secular education,
sometimes little money, English as a second language, and those
dealing with a great degree of trauma (from having left the greater
Chassidish community, from religious oppression, from molesta-
tion, which is unfortunately common in the heimish world, and
inherited from elders who survived the Holocaust). As Gabor Maté
has discussed at length, trauma is often at the root of addiction.

And yet, I've observed the downside of what Hart cautioned,
regarding drug use that gets in the way of meeting responsibility. In the coming years, I'd see kids from the heimish fringe go
in and out of rehab for heroin, or spend hours zonked out on
ketamine in some Monsey basement, staying up till sunrise, and
waking up in the afternoon, struggling to find purpose. I'd see
young, free-spirited festival girls get whisked up into predatory

situations, with little accountability or repercussion to the popular, charismatic boys at fault. And I've seen people close to me fall into manic episodes, that, if they weren't caused by psychedelic overuse in the context of difficult life circumstances, they were definitely exacerbated by them. I've made visits to the psych ward and have observed firsthand just how inept our medical system is at handling the very real spiritual and emotional crises that surface when special, brilliant, offbeat souls fail to adjust to the brutal realities of an economic system and social structure that works only for those who can successfully partake in the game of capitalism. And most heartbreaking, I've seen close friends succumb to homelessness and all sorts of instability—in situations where drugs like ketamine, meth, heroin, and acid played no small role—but still, I argue, were not the cause—just a progressive, self-perpetuating symptom.

◂▾▸

I came to observe that the glitz of the Magic Jews had a grimy shadow. Meanwhile, in my own professional life, I dug my heels into the grind on the flip side of what externally looked like a glamorous career in media.

In 2016, when *The Village Voice* was sold during my time working there, the new ownership fired my editors and installed a new staff (as is typical in the event of a sale). I was merely a fresh grad, vying for a long-term position as "staff writer," groomed by my editor Jack Buehrer, who helped me refine my skill and craft, while encouraging me to pursue whatever weirdness inspired me. He noticed my journalistic instinct and helped me find the confidence to hone in on it.

In a matter of months, I was hyperproductive, publishing an average of three stories a week, mainly on cannabis, but also on other cultural events and happenings around the city, from a feature on fashion designer Patricia Field's Bowery showcase to a breaking news story about a Bed-Stuy bank robbery to a trip inside a Bushwick shipping container where hipster culture maker Sheri Barclay ran a DIY radio station called KPISS.

I'd published my first cover story in November 2015—a profile on New York State Assembly Member Richard Gottfried, father of New York's medical marijuana program, who'd paraded the policy since 1996, when California initially legalized medical cannabis— and up next was a cover story on New York's then-burgeoning psychedelic scene. We hired a photographer to capture imagery for the article, which featured an inside take on where NYU's psychedelic research was vis-à-vis the movement on the ground, including the politics of the Brooklyn Psychedelic Society, the psychedelic salons and talks fueling grassroots efforts, underground therapy, and its aftermath for patients.

The story was nearly ready for press when a new editor-in-chief came in. He told me that my drug coverage was too cliché for *The Village Voice*, plus it was passé at this point (never mind that at around the same time, coincidentally, Michael Pollan had published his "Trip Treatment" article with *The New Yorker*, which would set the stage for his seminal psychedelic bestseller, and subsequent Netflix series, *How to Change Your Mind*). The new chief canceled the psychedelic cover story, and my dreams of becoming a *Voice* staff writer dissolved. (Within a few months, I felt vindicated to learn that the then-new editor-in-chief had already been fired; and within a few years, I felt sad to learn that the paper had gone out of print. Little did that editor know how much the cannabis and psychedelic beats would boom.)

There I was less than a year out of j-school, on my own in New York, writhing in existential angst, devastated, questioning why I hadn't gone to law school and pursued something more stable, or at least more lucrative. I was living off the remainder of my student loans, while simultaneously attempting, slowly, to pay them off. The trauma of all those times my mother told me we'd be homeless kicked in. Scared for my future, I was in survival mode.

But I wasn't the only one feeling challenged. There was an agitated energy in the air at the time, simmering within a handful of us. Aaron was worked up about the prospects of Bernie Sanders in the 2016 election, while social politics in the chevra caused divisions that would ultimately shift us all into a new era, which

I experienced as a lull in the magic. This moment in time felt like waking up the morning after a party to its grimy underbelly revealed in the light of day, unshowered, passed out, feral festie kids sliding off ripped leather couches, ketamine dust blanketing the coffee table, anxiously observing this reality as the flip side of fun, and wondering, *Now what?*

My last day at the *Voice* was a Friday, and it softened the blow when I got an invite from Aaron to come for Shabbos that night. He was apartment-sitting in Greenpoint, and had a massive loft and rooftop to himself. I got a little dressed up—as I often do when I feel like shit—donning a velvet top and skinny jeans. It was one of those heimish rowdy vibes, with a good, Aaron-style curation of frum-friendly, frum-escapist, and fashion-goyish invitees, with chitchat about the "problems" at Burning Man and the woes of capitalism, sympathetic ears to my kvetching over the *Voice*, and some jovial "Shalom Aleichem." At a certain point, when everyone began to trickle out, I was invited to stay. Really, I just wanted to feel close to Aaron, but it was also hard for me to see him struggle through heavy psychedelic use and housing instability, which he often balanced with heavy partying.

Channeling my worries into work, I hustled my ass off to meet as many people as I could to keep my career afloat. And yet, it worked; one thing led to another and I'd secured a gig freelancing for *Rolling Stone*. My first story was about the election and where each of the candidates stood on weed. Taking a national focus on cannabis policy—and a subfocus on Jewish culture—I set out to write for as many publications as I could, and filled out a freelance and "permalance" career with stories for *VICE, Playboy, The Times of Israel, Tablet Magazine, High Times Magazine, Merry Jane*, and others. I spent a solid two years writing anywhere between 5 and 20 stories a month, depending on length, working 9- to 15-hour days, making still not much more than $40k. Such is the state of the journalism industry.

Eventually, I'd moved from lower Manhattan to a handful of stops off the 2/3 line in Crown Heights, rode my bike everywhere I could (weather permitting), and spent my weekdays holed up at a dark and dingy cafe in Park Slope, where I'd write for hours, or take calls interviewing sources, and subsist on refillable cups of tea, and whatever meat-free lunch item on the menu would keep me full for the day.

I wanted to be there for Aaron during this time as well, but the edge that he lived on made me nervous—frequently tripping, coupled with challenging life circumstances, made for a tricky recipe. I remembered a guy from college who took something like 20 hits of acid and was tripping for two weeks, shaved off his long brunette mane that he'd worn in a ponytail, and claimed to be Jesus, or something like it, making most in his path deeply uncomfortable. Aaron wasn't taking so much acid at once, and thankfully the only thing he had in common with that guy was that they were both extremely intelligent. And yet I knew that it's the smartest people who are sometimes the most misunderstood. I've always wondered why that is, why someone else's mental disturbance perturbs us more than, say, the sight of someone in physical pain. Perhaps because we all have the capacity to lose our minds. And lord knows when or how it'll happen, which drugs will instigate it.

But there is something that tickles this mania. As Aldous Huxley writes in "Heaven and Hell," the follow-up essay to "The Doors of Perception," "Visionary experience is not always blissful. It is sometimes terrible. There is hell as well as heaven." In other words, just because something feels spiritual, or mystical, it doesn't always mean it feels good, or that it's a positive experience. There's black magic too, and the important thing is knowing the difference, and having the grounding and guidance to steer any mystical experience—be it through psychedelic journeying, or even Kabbalistic meditation—in a direction of contained light.

Chapter 19

"TOO MUCH LIGHT"

When life in New York (and later LA, once I'd briefly moved back there) took its lulls from time to time, I'd dip out and take a trip somewhere—usually Israel, or India on occasion—using the excuse of writing or researching a story as a means of gonzo exploration.

My early experiences at the Chassidish psytrance festivals upstate got me into the musical genre that's beloved by some, hated by many—heard as noise to those who can't get into it. The psytrance scene has something of a gnome-like and elfin flair, and is a bit nerdier than the techno or house scenes popular in the electronic music world. Psytrance can be rapacious and complex, an invitation to dance off angst, and crash into joy. It's a bit like punk rock, a bit like jam band psychedelic rock; more hippie than hardcore.

I love music, but I'm far from a connoisseur, and barely have the vocabulary to describe my own tastes; moreover, I'm equally as interested in the fans of the music as the music itself. It felt like psytrance in particular had dark undertones beneath the glowing, neon patterns of projector lights that often accompanied the DJ sets; and those with a lot of trauma—OTD Chassidim and Israeli veterans—seemed to feed off it the most.

There was something about getting swept up by its sinuous psychedelic beats that, at least in my experience, arrested the monkey mind and let the body shake out the rest. If trauma really does live in the body, then it makes sense that music that inspires dancers to bop up and down in some sort of ecstatic stupor might be unconsciously attractive to those needing that kind of release.

Still, there was a fine line and menacing allure to the whole thing: all at once you could get high from the music, the drugs, or both, and access a sort of lightness of being, a light in general that could massage out the weight of life upon your shoulders—and yet, like a massage with too much pressure, it could also crack your vessel, so to speak, and like a bulb that's burst, it could crack you out.

Observing the interplay of light and dark is really what got me interested in psytrance. And having noticed the obsession with artists like Goa Gil, I wanted to go straight to the source. My curiosity led me to the beachy hippie town of Arambol, on the northside of Goa, India—the psytrance capital of the world—where I met an Israeli traveler named Tomer at the Bayit Yehudit ("Jewish house," run by an Israeli Breslov family). He was one of those tripped-out guys who talks exclusively about lofty spiritual topics, as if he's peaking on acid at all times. If there are "two types of hippies," as Chaim Leib once explained to me, I took him for the party type, but in fact, he was the opposite.

You see, according to Chaim Leib, a Tzfat-based Na Nach who I first met at a Rainbow Gathering in Wisconsin, there are the "cracked-out" hippies who you see at a psytrance party or at the "Shakedown" of a Grateful Dead show—think dreadlocks, whippets, always on the road, and tripping till dawn—and the "sunrise" hippies who have their shit together—think essential oils, strict meditation regimen, vegan food with nutritional yeast, and waking up with the sun. Cracked-out hippies trip; sunrise hippies journey.

I'd falsely assumed that Tomer was a tripper because he seemed like a typical Israeli psytrance fan to me. After all, I met him in the nonstop party that is Goa, which might have the highest psychedelic consumption per capita on earth. But instead, he told me that he'd seen "too much light" and hadn't tripped in a decade. So what could explain his demeanor, I wondered—was he still "there," still in that trippy zone, still integrating it all?

This concept of "too much light" in religious terms, or "spiritual emergence/emergency" in psychological terms, is something both seasoned mystics and psychedelic therapists have cautioned about.

Psychiatrist Stanislav Grof and his wife, Christina Grof, first coined the term "spiritual emergence" in the late 1980s to describe "the movement of an individual to a more expanded way of being that involves enhanced emotional and psychosomatic health, greater freedom of personal choices, and a sense of deeper connection with other people, nature, and the cosmos." However, when this emergence becomes chaotic, confusing, overwhelming, or detached from reality, it becomes known as a "spiritual emergency" to describe this state of crisis. For those suffering from a spiritual emergency, their day-to-day functioning may be impaired or they may experience psychosis. "Occasionally, the amount of unconscious material that emerges from deep levels of the psyche can be so enormous that the person involved can have difficulty functioning in everyday reality," the Grofs write in *The Stormy Search for the Self*. Spiritual emergency could involve "one's entire being" cycling through non-ordinary states of consciousness, intense emotions, visions, sensory shifts, and unusual thoughts, which may revolve around spiritual themes like death and rebirth, oneness with the universe, and encounters with mythological beings.

Stan Grof also coined the term "holotropic" (which literally means "moving toward wholeness") to describe a state in which the ego dissolves and leaves room for the meta cognitive "inner healer" to shine through and do its work. ". . . many of the conditions, which are currently diagnosed as psychotic and indiscriminately treated by suppressive medication, are actually difficult states of a radical personality transformation and of spiritual opening," he writes. "If they are correctly understood and supported, these psycho spiritual crises can result in emotional and psychosomatic healing, remarkable psychological transformation, and consciousness evolution."

Breathwork, meditation, fasting, sleep deprivation, self-flagellation, ecstatic dance, chanting, and psychedelics are all ways to enter into so-called holotropic states, which I'd say might fall under the umbrella of "psychedelic experience." In fact, you don't need a psychedelic substance in order to occasion a psychedelic experience, or to get into a holotropic state; but at the same time, these states (occasioned by a substance or not) can heal on physical, as well as psychological and spiritual levels. So let me tell you about the time I dropped acid in Goa.

On that same trip when I met Tomer, I reread *Be Here Now*, as if reading the guidebook to the acid trip I was soon to embark upon, using its lessons to set my *kavanah* for the psychedelic experience: to intentionally be here now.

The thing about Goa is that it's already a trip: it's like Mecca for ecstatic dance and drum circles, healers and yogis, teeming with rustic cafes and fragrant shops full of incense, beads, spices, and colorful *shmatas*. Na Nach stickers are everywhere, and sometimes you'll find a menu in Hebrew, catering to all the Israeli travelers. Indeed, a whopping 70,000 Israelis visit India every year, and Goa is one of the hottest spots along the so-called "Hummus Trail." It is also popular among Russians, Western Europeans, and Indian tourists, and there are few Americans there, save for an expat crew including my dad's friend Mohan, one of the "originals" from Maharaj-ji's satsang, who hosted me and my friend Jenna and would spend hours kibitzing with us.

"People these days aren't having psychedelic experiences," he bemoaned. "They're simply getting high off acid." *What did he mean by that*? I wondered. How could you not have a psychedelic experience with a "psychedelic" substance? Sure, there's microdosing—the point of which is *davka* not to trip, but rather to take a sub-perceptible amount every few days to help with anxiety, depression, or general wellness. However, that's not really what Mohan was talking about. What he meant was taking enough acid (or your psychedelic of choice) to experience "ego death," to transcend yourself and become one with everything else around. A holotropic state, if you will.

What are we actually talking about when we say "psychedelic" anyway? The term was originally coined by English psychiatrist Humphry Osmond in 1956 in a letter to Aldous Huxley to mean, etymologically speaking, "mind manifesting" or "soul made visible." Albert Hofmann, the Swiss chemist who first synthesized

LSD, called it "medicine for the soul." And so, in my definition, a "psychedelic" experience brings out our true essence, connecting us back to our core nature—the soul or spirit—while enabling us to really feel what it's like to be in the body. When there's less ego, our neshama—that individual piece of collective divinity inside each of us—is more prominent. It's the experience of the soul, embodied

Germane to what seemed to be Mohan's concept of psychedelic, "ego death" plays a central role. Ego death refers to a temporary shift in cognition, from a self-centered to completely unbiased perspective. Scientifically speaking, it's defined by established brain networks losing localized integrity and increasing global functional connectivity with the rest of the brain. By the brain being in this state of entropy, previously established neuronal connections can rewire in the brain and establish new pathways that can redefine a person's sense of self. This is in part why some people, for instance, have been able to transcend their fixed patterns of thought in efforts to treat depression, anxiety, eating disorders, or addictions through psychedelic-assisted psychotherapy clinical trials with substances like psilocybin. If the ego is about boundaries between self and the outer world, ego death enables one to feel a sense of oneness or unity with other people, nature, or the cosmos. It's less about "you" and more about the collective. A feeling of safety, of being "held by the universe," as author and psychiatrist Julie Holland once put it to me, enables the nervous system to relax and allows healing to occur. The point being, "ego death" can be central to that feeling of oneness associated with the "mystical experience."

In religious terms, "ego death" might be called *bitul*, or self-nullification. It's a spiritual state associated with *chochmah*, or inner wisdom, and the experience of ayin, nothingness, in relation to G-d's infinite light and ultimate, singular unity. It's a form of spontaneous, ecstatic experience—a communion with HaShem. Scary as "ego death" may sound, *bitul* is a modality and meditation that conjoins with ultimate, deep-seated joy.

❧

A tab? Feh, Mohan might say. Try five. "So, you got any acid?" we asked him, mostly in earnest. He did; it was probably sitting somewhere in the freezer, but he wouldn't give it to Badri's daughter. So we were left to fend for ourselves.

One thing led to another and we stumbled into a grimy crash pad at a spot called Rihanna Guest House, a few steps from the beach, inhabited by an Israeli DJ and his friends, waking up midafternoon, smoking hookah and weed, ordering grilled cheese from the cafe next door. We drank a beer with them and tried to hold a conversation, but my Hebrew was as bad as their English. The DJ had acid and whatever else we might have been looking for. So in exchange for a couple thousand rupees (about $20 worth), we watched him extract liquid LSD from a bottle once containing eye drops, and use a dropper to place it onto a couple gummy bears (that somehow tasted like Indian food).

On a sunny afternoon, we *cheers*ed the gummy bears and took a walk from Mohan's place to the ocean. I remember we spoke to an Indian guy who was peddling something we didn't buy, but stayed to chat with us anyway. We got the feeling he was somehow already tuned in to the channel we were coming up on. There was a certain grace that he had, a certain grace that Hinduism, as I'd been exposed to it, seemed to present: Ram Dass and others in the satsang often talked about "Maharaj-ji's grace." As kirtan artist Krishna Das once explained it to me, grace—*kripa* in Sanskrit—"indicates the power of what is beyond us to help us." One doesn't deserve grace or earn it, he said. "Grace extends itself *naturally*. It's our natural state of harmony. . . . When the curtains part, and we get a little hint of the way things really are, we experience that parting of the curtain as grace."

And so, maybe on acid, the curtains were beginning to part. But it wasn't exactly a smooth process. We were struggling to "be here now." Jenna was playing with a baby she had met on the beach, but I was getting restless and wanted a change of scenery, maybe to walk a bit north, from the quiet of Mandrem to the action in Arambol. And so we journeyed along the wet part of the sand, first passing droves of Russians, where I picked up on an energy that made me feel like I was in Moscow, then passing a group doing tai chi when the acid really began to hit. I could literally see the energy that they were moving. It was all too much. I was seeing white halos reverberating around people, and the vibrations of colors and energy all around. It's as if I was seeing wavelengths of a radio channel that I hadn't previously known existed. I knew I would never be able to unsee the light that I was observing with my own eyes. And yet, I also felt light (as in, the opposite of heavy). I felt out of my body, like I was floating. Was this the "too much light" that Tomer was talking about, or that I'd been warned about by the trippy, yet sober religious types, like the Breslover who I'd interviewed years prior about Judaism and psychedelics?

Too much light, he told me, could shatter one's vessel—his point being that sober, daily practices, like prayer and keeping kosher, always trumped the psychedelic shortcut to illumination. A steady religious discipline in the end offers more light than receiving it all in a heavy dose that could be too much to handle. This theme of the dangers of spiritual experience without proper preparation or "vessels" to contain the light pops up throughout Jewish literature, from the Torah to later mystical writings.

A classic case is the story of Nadav and Avihu, the sons of Aaron, who were inspired to bring a fire offering to G-d, even though it was not the allotted time. For this spontaneous expression of inner devotion, they were zapped out of existence. From a psychedelic perspective, one might say that their "'set'" was right on; they yearned to connect with the Divine, but their "'setting'" was off—right place at the wrong time. Similarly, there is the story of the four Mishnaic sages who entered Pardes—through a method of spiritual elevation consisting of intense meditation on G-d's name—one died, one went mad, one became a heretic, and only Rabbi Akiva left in peace. Each of these rabbis was a massive Torah genius in his own right, and yet, the direct experience of the Divine unhinged them, all except Rabbi Akiva. The basic message according to rabbinic tradition is that direct spiritual experience is serious, sometimes even dangerous, and should be approached with respect and proper preparation. In seeing the light of heaven, only one of the four was able to grasp its unity; those who continued to grapple with duality—who couldn't integrate—had their minds blown open.

So there I was tripping, seeing more light than I knew how to handle. I knew I needed to get a hold of myself. Be here now; don't worry about *if* the vessel will shatter, or what *will* happen after this trip; just flow with it right *now*. Maybe even try to enjoy it? *Hineni*—"Here I am"—that's the response G-d asked of every patriarch he spoke to. As Torah teacher Nili Salem once explained to me: "If G-d calls, what are you supposed to do? Say *Hineni*, be here now." So sure, I was a bit overwhelmed, but at least I had an intellectual understanding of what was happening; nonetheless, I had to hold it together because Jenna was also struggling a bit.

She said she was having tunnel vision, and was losing a grasp on herself. She described seeing an Indian mother and her child, and *being* that mother and child. She got scared. Maybe we needed to get something in our stomachs to weigh us down, so we stopped at a beachside cafe, where we were so obviously disoriented that a British traveler took pity on us and helped us make an order of chai.

We were still feeling unsettled even after we'd figured out our way back to Mohan's. He was out of town and, in our acid-fueled frenzy, made a total mess of the apartment, rummaging through our stuff for whatever we could find to help us come down to reality a bit—essential oils, books, a change of clothes. Only after I'd taken two showers, stretched alongside Jenna into some yoga postures, and made a couple phone calls back home—"Hey, we're tripping hard and need some guidance"—to Matt in Israel, Daniella in New York, and my dad in LA, that we finally began to ground. We practiced some breathing exercises, exhaling longer than inhaling (a tip we read in a story that I edited for the second issue of *DoubleBlind* that, luckily, I had with me to give out), and I clutched onto my Hula-Hoop—my safe space, my most prized possession, and my lifesaver again and again and again.

I'd fallen in love with that hoop the first time I saw it in a smoke shop in Berkeley circa 2011. Its tubing was covered in hot pink and sparkly silver tape, and it was collapsible, meaning that I could fold it into an infinity sign, then into the size of two smaller circles, and bring it along on my travels—it's been on almost every one of my plane rides or road trips since. I wasn't in the market, so to speak, when I bought the hoop, impulsively out of pure instinct. And I didn't expect it to become an extension of me, spiritually and physically. But I took to it immediately and came up with a signature style, spirited and flowing all at once. Whether dancing with the hoop for hours, or even sitting still within the circle, it's been the greatest "medicine" I've ever had.

And so ultimately, at the end of that acid trip, we were okay—even better for it—eventually giggling our way back into blessedly sober consciousness. In that twinkle period after the LSD wore off—a solid 12 hours later—we headed back toward Arambol, slowly traversing the back alleys of the jungle, past fruit stands and hole-in-the-wall Indian food spots, before arriving at a quaint teahouse with an indoor swing and fluffy carpets, playing a combination of psytrance and Russian folk. The night felt clear, and so did I. A bit dazed from the trip, I was ultimately sharp and glistening.

And my back felt so very light. Something somatic had lifted. I felt like I'd been carrying a backpack my whole life, in the area of my back affected by the curvature of my scoliosis, and now that backpack was gone. It was surreal. And it lasted almost a year after that trip. Did I experience "too much light"? I'm not sure, but the point is that, whatever was happening, I used *practice*, like breathwork and yoga, as a vessel to harness that light, and guide the experience. Through such grounding practice, I broke out of whatever anxiety had burdened my trip—or maybe it wasn't just anxiety spurred by the trip, but a magnification of the anxiety that lives within me at all times, the strain that shows up in my spine. I remembered a quote I'd read once by Ram Dass, and now I could feel it in my body: "The game isn't to get high; the game is to get free."

Chapter 20

NA NACH TRANCE, CHASSIDISH MERRY PRANKSTERS, AND THE SOUL DOCTOR

The truth is, the most liberated and even joyful moments of my life occurred when I was sober. (And indeed, despite what you may gather from reading this book, all these trip tales are accumulated from sporadic psychedelic experiences spanning more than 13 years.) At the core of Reb Nachman's Chassidis is the quest for joy from the depths of heartbreak, as he preaches *there is no despair—the greatest mitzvah is to be happy.* Lesser known, however, is a Breslov teaching, which I read about in *Cannabis Chassidis,* that "it's very important to be happy, [and] the only thing more important is to be free." Because true joy is when we're free of needing anything at all to feel that way.

Easier said than done, of course. And I can imagine that if I'd been raised with the teachings of Reb Nachman, instead of with Ram Dass, I might have rebelled in the form of depression, rather than dissociation. Maybe they're two sides of the same coin: If only we could be present in the everlasting moment, we might be less depressed, more called into joy; if only we could draw forth from our soulful core an inner capacity for joy, we might be less dissociated, more called into the present moment.

Of course, the most present moments of my life have been the most joyful, and vice versa. As Carl Hart once told me during an interview for my podcast *Set & Setting* on the Be Here Now Network, "Being present is an altered state."

Perhaps the most explicit experience I had of this was in Jerusalem with Jenna, on another one of our trips together, this time working on a story for *Tablet Magazine* about the shared love for trance music among Charedim and Chilonim in Israel. As much as the topic interested me, in essence, reporting the story was an excuse to go riding around in a Na Nach trance van—arguably and appropriately, one of the most joyful days I'd experienced.

There wasn't much to it; I was just happy to be there then. Maybe if I had the same experience years later, it would've hit differently because at that point in my life, I was still in what you could call an "exposure" phase with Na Nach: amounting to some of my most inspired and inspiring moments. I'd taken a handful of trips with Aaron to visit his Na Nach sister Dena, who's just a few years older than I am, with a baby face underneath a big colorful *tichel*, and her family in a small village down the road from Rebbe Shimon Bar Yochai's kever at Mount Meron. Her children shone with a certain light, and they all lived simply—a family of six in a two-bedroom house, down a dusty road that branched off into other parts of a neighborhood featuring a tiny winery and vineyard, a chicken coop, and children's toys scattered about. To this day, they might still be the happiest people I've ever met. Her husband, Ron, had put out a reggae album of *Tikkun HaKlali*—ten psalms of poetry written by King David, but arranged by Rebbe Nachman in a particular order that he claimed had the power to repair every breakage and blockage and to serve as *teshuva* for sin.

The glitz and glam, grist and grind, hustle and bustle of life in America paled in comparison to the richness of life on this mountaintop. Emunah just came easier here, G-d felt closer; maybe it was just the altitude—physical and spiritual. The Ron and Dena life became my North Star—my "plan B" if life in the media game, in the competitive, complicated, capitalist American paradigm failed to serve my highest purpose. And to this day, I still struggle with why that life isn't already just my plan A. Maybe I needed to finish writing this book first.

Back with Jenna, sitting outside a cafe behind Jerusalem's shuk Machane Yehuda waiting for our interviewee to show up (now hours late), I'd still had limited experience in the Na Nach-specific trance scene, despite these soul-kindling moments with Aaron and his family, such as on Shabbos, where trance was totally absent. In the past, I'd have fun enjoying the music from the colorful Na Nach vans when they'd park outside Tel Aviv's shuk HaCarmel at random, but that was it—I hadn't yet spent time living among them in Tzfat; I hadn't yet gone to Pushkina (a Catskills Na Nach festival named after the main drag in Uman, Ukraine, where pilgrims visit the Reb Nachman's *kever* every Rosh HaShana, amounting to what *VICE* once called the "Hasidic Burning Man"); Spotify hadn't yet recommended to me a playlist called "Rebbe Nachman"; I hadn't yet danced wildly enough to cause a Na Nach van to stop its music and announce a reminder that there was a women's section; and I hadn't yet found my way in a Prius decked out with Na Nach stickers to a trance party in Tiveria to celebrate the yahrzeit of Na Nach mascot Saba's own rebbe, Yisroel Karduner.

And so this experience still phased me in that first-time sort of way. But to this day, I'm sure if I had to relive it, I'd have just as much fun.

So there we were slurping smoothies from the Etrog Man, then blended ice coffees from Aroma (Israel's Starbucks), listless in the early summer heat, when finally Jenna and I began to hear trance music coming from down Agripas Street, followed by the sight of a psychedelic, multicolored, Merry Prankster–style van painted with swirling rainbows and flowers, a boom box attached to its roof, attracting stares as it slowed to a halt behind the bustling shuk, and a cohort of teenagers and 20-somethings hopping out to dance in the street. In the spur of a second, we picked ourselves up and excitedly hopped into the open doors of the van (a novelty and rarity that they even let girls in to ride with them).

I was so caught up in the moment, I couldn't help but smile. How do we access joy? Be here now. And in those moments of joy, presence just comes easy. A high-tempo electronic melody aptly titled "Happiness" blared through the speakers. I wondered if that was an intentional choice.

To the rest of the world—even to most other (mainstream) Chassidim—Breslov, and especially Na Nach may come off as crazy, and even some Breslovers frown upon Na Nach and all of their performative antics. Indeed, as one Breslover named Aryeh put it, "Na Nach is a kind of understanding of the world." The philosophy is that it's better to be happy, even if it means being a fool, than to be unhappy and "normal." As he is sometimes referred to as doctor of the soul, "Rebbe Nachman said to release the mind," one of the passengers in the van told me. "So there is something in trance that releases the mind."

Squished into a corner of the van's back row, we began noticing a change of scenery as, after a few stops to dance at red lights, we were now headed up a winding mountain dotted with olive trees, until we arrived at Har HaMenuchot. The hilltop cemetery is the largest in all of Jerusalem, and where, among other notables like Shlomo Carlebach, Saba is buried. It's easy to spot his kever because the entire area surrounding it is all decked out in Na Nach: stickers, books, some Breslover crying his heart out . . .

It's hard to describe what I was feeling at that moment. Some form of ecstasy, spurred by the excitement of it all, the music, the joyride, but also this sense of equanimity and rightness. There was a certain calm at that mountaintop, removed from the chaos of downtown Jerusalem, and with views of the Land in every direction. The ride back to the Jerusalem city center was quieter, everyone a bit dazed and muted. But the silence was only temporary, because before long, we parked at the square nearby the Tachana Merkazit on Yaffo Street, where the guys set up folding tables full of Na Nach stickers and books, attracting attention once again with the van's vibrant colors and sounds.

On that same trip, when Jenna and I first met up in Tel Aviv, we connected with Shahar Zirkin, a biochemist and founder of one of Israel's largest psytrance festivals—Doof—who took us to a tiny, off-grid forest party down a dark, wooded road near Afula—a city just north of the West Bank. We'd been driving in circles, looking for clues as to the party's location, when finally we spotted a piece of toilet paper strung delicately among the branches of a tree. Zirkin turned left, driving slowly, eyes peeled for more discreet "signs" until we could hear thick, sub-bass frequencies punctuated with synthesized audio effects in the distance, absorbed by the thicket of trees between our car and the sound system. To the untrained ear, it might have sounded like the soundtrack to an intergalactic space journey; to anyone familiar with the genre, it was the beckoning beats of psychedelic trance. As we approached the party, the beats reverberated through the woods from the underground, neon-lit party reminiscent of festivals in the wide-open Negev Desert, or deep in the jungles, or on the shores of Goa.

From the nature parties to the square in Jerusalem, from the heimish festivals in the Catskills to the nightly trance parties in Goa, what I've observed is a shared ritual and affinity for psytrance, a lubricant for bodily transcendence. From secular to religious, despite seeming worlds apart, the music doesn't discriminate in offering a common ground where somatic integration is possible, where a sense of unity within oneself can happen, even if momentarily, amid the dance of simply shaking it all out, all the pressure, all the fears and expectations and traumas of the past generations and the present, of living in a land that's constantly at war, of living within a paradigm defined by external pressures, be they halachic, cultural, capitalistic, what have you.

Oddly popular across the Jewish world, psytrance is its own type of creed—spiritual, if agnostic. "You get into this trancey kind of experience. You feel like you're not part of the lower world anymore and you're one level up," Zirkin told us for that story we published in *Tablet*. "Psytrance gives you the ability to change the awareness of your mind."

The Israeli connection to trance really got going in the '90s, world-renowned psytrance artist Goa Gil told me in an interview. Israeli musical acts like Infected Mushroom or Astral Projection gained popularity around the globe, propelling what Gil calls "an ancient tribal ritual for the 21st century," and the dance that goes with it "an active meditation."

"When we dance, we go beyond thought, we go beyond the mind to become one with the cosmic," said Gil. "It's that experience of oneness with the whole environment around you." In other words, trance dance could lend itself to a partial "mystical experience."

It didn't take long for the psytrance genre to take root in the Middle East as DJs like Zirkin began producing festivals. Starting around 1995 as an underground party in the Negev that drew fewer than 500 people, the Doof Festival blossomed into a permitted annual festival of about 8,000. Other parties are even bigger, drawing up to 12,000 people, said Zirkin, sometimes running three days straight. It's all in the name of that release. Doof's tagline reads: "Everybody needs a place where they can go insane peacefully."

For the Na Nachs, that's just the point: a peaceful, free-spirited silliness grasping at joy as ultimate truth, not altogether different from the insanity found in nature parties and espoused in Doof's tagline.

"We are a generation of trance," said Aryeh. "Before I tried to believe, I found trance. And when I heard trance with religious people, I felt comfortable because it was the same as before." Not only an entry, trance is also a point of return: "Go where you had been before you did teshuva, to the place where you made the sin; go back there and go fix it." For Na Nachs who came of age along with psytrance, returning to familiar music from the vantage point of their new religious way of life is an opportunity for that teshuva. Rebbe Nachman also teaches to take the clothes of the outside world, to capture that light and make it holy, make it your own, Aryeh added, and that's just what the Na Nachs have done with trance.

For those who are secular to observant, and anyone in between, psytrance can both bring one back into religion, or liberate one from its grip. Essentially, it's the other side of the same coin: for everyone, it equals liberation, but from what and toward what is more subjective.

At its core, it's an escape—whether it be from the pressures of life in the Holy Land, adherence to a strict religious lifestyle, or even the irreverent humdrum of the mundane—before breaking free into someplace more spiritual.

For me, officially belonging as neither a secular Israeli nor an OTD Chassid nor a baal teshuva Na Nach, but still party to all these groups, psytrance simply helps me feel ecstatic, shaking out raw feelings and detaching from the constant flow of thoughts that plague my mind, offering a type of clarity. Imbuing a "secular" genre with a kiss of the sublime, atheists and believers alike agree the music may even be holy unto itself.

Chapter 21

ON THE CALIFORNIA– NEW YORK– ISRAEL TRAIN

Back in New York, the initial magic that had once enchanted me began to fade, or at least took a temporary lull. Social dynamics shifted, everyone moved out of the Park Slope brownstone, dispersing the scene, and I started spending more time in California as reporting on weed picked up around legalization. Meanwhile I'd been shuffling between apartments, from a dingy spot in Crown Heights with two queer hipster roommates and a slumlord who refused to fix the oven, to a nicer spot nearby with a kosher kitchen and five roommates, until one thing led to another and I moved into Aaron's bubbe's place in Brooklyn.

We'd known each other for three years by now, and had been officially dating for about one. Despite the fact that I once thought he lived too much at the edge for me to fell 100 percent safe partnering with him, he was still one of my best friends, and I couldn't distance myself. Our relationship was sweet and familial (and continues to be even to this day) and there was a certain charm to exploring New York with Aaron by my side, or practicing a blended type of Judaism he introduced me to: singing "Azamer

Bishvochin" on Shabbos, or feeling the energy of Purim (my favorite holiday) while candy flipping through Jerusalem.

Within a few years of our friendship, Aaron's grandmother passed away, and he moved into her large three-bedroom apartment in the Chassidish, south Brooklyn neighborhood of Borough Park. Inside was Bubbe's furniture—a marble coffee table and her hardwood display case full of old china; mold on the walls where her hospital bed was drilled in; linoleum kitchen floors from the 1960s; and outside on the balcony, where we'd smoke spliffs every night, Aaron had hung a Mets flag beside a Bernie poster overlooking a right-wing, tree-lined block.

I made friends with the Latino guys who worked at Fallsburg Bagels around the corner, where I'd go for blended iced coffees, and I'd generally put on a skirt to go anywhere else within the neighborhood—16th Avenue Glatt to buy tomato dip and kugel for Shabbos, Schwartz's to buy challah, and the Nuttery, where I'd get our favorite snack, maple-glazed Chinese pecans. It's not that in dressing *tzniusdig* I was pretending to be one of the Chassidim— no matter what, it was obvious I was an outsider—but because I "knew better" I therefore felt guilty dressing in a way that would be alienating at best and offensive at worst. It was bad enough I'd ride my bike in jean shorts through the neighborhood on my way to literally anywhere else that felt relevant to my life. I'd cruise through Prospect Park on my way to Park Slope, to and from Williamsburg, or, my favorite, over the Manhattan Bridge into Chinatown. Other times, Aaron and I would bike toward Coney Island or into Bay Ridge, exploring the diverse neighborhoods around us, trying authentic Russian, Uzbek, Pakistani, or Palestinian food.

But the truth is, I felt so far and disconnected from the New York that I'd fallen in love with a few years prior. South Brooklyn was unfamiliar and, without a car, it took so long to get anywhere else, even Crown Heights, where most of my friends were. The only familiar thing near Bubbe's was Cholent, a decades-long gathering of fringy frum-ish oddballs and misfits who'd come together in the wee hours of dawn on Thursday nights to read poetry, kibitz, jam, and eat the classical Jewish stew known as cholent. The founder and "host" of Cholent, if you could call him that, was Isaac Schoenfeld, a tzadik in his own right who'd shepherd lost souls from *the community* into a community unto itself. Since its inception in the '90s, Cholent had been through various iterations and locations, including a longstanding stint at the Millinery Shul, a freestanding old school chapel in midtown Manhattan (in the attic of which longtime cannabis and ibogaine activist, and former Yippie, Dana Beal had resided for years).

Even though Bubbe's was free, the point, for me at least, wasn't to then relax into working less, but to try and save money by working the same amount, or even more. I remained as stressed as ever, and on busy weeks almost never left the house.

Yet, my writing was blossoming. I wrote one of my all-time favorite stories in that period—an article for *Playboy*'s print magazine about the role of trauma in the Israeli–Palestinian conflict, where I drew on experiences I'd had drinking tea with peace activist Antwan Saca in Bethlehem, attending medical cannabis hearings at the Knesset (Israeli parliament), having phone calls with MAPS founder Rick Doblin about his organization's MDMA-for-PTSD research, and doing street interviews in East Jerusalem about cannabis (also as a PTSD treatment). The story tickled within me a yearning to not just understand the conflict better, but to spend more time engaging with it—not necessarily from a political standpoint, but a human one, where addressing trauma on all sides of the equation was top priority, and one which could transform the politics. The bottom line was, I knew I needed to get back to "the Land," as Antwan taught me to call it—maybe one day, even to live.

But meanwhile, I was in Brooklyn. My relationship with Aaron had its ups and downs, and to confront things and build from there, he routinely suggested that we take acid together; but I almost never wanted it at that time. I was scared for some reason, didn't feel completely safe in it, or just was not feeling called. The constellation of these factors—my workaholism and resistance to tripping at the time, which meant my rejection of what he hoped could be opportunities for growth and connection in manifesting a deeper relationship—grew into points of tension. When I ended up typing so much that I developed tendinitis in my wrist, I was forced to take a break. I booked a ticket to Tel Aviv, where I went to report a few stories, attend a friend's wedding, and get some soul nourishment.

Not long after I returned, Aaron and I "moved" to LA after the summer. I was mostly writing about cannabis those days—science, policy, industry, culture—and was getting invited to speak on conference panels at places like the Skirball, in West LA, or the Ace Hotel downtown, or to cover weed parties in the Hollywood Hills. In New York, I was tucked away in Borough Park; in California, I was a cannabis "socialite." Sometimes, Aaron and I would go up to the Bay, to party with the old-school Jewish crew behind the Doc Green's cannabis brand, or check out the outdoor bud and legacy farmers at the Emerald Cup. The industry at this time was booming—although it would take a dip within a few years, once the persistent black market basically eclipsed it. (Who wants to pay high taxes? And what small-scale farmer has the capital to compete against multistate operators?)

My official "excuse" for moving back to LA was that I'd secured a "real job" (benefits, 401k, health insurance) as an editor with a cannabis media start-up off Abbot Kinney in what was the nouveau chichi version of Venice that made me miss the rootsy, grungy Venice of my childhood. It was a far cry from the old-school hazy stoner culture that I grew up with, that pioneered the cannabis landscape into what it would become, into the movement that would garner enough capitalist attention to render it palatable in the eyes of the Silicon Valley and Wall Street suits who'd swoop in with their squeaky-clean criminal records and rebrand cannabis as an industry, built upon the backs of the growers and old guard hippie activists who risked their freedoms and reputations for the political reforms that the new school came in to capitalize off of.

Because I was burnt out on freelancing, I appreciated the perks of having a Job with a capital J, of making peace with my family, seeing old friends, and of scratching the desperate itch to settle into a space that looked and felt like mine—a cute studio in Los Feliz, right by Griffith Park—but ultimately, I'd fill up on "soul food" during trips to Israel, India, or back and forth to New York, because in truth, as I would learn, this new life really wasn't for me.

And it certainly wasn't for Aaron. He'd put in a good faith effort to make LA work so that we could work, and got a job at *High Times*, but ultimately he's a New Yorker through and through, with no tolerance for the way "you California people" do things. Our relationship was ailing and became a messy on-again, off-again merry go-round once he returned to Brooklyn, and I straddled the coasts. As they say, LA is easy on the body, but hard on the soul, while New York is hard on the body, but nourishes the soul. If I was going to make LA a viable place to live, even if it was ultimately a temporary move, I knew I'd need to give attention to my soul. This time, however, it wouldn't be through my ecstatic hippie heimish escapades, but through sobering internal soul-seeking, integrating everything I'd learned along the way.

PART 3

INTEGRATION

*"Only joy enables a person to direct the mind
as they please because joy is in the
realm of freedom . . .
Through joy, a person becomes free
and goes out of exile"*

— REBBE NACHMAN

Chapter 22

LECH LECHA

The forests surrounding places like Tzfat or Jerusalem are alive with the soundtrack of Breslovers howling into the trees, doing their *hitbodedut*: literally meaning "seclusion," the practice consists of talking to G-d as you would a best friend.

As Reb Nachman described it, hitbodedut is a free-form conversation with HaShem, in one's native language. It can include complaints, excuses, praise, pleading, anything really, in order to become closer to the Divine. Pour your heart out; nothing is too mundane to discuss. Sometimes it's common to simply scream out loud.

The thing with Breslov is that there's no barrier to entry; G-d meets you where you're at, as one baal teshuva Na Nach once told me. Rebbe Nachman says so himself: "[Hitbodedut] is accessible to all people, from the least to the greatest. For anyone can make use of this practice and thereby reach a higher level." He prescribed hitbodedut for at least an hour a day, alone in nature or a room, and ideally in the very early hours of the morning while people are still sleeping. Out in the fields, he wrote, "all the grasses join in [the] prayer and increase its effectiveness and power."

No matter where you're holding, how distant you feel, how crazy it might seem to talk to yourself in an attempted chat with G-d, the point, Reb Nachman says, is to simply talk to your Maker about your life and ask Him (or Her or Them) to bring you closer. Even if you can't bring yourself to say anything at all, he says, the mere act of showing up with a "yearning and longing to speak" is a step in the right direction.

Historically, I've always been shy to make my voice heard in such a way, even in the privacy of nature. Only once I was living in LA was I desperate enough to utilize this practice that I'd observed, reported on, and read about. I missed the ecstatic Judaism I'd experienced in New York and the heimish *velt*, which felt so thick back East and inaccessible from the posh hipsterville I'd moved to in LA. I was in daily, tearful agony over my never-ending breakups with Aaron, but found solace co-working with my old college friends Angelica or Daniel, both of whom I lived with in the Berkeley co-ops, or when Daniella, who'd taken her own sabbatical from New York to travel the world, came to stay with me for a month or two, bringing life to my otherwise lonesome studio apartment with her enviable kitchen skills, comedic seltzer addiction, chit-chatty flair of a JAP from Queens, and deep commitment to sisterhood.

In a fit of doomscrolling one night on Instagram, we came across a video of our friend Elana Brody, a highly spirited musician and Cohenet we knew from Brooklyn, and raised by earthy hippies in Appalachia. Charismatic even in her rawest moments, Elana had filmed herself in the throes of her own heartbreak, out in a forest, taking dead branches, breaking them apart, hurling them through the air in rage, screaming to HaShem, her cheeks rosy with tears and ruach.

So on a weekend road trip up to San Francisco, Daniella, another friend Devorah, and I took some mushrooms and channeled our inner Elana on a majestic afternoon in Golden Gate Park. We were half serious, half cracking up, but it was still cathartic— and laid the foundation for me to keep up the practice on my own.

Just a block from my apartment, alone among the dry, Southern California foliage and in the hills of Griffith Park, I'd scream and cry and beat up sturdy tree trunks. The way an old, tired dog takes punches from a puppy, stoic yet nurturing, the trees offered compassion toward my anguish. And even if I felt disconnected from the Jewish world that surrounded me in New York, here I was forced to resource myself from within, reaching into my own inner world to find the vocal cords that tethered me to G-d. Plus,

LA's mild weather gave me the opportunity to sprint up the mountain to the Griffith Observatory, or Hula-Hoop on a more regular basis than I ever had in New York, where the winters made it impossible to spend time outside—I'd bring my speakers to a clearing in the trees and hoop until the moon had traversed its path halfway across the sky. Sometimes an Argentinian medicine man, Shalom, would come hang out with me there, giving me cacao, *rapé*, or *sananga* eye drops on occasion, discussing *la revolución* since word on the street, he said, was that *Moshiach* was right around the corner. (Of course people have been saying that for literally thousands of years. Maybe it's a really big corner?)

LA also had its tender moments, like taking hikes with my dad at Franklin Canyon; getting manicures and Bigg Chill froyo with my younger sister—my "favorite person" ever since I was 14, when she was born; rekindling a close relationship with her mom/my stepmom during visits to the chocolate shop she had opened with her new husband; receiving "life coaching" from my tween-age niece; and of course, late-night pickles and rugelach at Canter's—a 24/7 Jewish deli with an adjoining dive bar called the Kibitz Room, drawing (and I say this with only respect and endearment) the highest quality freakshow in all of Hollywood.

While I was still at the cannabis media start-up, I also co-founded *DoubleBlind*, an artsy psychedelic magazine and online media start-up, and despite having been burnt out on freelancing—which inspired me to take that 9–5 in LA—there I was working round the clock (again) at two jobs. My passion and excitement over the then-nascent *DoubleBlind* and the promise of revitalizing print journalism sustained me in what was otherwise a grueling hustle. Right time, right place: Things picked up quickly with *DoubleBlind*, and within a year my co-founder and I were constantly invited to speak on panels at conferences or as guests on podcasts.

Once the weed start-up folded, my weekdays were spent tapping away at *DoubleBlind*, often working overtime to meet the start-up's needs, publishing SEO articles on ayahuasca rather than doing it, eating kale salads alone in my apartment, processing my relationship with Aaron—a lot of love, a lot of mess—and biking to yoga in between café hopping at Stories or the Bourgeois Pig.

It wasn't a bad life, but it didn't feel entirely like *my* life, whatever that meant. I tried dating a little—a hipster musician whose Judaism began and ended with his last name, a Persian Chabadnik who tried to marry me after three dates, and a Bu-Jew from Boulder by way of Monsey who turned out to be more of a brother than a boyfriend—all only to further validate my intuitions that I wouldn't be "settling down" in Los Angeles anytime soon. I knew this moment in LA—like all moments—was ultimately ephemeral.

Instead, that chapter of my life showed me that I was there to make a *tikkun* on (eventually) leaving LA (again). In order to do that, I needed to return home first, then leave not because I was running away from my family, but because I was running toward making my own. And in the middle of the pandemic, I restarted an application for aliyah. Despite my complex feelings about the politics in Israel—Palestinians in their own diaspora don't have such a right to citizenship in the Land—personally and professionally, I knew I would have the most going for me in Israel, plus I wanted to further explore psychedelics and trauma-informed perspectives in relation to both Judaism and the Israeli–Palestinian conflict. Although, as I made "my" plans, G-d made his, and at the time of writing this I've yet to actually become a citizen.

In the meantime, I began spending Shabbos more often in Beverly Hills, going with my mom to Kabbalat Shabbat at the local Carlebach shul Happy Minyan, inviting friends over to eclectic Shabbos dinners at my dad's house, meal-hopping around Pico-Robertson for Shabbos lunch or *shaleshudis*, and discovering a thriving, magical, Breslov-flavored chevra underneath an orange tree in the Ben Yehuda family's backyard. The boys all had long, thick *peyos* like the hippie kids in Israel, while the family had roots in the legendary Moshav. Having community in the vicinity of my parents' neighborhood somehow helped me reconcile where and who I came from. There was something sweet about having my dad show up to *melave malka* or hosting a Nili Salem *shiur* at his house, especially once the old-school kirtans became more seldom as the satsang matured and people dispersed over the pandemic.

Still, I missed the chevra in New York, I missed getting around by subway, and I missed Aaron. Back in New York, he founded a "heimish entheógenic" nonprofit called Darkhei Rephua (Paths of Healing) and pursued activist work in state and local psychedelic policy reform. He "owned" his time, and had always encouraged me to do the same. Yet, it took years for me to internalize that lesson.

Despite being a co-founder of *DoubleBlind*, I rarely felt like my own boss and fell prey to a common work culture that pedestaled burnout as a virtue, as if working *too* hard was the only way to keep the start-up afloat—at the expense of what felt like my own well-being. I tried to go with it, make the necessary sacrifices I thought I was supposed to, but my neshama was in agony, and my physical health was fine, but not thriving. My body—my skin, my digestion, my backache—was trying to tell me something, and it only got louder when I contracted Lyme disease one summer at a Rainbow Gathering in Pennsylvania. I sensed an integrity issue: I couldn't engage in journalism about psychedelic wellness, while simultaneously feeling "unwell." I strove for work-life balance, but such efforts became a point of tension at work.

In LA, it felt like I had stopped "living the story" for a bit; in that moment of existential pause, I began a process of integrating everything I'd experienced and learned over the course of the last decade. That's not to say my story "stopped," but all the fun, weird, trippy, Jewy experiences that I drew on as my muse were mostly happening in New York or Israel.

When I tried to recreate them in California, my psychedelic trips were often more trauma-focused. One particularly difficult mushroom trip with Aaron and my "brothers" Lee and Jared, in Carmel Valley during the pandemic, showed me just how dissociated I'd been. Even though the symptoms of my high school eating disorder had long subsided—starving myself out of my gut feelings—I realized during that trip that I still struggled to come home to myself, to literally feel my body. Okay, fine, so by now "somatic" was a buzzword in the psychedelic discourse, and I'd interviewed all the right therapists about other people's embodied trauma, and I knew intellectually this probably applied to me as well, at least to some degree. I mean, I knew this, at least on some level, one level that I all but forgot about, when a therapist once told me I had some form of complex trauma and tried to get me to do tapping exercises that would help me with my indecision—but it didn't stick, and I "moved" to Israel instead of continuing therapy in LA between college and grad school.

I've always had this restless urge in me, this impulse to just run; and at times when I'd felt stuck, especially during the pandemic, I'd ask myself from where and to where I was running and returning—*ratzu v'shuv*, in Hebrew. The answer has always been one and the same: home.

◄▼►

I've always been "at home" within Judaism—the familiarity of the Hebrew alphabet, the miracles and muck defining our narrative, the worry, the joy, the pickles, and the preciousness of our customs, like saying the Sh'ma every night with my parents. Even when they divorced, they each upheld the tradition. And then of course, in Judaism and in Jewishness, there's the classic "wrestling" with this figure we call HaShem—an ever-so-complicated relationship of exile and ecstasy, enmeshment, conspiracy, codependence, comfort, and faith. Lest we forget, Yisroel, or "Israel" in English means "to wrestle with G-d." But when I learned this, I interpreted it to mean wrestling with oneself—as in, all the times I wrestled with myself, my body, to feel at home within it (mostly because throughout my teenage years, I didn't feel that way). At the time, the idea of Judaism in the body, as a means of experiencing the religion through experiencing somatic sensation, was still new to me.

As the story goes, when Jacob (had a dream that he) wrestled with a man—or an angel—and prevailed, he was given a new name: "Israel . . . for you wrestled with G-d." I don't remember learning this in Hebrew school, and even if I had, it didn't register. What could this mean? To fight with G-d? To fight with yourself? To engage in some sort of internal or external mystic battle with an all-powerful opponent? Why would we be in opposition to G-d anyway?

In general, I always had a hard time connecting to Torah stories, the same way I could never connect to a period piece with the characters speaking in thick Old English accents, wearing corsets, going to war on horses to fight (political) battles I couldn't relate to. Similarly, the way our foremothers and forefathers were presented to me as a kid felt distant from my own experience (despite feeling a deep connection to my middle name, Rachel). Before I'd been to Israel or had ever gotten high, they seemed like flat, illustrated characters in children's picture books wearing white robes and sandals, walking through dusty stone pathways or traversing the desert—imagery I couldn't relate to as real back then. Plus, their struggles of fraternal strife, infertility, or sparring with the Romans felt too irrelevant for me to connect to the deeper emotions behind them.

So it wasn't until I smoked a spliff with Natalie Ginsberg on a weekend trip to Desert Hot Springs, where we shlepped all the books about trippy Judaism we could fit into the car, that I could finally appreciate the story of Jacob-turned-Israel.

I'd known Natalie for a few years at this point. The first time we met in person, we visited a pot farm on a moshav in southern Israel. Originally from Manhattan, she had an Ivy League education and worked in policy at MAPS; she also had a creative and sophisticated style sense, always dressed in colorful couture while advocating for psychedelics around the globe, including at the UN and eventually the Jewish Psychedelic Summit that we'd come to establish together with Rabbi Zac Kamenetz (a subject in Johns Hopkins' psilocybin study on religious professionals, who'd eventually found the "Jewish psychedelic support" nonprofit Shefa).

But our weekend retreat to the desert was before any of this. Natalie and I wanted to do some further research into the topic of "Holy Plants," having been inspired by a talk about psychedelics in Torah that we'd co-hosted many months prior with Rabbi Harry Rozenberg at a colorful church-turned-Chabad house in Venice Beach. In the talk, he spoke about topics like acacia, a native Middle Eastern shrub containing DMT, and how on Yom Kippur, the high priest of Jerusalem would hotbox himself in a chamber, the Holy of Holies (Kodesh HaKodeshim), with entheogenic incense burning on acacia coals. It's also suspected that cannabis was part of the concoction.

Whenever I tell people I write about Judaism and psychedelics, the stuff about entheogens in Jewish text is often what they think I'm getting at—and in truth, I had a whole chapter on it that I cut from this book—because psychedelic Judaism isn't only about proving that our biblical ancestors altered their consciousness with plant medicine, but rather about using the religion itself as a vehicle to have and to hold such an experience.

So there I was in Desert Hot Springs, a bit high from the "sacred herb" stuffed into that spliff I had smoked earlier with Natalie, as I sat by the fireplace in the early morning hours, and read a chapter on "unity" in one of Aryeh Kaplan's books on Jewish meditation. In it, he beautifully describes the essence of Judaism's most basic prayer, the Sh'ma, which translates to "Hear, Israel, the Lord is Our G-d, the Lord is One."

As Kaplan explains, it was only once Jacob was in a meditative state that he could access the angel—and therefore, it is only through such a state that we too may access the Israel inside each of us, as in the part of us that connects to and wrestles with G-d. In the Sh'ma, first we must ready ourselves with meditative consonants and an elongated vowel sound, "shhhhhhmmmaaaahhhhhh" (translating as a command: "hear!") in order to clear the mind and listen up, before coming to engage with the Divine—at which point, the part of us (i.e., the Israel within each of us) that comes before G-d is then privy to his wonder, to the basic, psychedelic, mystical-unitive fact of existence that it's *all one*. G-d is one. When I first read this, I thought instantly of the criteria for the Mystical Experience Questionnaire, with the first among them relating to oneness. And then I thought of one of the bumper stickers that Maharaj-ji's satsang put on their cars—"All One"—because for the guru too, G-d, in various names and expressions, was all One, just One. *Adonai Echad.*

There was something validating about making this connection because the prayer that was so central to my feelings and experience of "home" was now relevant to another "home" of mine: drug culture. Because my whole life, I've always held these two motifs in my heart: Judaism, naturally, and a certain faith in what's fringe. Jewish thought shared the same edges with psychedelic discourse, and it was here at the intersection—the everything in one—that the kaleidoscope of what "home" means began to fractalize into a singular whole.

And it was at this point, once I was back "home" in LA, the home that I told myself I would never end up in, that the connections I began to see in psychedelic experience and the experience of being Jewish—in the stories of our Torah, in the intellectual play of learning a text, and the physical experience of shuckling, dancing, and certain mitzvot—began to express as, well, *one*.

The Jewish religion, at least for me, all of a sudden became one giant trip tale, a collective psychedelic journey of a people thrown into the trippiest of all trips—a never-ending wrestling match with the guy in the sky, "chosen" for a struggle that would teach us to strive to thrive, rather than just survive.

Through psychedelic consciousness as a lens, I began to learn more about Judaism in a way that now felt like it not only applied to the details of my own life, but also helped me integrate and make sense of them. In this process, I began to realize that Judaism itself—as a religion, and a quality of the soul—could offer a set and setting through which to engender an altered state, with or without a psychoactive substance.

Learning stories like Jacob's through teachers like Kaplan, I sensed that the development of the Jewish religion itself expressed the psychedelic moments experienced by the original Members of the Tribe, and that the practice of Judaism was a container for them to be transmitted through the generations. With ancient technologies like prayer and ritual, used by our ancestors for generations, perhaps we could tap into those timeless states of consciousness experienced by those at Sinai or in the

Beis HaMikdash. And yet, through contemporary psychedelic experience—especially in conjunction with ritual or in the context of Jewish framework—I also sensed we had a growing opportunity for totally novel moments of revelation giving way to new practice, rooted in ancient consciousness.

And so, I got a kick out of every time I learned about the litany of psychedelic moments in Jewish narrative—sometimes, but not always involving an entheogenic plant, which wasn't really the point anyway: It's not the substance that elicits a spiritual or healing experience; it's G-d. The "medicine" simply offers instructions for how your mind and body can operate differently, in the event of emotional, spiritual, or physical need. I think of it like tuning your neshama to G-d, getting aligned with the Source of all that is holy and healing. But to think that *the thing* or *the vehicle* is the thing that heals, that spiritualizes, and to expect the same result every time—that's *avodah zarah*, or idolatry, according to Rebbe Nachman.

To put it another way, when I saw the headline to a psychedelic trend piece giving credit to ketamine in couples' therapy for saving marriages, I thought to myself, *That's what Reb Nachman is talking about*: It's not the ketamine that's saving these marriages (because any other method might be able to do the trick, as well); it's whatever these couples are tuning into together that's saving the relationship. While some are more effective than others, the means to the end is just that, not an end in and of itself.

According to old Kabbalistic tradition, every blade of grass—every herb, every plant—has its own unique *mazal*, its own song, its own healing powers. As the Talmud says, "There is not a blade of grass below that does not have a star and an angel above, which strike it and tell it, 'Grow!'" Every plant has a particular essence, its own distinct spirit. No one necessarily *needs* it to commune with G-d, but it's there, maybe even to help with that purpose.

I once wrote an article about a Philadelphia start-up called Cannatunes, whose founder, "acoustic ecologist" Loretta Maps Bolt, would hook up an electrocardiogram or EKG device (typically used to monitor a patient's heart rhythm) to the fan leaves or stems of cannabis plants in order to read its electrical signals. Each signal would correspond with different frequencies on the Hertz Scale, and therefore different notes. The result? Every plant had its own song, literally. A plant's electrical system is like its brain, she told me. "These plants are making conscious decisions to communicate or not communicate with each other and the environment around them."

Now put that in your pipe and smoke it.

Or rather, first put it on your plate and eat it. Because what's a wellness-oriented "plant medicine lifestyle" that doesn't start with fruits and veggies, or at the very least end with picking up the habit of healthy eating as part of the integration (including the preparation) process? It's not just what we put into our bodies, but how we use our bodies—through physical practice—as a vessel to hold the psychedelic experience and walk the path of incorporating its lessons into our everyday lives. At best, we'd have those practices in place before the psychedelic experience, so that we can harness the high through the *keilim* of our discipline, so that when the body of the medicine leaves your own, at least the consciousness it helps us uncover—that spirit in the blade of grass—can stay.

Chapter 23

TRAUMA, TRUST, AND TOAD VENOM

One of Reb Nachman's most famous sayings goes something like: "The world is a narrow bridge, and the most important thing is to not be afraid." So when fear lives in your body from generations past, not being afraid becomes a process of learning to regulate the nervous system, so much as it is a conscious decision of emunah in daunting moments that call for a leap of faith. It's one thing to know G-d has your back, it's another thing to feel it. My experience with 5-MeO-DMT (a.k.a. the "G-d molecule") was a lesson in all of the above.

On a cloudy Sunday morning in late spring, I Ubered from Los Feliz to Topanga, taking winding canyons through the Valley, as I clutched onto *Aneni*, the little blue and silver hardcover, reading prayers in Hebrew and English for healing, journeying, health, and so on.

I arrived at a chic, rustic home tucked away in the hills, with wooden decks boasting views of the mountains, and pebble floors inside. Because my guides told me I shouldn't drive myself home afterward, I arranged to get a ride from my friend Roxanne, who'd helped me through challenging trips in the past, and lived with me on the third floor of Cloyne's west wing, in a glittery pink bedroom known as "W3H" or "W3Happy." Knowing she would be there to greet me after the session made me feel better. I was a ball of nerves.

As I got comfy on a cozy, blanketed floor cushion, my guides explained how this would go down: first, a baby dose of the venom inhaled through a fancy vaporizer, to get acquainted with the medicine, then a full dose (which would last about 25 minutes), and if I felt like it, I could do a third, smaller dose after that.

I don't know how long it took after the second dose for me to start freaking out as the medicine began to slaughter my ego and any sense of time. I discovered that once the toad hits, you're not "there" anymore. "You" dissolve within a matter of minutes, if not seconds, and what's left is pure, boundless, consciousness. Meanwhile, your body's nervous system is left to its own devices.

"Am I okay? Am I okay?" I repeated the question over and over again as I was coming up on the second dose. I don't even know if I was conscious that I was talking. I was so *scared* of the medicine, of losing myself. I was just, *stam*, scared. And I realized, my fear of the medicine was just a proxy, a surface-level fear, an opportunity to be afraid of something in my actual life to justify the fear that already lived within my body. I wasn't just scared of the medicine, I was scared of life itself. My genes were programmed to be fearful, to be vigilant, to wonder incessantly, *"Am I okay?"* or, in other words, *"Am I safe?"*

The trauma living within me from my own life, and it seemed, from generations past, bubbled up to the surface. I never felt so innately Jewish as when I did 5-MeO-DMT. This time, however, rather than the flavor of Yiddishkeit coming from the outside in— the niggunim as medicine music in ayahuasca ceremonies, the mystical teachings, the community of kindred spirits, encouragement to *pray* under the medicine—here my sense of Jewishness came from the inside out.

In the experience of my own lifetime, my parents' divorce triggered the trauma of insecurity and abandonment. The phrase "worrying is praying for what you don't want" rang especially true for my mother, whose distress over money was manifest in hyperbolic threats of homelessness; while my father on the other hand, who never quite got over losing his own father and older brother, carried the tendency of emotional shutdown when it came to needs of the heart. His own mother, naturally, had grown distant in the aftermath of losing her son and husband, not to mention having grown up an orphan herself.

My ancestors too had fled the Spanish Inquisition (on my father's side), heading east, where on all sides of the family they survived pogroms in places like Belarus, Lithuania, Austria, Poland, and Ukraine—back then, known as Galitzia—until they eventually immigrated to New York through Ellis Island. They had Yiddish names like Shloime, Rochel, Arel, and Sora, and took on English names like Solomon, Rose, Harry, and Sylvia, to fit into American society. The family they left behind in Europe all perished in the Holocaust.

As a child, I was obsessed with and terrified of anti-Semitism. I wondered if I *looked* Jewish enough to be targeted and was an avid reader of YA (young adult) Holocaust literature. I connected deeply with Anne Frank because she was a writer and a little rebellious. These things stick with us, often in ways we're unaware of.

And so, as the toad venom was not so subtly revealing to me, my body leans toward hypervigilance, ready for the moment in which the answer to that aching question "Are you okay?" is "No, I'm not okay." Perhaps adaptive behaviors, like hypervigilance, enabled my ancestors to survive, but now it was working against me. In the context of all the race-based, systemic trauma out there affecting populations of Native Americans, African Americans, and so forth, was this my own psychedelically triggered experience of what's considered "Jewish trauma"? It was certainly an expression of a type of anxiety that lives inside me, within my Jewish body.

At first, I was so dissociated, I didn't even register the sound of my guides telling me to breathe. Somewhere in the ether of my ego's nonexistence, I dissolved into everything and nothing. I can't fully remember what was going on "up there," but when I came down, I was relieved. Mainly because I was okay. Of course I was. But I still hadn't quite grasped the gravity of what my guides meant when they said "breathe," thinking they were maybe just trying to get me to relax; instead, they meant something more specific.

The guides offered me a final dose. And with it an opportunity to practice the breathing exercises that they tried to get through to me during the blast off. Maybe this was a chance to do teshuva with the toad. With *breath* in my tool kit, I gave the venom another shot, albeit at a lower dose than before. I inhaled and exhaled as they instructed me, feeling the rhythm of air enter and leave my body—and finally, I tasted just a little bit of bliss.

Lying down, knees bent, one hand over the heart, the other over my gut, I took three big breaths into the belly, then three into the chest, and did that three times in succession. A sense of relief came over me like a wave as I stayed with the breathing technique while the medicine wore off and I reentered my body. I was home. *I* was home. That's what tripping is about anyway: you take a psychedelic and you journey into another realm, all with the intention of returning home to yourself, your soul comfortably and sensationally in the body.

Each breath, according to the sages, merges in connection with the Supernal Breath that enters a person's body at all times—the neshama praises Source through the *neshima*. In other words, Rabbi Dovber Pinson explains in *Breathing and Quieting the Mind*, "Here there is no longer any I. There is no more separate self, no independent existence, no yesh. There is no-thing to experience. There is no experience, no I to register the experience. One is one with the One and is so with no awareness of such unity. The experiencer is one with the experienced."

This is almost exactly what I—or, well, the not-I—experienced with 5-MeO. And it was through the breathing techniques—literally feeling the expansion and contraction of my belly and chest as air moved in and out of my corpus—that I was able to embody the rhythm of creation itself, reflected in the expansion and contraction process known as *tzimtzum*, the very method by which G-d created the world.

I left the session with homework to practice the breathing exercise at least once or twice a day going forward. Like learning a word in a foreign language that sheds light on a concept unique to that culture (e.g., hygge), the exercises made me more aware of the way I breathed in the context of stress.

Chapter 24

LEARNING TO BREATHE AGAIN

To be completely honest, I've never had the attention span to sit down and *just breathe*. Never mind that I could read volumes on what Jewish thought says about breath. I'd rather sprint up a hill or take a *shvitzy* yoga class—forcing me, subconsciously, to focus on the cycle of inhalation and exhalation—than sit still and practice that cycle on purpose. It's an *avodah* for me to do it in my regular life, and only if or when I hit challenging (psychedelic) moments am I naturally drawn to conscious breathwork. Yet, maybe that's the point of a "practice"—putting in the work, even when we don't want to or don't feel like we have to—so that we have the vessel when we need it.

As Krishna Das has described, practice is like dropping an anchor into the ocean. Waves and weather may still rock the boat, but ultimately it's stable and not straying too far from its anchor in the present. Practice, he once said, is "becoming familiar with *being here*."

It's at the intersection of here and now, where I often find the answer to "Am I okay?" Because if at that intersection I'm still breathing, then at the most basic level of life and death, the answer is some version of yes. Under the influence of a psychedelic, it's not uncommon to feel like you're dying (maybe on account of ego death, or some somatic experience that sheds light on the vulnerability of being human). And it's been in these moments that I'm forced to reckon with just how much emunah I actually have: because if I truly believe that my fate is all from HaShem, and if I believe that G-d is good, then shouldn't I also trust that it's all for the good (bitachon), and therefore *everything is gonna be okay*? These are questions that psychedelics have inspired me to ask. And yet, in the context of vaping the toad venom, I felt like I was the character in that meme, where G-d simultaneously pushes you off a cliff (or perhaps, in alignment with Divine will, you opt to jump), and then you land in G-d's hands. There's another meme about emunah: traversing a dark tunnel with the knowledge that eventually there will be light; you can't see it, but you know it exists, that there's always light at the end of the tunnel. As Reb Nachman teaches, faith only starts where knowledge ends.

As a kid, I always wished my mother would just tell us that everything would be okay. She never did. Instead, I used my iPod to play Bob Marley's "No Woman, No Cry" on repeat, because it featured the line "Everything is gonna be all right" and reminded me of the soundtrack to dozing off with my siblings in the back row of my stepmother's Lincoln Navigator on the way home from kirtans or barbecues with family friends by the beach. But emunah wasn't yet a word in my mom's vocabulary, and the way she approached life reflected that, even more so in times of crisis. The mentality was that life happened *to* us, not *for* us, and she, especially, seemed to be enslaved by her circumstances.

Rebbe Nachman teaches that breath itself is emunah, while shortness of breath is lack thereof. During their slavery in Egypt, the Hebrew tribe lacked the emunah that Moses would lead them to redemption, and thus they experienced shortness of breath—*kotzer* ruach.

In elementary school, I was diagnosed with childhood asthma. Despite the fact that I sometimes used an inhaler when we had to run laps around campus in P.E., I grew out of it, thank G-d, and basically forgot about it, maybe even blocked it out, until a two-night ayahuasca ceremony during a more recent Chanukah, when all of a sudden a struggle to breathe crept up on me. I felt a tightness in my chest that brought me back into the body of my younger self, as if reinhabiting a layer of an onion stored deep inside my somatic memory. I was uncomfortable but I didn't freak out. In fact, I wasn't even scared. My chest was tight, but I'd learned in a previous ceremony a few years earlier that I could "hack my health" by getting *behind* the ailment to the ruach that sustains our life force.

Like a baby who cries when taking its first breath (ruach), G-d knew the time for salvation had come when the Israelites sighed and cried, screamed and howled on account of their bondage. They cracked open, and the life of the Jewish people began anew. Emunah absolved their fears. It's said that, rather than part the Red Sea all at once, the Israelites walked headfirst into the water, up to their necks, as G-d only parted the sea in conjunction with their faith put into action. I can imagine the fear they faced as they entered the water, as much as I can almost hear the beating of the tambourines as Moses's sister Miriam and the women held down the vibe to keep spirits high. Overcoming fear is a choice, as much as choosing to have fun, to be fun.

If you let it, fear might kill you—even if it's a slow death by anxiety and the physical breakdown that comes along with it—but if you hold faith, or know in your bones that "everything will be okay" then I think it's possible to neutralize the fear, even if just by an iota. That's emunah (at least some form of it), but it's taken years for my body to catch up with and latch on to my intellectual understanding of it. And to this day, I'm still figuring it out. So there I was, reliving the me who had asthma, and relearning how to breathe. I tried clearing my throat, breathing in what seemed like circles, feeling into my stomach and my chest. Eventually I could breathe clearly again—and I didn't take it for granted. I let out a deep sigh of relief and gratitude.

The Talmud teaches that "sighing breaks a person's body," which, according to Rebbe Nachman, means that with breath we can overcome our physical limitations, strengthen the soul, and achieve spiritual elevation.

I've found yoga to be a good example of this: "One breath, one movement," a good teacher might say. Focusing on the breath, tethering our inhales to one asana and our exhales to the next not only quiets the mind (and ego), but also enables us to do things with our bodies that without such presence would be impossible.

Indeed, every sigh fills a want or a lack, according to Rebbe Nachman, because, since "the world was created with . . . the breath of G-d [who's compared to a glassblower]" then no breath means no life, but with each new breath life is renewed, exhaling impurity, inhaling vitality. A *krekhtz*, otherwise known as the "oy breath," he says, "provides wholeness [in place] of the lack."

It's ironic for me now to see the value in a sigh because I always resented it when my mother would take one of her long, audibly vexed sighs to preface a gripe, or in response to an inconvenience. But I can appreciate now that her tired sighs, on some level, signified her own version of optimism, as if she yearned for things to be better. Despite the fact that her attitude was usually glass half-empty, and despite what seemed like her lack of faith or trust, I also knew she spoke to G-d every night, asking for us all to be blessed. Maybe her sighs were just nonverbal prayers.

◂▾▸

The first night of that two-night Chanukah ceremony, I'd worked my way through breath, through tears, through dance, eventually bringing myself to a white shag carpet where I'd flow through yoga postures. But before that, I was brought back to the 16-year-old anorexic raging over the scale that defined her worth, crying hysterically to my distraught mother, who was helpless in helping me, and my father, mostly absent in these moments. All these years later, I guess I wasn't done crying. I hugged my knees to my chest, sobbing my heart out, before I slouched back in my seat, a tween lying awake at night, compulsively swallowing her tongue, afraid to be heard, afraid to suffocate. I took a sip of water. Maybe I was just thirsty. *I should drink more water*, I thought to myself, remembering the time a gut doctor once told me I was "chronically dehydrated." Then I became the asthmatic schoolgirl, tight in the chest. I didn't have the vocabulary or awareness at that time of my life to appreciate my body's part-somatic, part-genetic response to trauma, but two decades later I was able to draw on what I'd picked up later in life to help that girl heal.

When I thought of Tzfat—city of air, city of refuge—I could breathe easy. Tzfat: a psychedelic unto itself in the form of a city, where (to me, at least) G-d just feels more palpable. Tzfat is known to be a place of healing; no wonder so many holistic practitioners flock to its stone alleyways, ascending the staircases that define its topography—who needs chemical help when you have connection to HaShem? Who needs to get high when you're already at the mountaintop? Yet, if we can use breath alone or other mundane means to embody our relationship to G-d, I thought to myself, who needs "medicine"? Why run to ayahuasca, I questioned internally (while under the influence), when you can just run straight to HaShem?

In an effort to get close to G-d, I grabbed a velvet pink pouch once used for jewelry, where now I kept a little rock, painted gold with the letters: יאהדונהי (two names of G-d braided together into one). Rabbi Greenberg, a Kabbalist in Tzfat, had told me, in his thick Brooklyn accent, to look at this configuration every day for at least a minute, in order to get aligned and to clear out indecision. So I commissioned an artist to paint it on a rock that I could carry around. "Be very careful," she cautioned me when she handed over the finished stone art piece. I wasn't sure what she meant; maybe something about treating the object with respect because it carried G-d's name? I returned to New York a few weeks later, excited to show the rock to Eilish, the psychedelic Satmar unicorn with a Breslov flair who I'd been dating for about a year, some time after what seemed to be my final breakup with Aaron. A medicine man at his core, Eilish had his first psychedelic experiences as a young child in Williamsburg, taking in Shabbos, or by simply being in Tzfat when he got older and left home; therefore, I knew he'd probably explored this configuration in his own tripped-out teenage deep dive into mind-altering Chassidis and mysticism. "Wow," he said reverently, when I showed him the painted golden stone with blue and purple flourish. "This is a portal." As with the artist, I wasn't exactly sure what he meant, either—until I did.

It wasn't just a cool name of G-d, it was a portal *to* G-d. With the entheogenic brew coursing through my veins, I couldn't so much as hold the rock, let alone look at it, for more than a few seconds when the letters began vibrating into a spin, my whole body reverberating with electricity. I felt like I'd been zapped, and even after I put the rock away, I couldn't even look at the light of the fireplace or the candles at the center of the prayer circle. It was too much light. I felt like I'd brushed fire. I thought about the sons of Aaron, Nadav and Avihu, or the Four who entered Pardes. I begged G-d for mercy, apologizing profusely for being too nonchalant about the rock, too flippant about the power of the medicine. I felt like I'd been metaphysically electrocuted, and prayed that I shouldn't sustain any burns.

I'd never simultaneously experienced so many expressions of G-d as I did that night. There's the G-d who gives and who takes, who's nowhere to be found and everywhere, who is the light and the darkness, who is the sun, the moon, the stars, the earth, the universe, and simultaneously the mastermind and consciousness behind it all. It's G-d the father who, Judaism teaches us, protects us and lays down the law. He knows the best and worst about us (he created us after all) and so we aim to dedicate our lives in service of him, to get aligned with his will for us, and plea to him for blessings and redemption—since we know, after all, that he loves us. G-d the mother, on the other hand, is the *Shechina*, the Divine feminine, who soothes, who nurtures, who's there for us when Dad gets angry, who cradles us amid our tears and wipes them away with her love. She's a warm and cozy blanket on Shabbos, always there to catch us when we fall.

But the thing is, even in this diversity of expression, in the many names of G-d (HaShem, Adonai, Elohim; Krishna, Rama, Durga, just to name a few), the Lord really is just One. *All One.*

Since the episode with the rock, I'd kept my eyes mostly closed or squinted, sensitive to light (even in a dark, otherwise candlelit room), until I heard Eilish begin to sing a *bracha*. I opened my eyes to watch him light the menorah, and I settled into a calm. It was the fourth night of Chanukah. I gazed at him, remembering how earlier that night we'd lit the candles with his kids—an adjustment in and of itself, dating a *tatti* of three, but also an opportunity to uncover a redeemed sense of family.

I looked at the candles, considering how all the flames were actually from the same source. They were the same flame, now on different wicks. But they were one—the same way that certain loves can feel like a split flame, or soul, in two bodies.

The rock had put me through a spin, but like the garments spun through a laundry machine, I came out feeling a little more clear. The woes I'd brought to Rabbi Greenberg, the mind games I'd played with myself over the years, the doubts, the worry, the love, the excitement, the fear, the misalignment, the supposed *b'sherts* I so far didn't end up with? In that moment at least, something clicked into place; maybe an acceptance that G-d ultimately runs the show, an okayness with what is. My life had spiraled into this very moment, this calm, this present—in all senses of the word (it was Chanukah after all, a holiday of gifts and of light).

Chapter 25

DESCENT FOR THE SAKE OF ASCENT

At the heart of Judaism is the concept of descent for the sake of ascent—our slavery in Egypt for the sake of liberation, the darkness of Chanukah so that we could have the miracle of light, narratives of trauma baked into stories of resilience. Our souls descend into our bodies on earth so that we may use the physical as a vehicle for spiritual ascension.

We see the convergence of descent and ascent in the shared gematria (358) of the words for snake (*nachash*), representing the lowest low, and Messiah (Moshiach), representing the highest high. As Nili Salem once pointed out to me, looking into the eye of the snake (a motif not just in the Bible, but in all religions, including and especially ayahuasca imagery and ideology) is where you meet your healing. Face your demons and they cease to be; the only thing to fear is G-d himself.

In my own life too it's been through my embrace of heartbreak, through the cracks, that light's crept in. Indeed, during some of the toughest, darkest moments, I've had the greatest spiritual highs, and glimmers of opportunity to connect with paths and people for my highest good.

◂▾▸

I was en route to Israel, one step shy of getting my immigration passport, when I came back to New York from LA to visit friends before my "move." I was working to heal my Lyme disease, but more so working to fix that thing inside me that kept falling for toxic relationship patterns. "You say you want a family," my friend Yaakov, a therapist in training, told me a few months earlier during a shroomy Shabbos camping trip in the mountains east of LA, "but you're not acting like it." I needed to embody a different version of myself; what could it possibly feel like to be healed enough from the wounds of the family I came from, in order to have my own? Eilish was tall and beareded, with dark brown hair, pale white skin, and gentle blue eyes. When we first met, briefly, a few years before dating, we talked about Ram Dass (who "left his body" a few days later), and I thought he was cute, but otherwise didn't think anything of it. He had *peyos* and car seats, which I later noticed, as Tsiporah, Esther, and I piled into his car headed into the sunset before Shabbos.

When I first started seeing Eilish, I thought I was on my way to becoming a resident of Israel, and hadn't foreseen that becoming a "stepmom" (or some version of it) in Monsey would come first, bringing all my "stuff" to the fore. But as the adage goes, *Mann tracht, un G-tt lacht* (Yiddish for "Man plans and G-d laughs"). And yet, if my childhood was good for nothing else, couldn't I relate to children of divorce as a grown-up stepdaughter myself? In a newfound moment of appreciation and empathy, I came into a different sort of love for my own stepmother, who in truth—like my mother—has been one of my greatest cheerleaders, and out of all my parents, takes the prize for greatest concern over a *shidduch* for me and grandchildren for her.

Contracting Lyme disease six months prior to the start of that relationship had woken me up to the way stress now affected me, as I was on-and-off sick for months. Whereas once I almost never even felt my body at all, now I was forced to tune into my body, as regulating my nervous system wasn't a luxury but a necessity. And it was for the good: what happened for the first time ever was that I prioritized my physical and mental health as a path to ultimate wellness—and in doing so, I had the spaciousness, at least in those early days, to explore a new connection from a standpoint of mind-body attunement I hadn't previously experienced. In a relationship, I was looking to feel safe.

Descent for the sake of ascent: Did I need to endure heartbreak so I could feel the high of transcendent sadness as the foundation for better understanding love, family, and relationships? Did I need to slump into Lyme-y affliction just so I could rise to the occasion of treating my body better than I ever had before? Did I need to end up in suburban Monsey before I could end up in psychedelic Tzfat? (Still working on that one.) It was one thing to read about the nervous system in popular science-y books about trauma; it was another to take that information and integrate it into a real-life sensitivity toward my own.

Through breath, we can access the autonomic nervous system (ANS), which regulates physiological processes like heart rate, blood pressure, digestion, respiration, and sexual arousal. The ANS is synchronized by its two branches: the sympathetic, which acts as the "body's accelerator," and the parasympathetic, which serves as its "brake." The sympathetic activates in a state of fight-or-flight, while the parasympathetic ("safe mode") activates in a state of rest, digestion, repair, and relaxation.

Inhalation activates the sympathetic branch, and exhalation activates the parasympathetic. That's why mindfulness instructors will tell you to breathe out for longer than you breathe in. Meanwhile, heart rate variability (HRV) measures the balance between these two branches of the ANS: "As we breathe, we continually speed up and slow down the heart, and because of that the interval between two successive heartbeats is never precisely the same," Bessel van der Kolk writes in *The Body Keeps the Score*. "HRV can be used to test the flexibility of this system, and good HRV—the more fluctuation, the better—is a sign that the brake and accelerator in your arousal system are both functioning properly and in balance."

A lack of coherence between breathing and heart rate, he explains, makes people vulnerable to physical illnesses like heart disease, cancer, depression, and PTSD—whereas harmony in the HRV system, aided by practices like yoga, can reduce anger, depression, high blood pressure, elevated stress hormones, asthma, and back pain.

Because "man was made in the image of G-d," each aspect of human physicality has its spiritual correlations. Therefore, while medical doctors might focus on respiration in the context of the ANS and HRV, soul doctor Rebbe Nachman evaluates the rhythm of breath in terms of ruach and *chayos* (angels), teaching that the blood vessels in the heart correspond to living angels, and that the lobes of the lungs, or angel wings (*kanfei rei'ah*) use ruach (oxygen) to regulate the flame of the heart. Think of the neshama like a flame: you can fan the flame to make it bigger, or blow on it to put it out. Respiration regulates the heart; breath connects to the neshama.

And it was in the safety of this refreshing paradigm that I initially experienced when I dated Eilish that I could breathe a little easier. I felt safe to acknowledge wounds around home and family, love and money, that had previously, subconsciously held me back. I wasn't defined by my trauma, but I tried to actively notice when it showed up.

◂▾▸

Nowadays, "trauma" has become something of a buzzword, almost emblematic of our times—especially when the zeitgeist has been characterized by a global pandemic, the rise of fascism, the increasing threats of climate change, and other consequences born from a society built on distractions from *being here now*—because "be here now" isn't just about sitting on a pillow and relaxing into a state of presence, but about waking up to everything we do and don't want to see within the here and now, such that this heightened awareness motivates us to address the points of injury most in need of individual and collective tikkunim. Society can't be well unless we're individually healthy, and we can't be well when we've adjusted to a sick society. In the words of trauma expert and Holocaust refugee Dr. Gabor Maté, "So much of what we call abnormality in this culture is actually normal responses to an abnormal culture. The abnormality does not reside in the pathology of the individuals, but in the very culture that drives people into suffering and dysfunction."

But as Maté defines it, "Trauma is not what happened to you. Trauma is the wound that you sustained." It's "what happens inside you as a result of what happens to you"—and perhaps, as a result of what happened to your predecessors too. In fact, the theory of epigenetics holds that the trauma of your ancestors impacts the way your genes function.

Contemporary discourse highlights that "trauma lives in the body." It manifests not only in our thoughts, dreams, memories, and feelings, but also in the health of our physical being—in our backaches, our ulcers, our sleeping and eating habits, our brains' anxiety disorders, compulsions, and addictions. We may not always be consciously aware of the traumas that we're holding on to and carrying around with us, but such injury, when not processed and integrated, will continue to express itself through the language of our bodies, rather than in clearly articulated thoughts or words. Therefore, it's in the body where we must often encounter and embrace our deepest brokenness or wounding.

"Trauma triggers a physiological process that needs to be 'worked through' the body," psychiatrist and author Julie Holland once told me in an interview. As she explained it, the same way a goose might shudder after a confrontation with another goose, or a deer shivers after it's been startled by a person, before the animal can resume its regular life and go back to, say, eating, "a mild tremor goes through the body." This is a normal, necessary response, allowing an emotion, like fear for instance, to make its way through the body and be released, rather than getting stuck. Cementing into the fight, flight, or freeze response does no good for the nervous system.

To varying degrees, all of us have experienced trauma within our lifetimes because "every childhood had trauma; at some point, you had needs that weren't met," Julie has said. "To heal from trauma, you need to do the hard work of standing your ground, getting into your body, feeling your feelings, and allowing the muscular tension to release, just as you had allowed the trauma to exist in your narrative. Make space for it."

When we look at all these other ailments—addiction, depression, anxiety, chronic pain—trauma is sometimes the suspected root, despite being, as psychologist Peter Levine has called it, "the most avoided, ignored, belittled, denied, misunderstood, and untreated cause of human suffering."

But is suffering the worst thing to happen to us? To quote Maharaj-ji, as Ram Dass did in a 1992 lecture about Judaism, "I love suffering, it brings me so close to G-d." This too is central to Reb Nachman's Chassidis: From the lowest lows may we garner momentum to soar to the highest highs, like pulling back a bow and arrow to its farthest point so that it may shoot as far as possible. Through a broken heart we have the greatest capacity to connect to G-d; through the cracks there's an opening for light. Or as the Kotzker Rebbe once said, "There is nothing as whole as a broken heart."

And it was precisely this that I've observed over the years in the "heimedelic" fringe. It's sometimes easy to see Chassidis articulated in real life, when you observe it embodied in actual Chassidim—and in yourself.

In one ceremony to honor Tu B'Shvat, I remember prostrating myself to G-d, at the time not even consciously realizing that's what I was doing, because it also felt so natural—taking the position in my spot on the women's side of the room (as it's common to put the genders on opposite sides in frum ceremonies), where I sat between a yoga teacher from Crown Heights and a Chassidish woman with a *tichel*, thick tights, and shin-length skirt, who'd later dip out to use a breast pump.

I could feel my heart beating in my fingertips, an electric pulse emanating from the soft padding beneath my nail beds, and I became aware of the race happening within my chest. *Am I always like this*, I wondered, *and only now am noticing it?* My grandfather died of a sudden heart attack in his 50s, leaving my mother, a young and wild 26, to navigate the perils of life and men without his guidance. I never met Howard Levin, but my mom spoke to us about him, and I know he and my grandmother were madly in love and she never quite got over his death. Considering the heartache in my family, I pondered whether I had inherited this fast-paced beating from my mother—she runs on an even higher decibel—and who knows, maybe I even picked up the speed in gestation, as a fetus co-regulating with the high-strung pace of her own body.

I recreated *the womb*, so to speak, and crawled into "child's pose"—a form of prostration—my *keppele* on the floor, creating a cavity between my torso and the ground, as I reached my arms out in front of me in surrender. *"Kish in the keppele,"* my father would call it when I was a kid, and he'd plant a kiss on my forehead. I thought of the people I loved, such as Daniella, who was *always* there for me, who always dreamt of us all living together on a "mommune." I called in their presence for a moment, but ultimately, calling in the love energetically launched me into a love affair more so with Source. In that space beneath my belly and above the floor was G-d. Literally, *dveykus* embodied, as if I were hugging HaShem, cradling him with my body. And it was from that position, in combination with focusing on my breath (aligning with Source to reproduce the moment), my nervous system began to calm down. In the following six months, I'd pay extra attention to what made my nerves tick and what quelled them; it wasn't severe, but I was struggling with monthly Lyme flare-ups and needed to get them under control.

Judaism holds that physical health is a prerequisite to spiritual pursuits. According to the medieval Torah scholar known as the Rambam, "A healthy and complete body is among the ways of G-d because it is impossible to understand or have any knowledge of the Creator when one is sick."

If psychological issues like anxiety, depression, or trauma can dysregulate the nervous system, putting us at risk of heart disease, cancer, or PTSD, we then, as the Rambam might say, have a responsibility first and foremost to address it. In simpler terms, if the mind is sick, the body follows—but we can also start with the body to heal matters of the mind.

Even the Baal Shem Tov—an herbalist, healer, and shaman in his own right—recognized that his primary task "was to heal the body of Israel, and later to heal the soul of Israel," as author Yitzhak Buxbaum put it in *Light and Fire of the Baal Shem Tov*. Indeed, the most basic of shamanic wisdom hinges on a nourishing, symbiotic relationship among body, mind, and soul—the physical, emotional, and spiritual.

But psychedelics, if used for healing, can help speed up this process—not by curing us overnight, but by showing us in stark relief what needs attention and setting us on the path to heal it on our own. If anything, psychedelics wake us up to what those in the field call our own "inner healer." With my racing heart and questions of existential security, I've found that psychedelics can offer a kind of artificially initiated trauma experience, during which, with help, we have the opportunity to move through the body's programmed responses, transforming fear, resistance, and discomfort into healing. But equally or even more important is that, in acute moments of fear or discomfort, gratitude or love, psychedelics have helped me refine my prayers.

Psychedelics can offer us a kind of (dis)embodied experience where one is both subjectively immersed within and objectively witnessing their own experience. From this simultaneously in- and out-of-body perspective, it becomes easier to identify where emotional or physical injury lives within our soul-body-mind field, and then to play and work with it in order to move it around and release its hold on us. And the only way out, as they say, is through: to acknowledge anxiety, breathe into it, and release it, until the tension simply dissolves—not from avoidance or escape, but through encounter and acceptance.

As the saying goes, what you don't transform, you transmit. "Being aware that the things that happen to us can affect us is ultimately very positive, even if at first, it is painful to take in," Dr. Rachel Yehuda, director of the Center for Psychedelic Psychotherapy and Trauma Research at the Icahn School of Medicine at Mount Sinai, told me in an interview. "The word 'trauma' has a very negative valence, and it often doesn't make room for some of the positive consequences of trauma exposure that can occur once these events are processed and incorporated into our narratives about ourselves. These consequences could include learning from experience, having a challenging experience shape us in meaningful or positive ways—this is what is often referred to as posttraumatic growth."

In Jewish terms, "posttraumatic growth" is the transformative potential that lies in our pain. As the Baal Shem Tov said, "In the place of the king [G-d] there are many chambers and each door has its own distinct key. The deeper Kabbalistic intentions are the keys to the rooms. There is, however, a master key that opens all doors, and that is a broken heart."

Chapter 26

ARE YOU
MY GURU?

For my father, it was a broken heart that opened the door to India.

Judaism had failed him in the wake of life's hardest moments—losing his oldest brother (who was also his mentor) to leukemia, and six years later, at 19, losing his father in a fluke accident during an operation. Both my grandmothers had been widowed in middle age; neither remarried. My grandmother Pearl, who I'm named after (in Hebrew, *Margalit* means "pearl" or "gem") had emotionally shut down. Unable to find solace in his family, my father went on a journey of existential angst and spiritual seeking. But because Judaism, as he'd experienced it, had little to offer, he looked elsewhere.

Those who came of age in the wake of the Holocaust were deprived of "the ecstatic high religion that had been, [because] we were too wounded," writes Yoseph Needelman, summarizing Shlomo Carlebach, so instead many Jews went to the Far East to learn from spiritual masters who, unlike many of the rabbis or religious leaders of my father's generation, were not "contaminated from the Holocaust [about] the way we could let G-d into our hearts."

My father might not be Jewishly "observant" in the typical sense, but he is, without a doubt, one of the most religious people I know. He's a believing Jew whose daily spiritual practice includes elements of Hinduism and Buddhism. The anger he felt toward G-d in his youth ultimately inspired him to seek a closer relationship to the Divine (which until his most recent years, he found mainly through traditions other than Judaism). Besides, being so angry with G-d is predicated by a strong belief in Him—and that, my father has always upheld.

"I drove Allison nuts talking about G-d all the time," he recalled of his time single-parenting my older sister before he had more kids. "I was obsessed with trying to find meaning in the religions of the world." On his bathroom mirror, my dad once taped a Post-it note on which he scrawled, "Whatever happens to me is the best possible thing that could happen to me." At times, when I've worried about money, or about his decisions to take on another family, or to have another child at the age of 64, he's told me, "The Lord will provide." Despite his standard "Jewish anxiety," emunah and bitachon always seemed to come naturally to him. Maybe the heartbreak of the losses he suffered early in life launched him into a deeper level of connection with G-d, even if it was at times colored by anger.

G-d always made his way into any conversation with my parents. For my mother, it was usually in the form of a "G-d forbid," sometimes followed by a superstitious trio of spitting "pu pu pu," should the potential of something especially horrendous (*G-d forbid*) get her all perked up. "G-d willing" was also a popular one among both my parents, and of course "Thank G-d." Plus, it's thanks to my parents that I wouldn't spell out G-d with an "o," or get a tattoo for that matter, either. They're religious about certain things, even in Judaism, despite their lack of halachic commitment.

In fact, it was the Baal Shem Tov who popularized inserting G-d's name into moments of everyday speech, with phrases like those my parents use, as a way to bring G-d into our consciousness throughout the day, not just in prayer and study. The idea, as I interpret it, is to see G-d in everything: To casually tell him what we want, what we don't want, and what we're grateful for. My dad has the soul of a Chassid, and I've always related to him from that place—free-spirited, G-d-curious, and a *bissell* anxious. So much of what I've learned about the philosophies of the Besht or Reb Nachman I see in my father's own practice. And so much of what motivates him comes from a place of Divine inspiration, devotion to his guru (almost exactly the same way Chassidim follow a rebbe), and the pursuit of a good time. But only through meeting others who reminded me of my father, or with a similar spirit—this time through my own journey, rather than through characters I met through his—did I come to appreciate him in a different light through expanded context.

◂▾▸

Within four years of founding his legal practice in 1967, my dad had defended more cannabis cases than anyone else in the country. For what could be called the very antithesis of corporate law, he had built a large practice of about six lawyers and 15 total employees. He drove nice cars and lived in a big house, where he threw fabulous hippie parties, featuring bands like Fleetwood Mac, Canned Heat, and Steve Miller. Then, in 1971, he decided to take an indefinite sabbatical. "I wanted to try to get some answers while I was still young," he told me, "as I saw my brother passed on early and my father was not even sixty when he passed. I saw that life was short, and I wasn't going to wait till I was seventy years old to start davening at a temple to figure out what life was about."

He was 29 when he consulted with a psychiatrist, Dr. Harry Siegel, who told him, "Life is a mystery to be lived, not a problem to be solved." After about six weeks of therapy, my dad made the decision to go off into the world. "I left my house, I left my car, I left my dog. I just had to go," he says. The doctor had given him several books on spirituality and consciousness that he said helped him on his journey, including Ram Dass's then-newly released *Be Here Now*, Carl Jung's *Man and His Symbols*, Robert de Ropp's *The Master Game*, George Gurdjieff's *Meetings with Remarkable Men*, and others. "I know where you are going," Dr. Siegel told my dad. "I only wish I was going with you."

He began his trip in Greece before making his way south and east, covering Egypt and then a kibbutz in Israel, before finally arriving at the other promised land of India. There, in Rajasthan, he signed up for a silent meditation course with S. N. Goenka, a Burmese master of the Vipassana method. During the 10-day course, students were required to wake up at 4 in the morning, meditate for repeated three-hour stretches until 9 at night, and never speak unless spoken to. At first it was "torturous," my dad recalls, thinking he had better things to do than "contemplate my breath," but by the end of the course, as he writes in his memoir, "I felt mentally very strong and that I had a grasp on the limits and the potential of my thoughts. My body was strong and healthy, especially as I hadn't eaten meat for a long time—I had given it up as a *tapasya* during the [State Assembly] primary campaign [of 1970]. All my energies were really high. I was ripe."

As it turned out, many of my dad's fellow Vipassana students knew Ram Dass, who had taken the previous five courses with Goenka. And so after the Goenka course, my dad trekked to New Delhi. On the roster of a hotel he decided to stay in, he noticed Ram Dass's name. My dad wasn't attempting to meet Ram Dass, let alone know where to find him. Going around Delhi asking for Ram Dass, my dad jokes, would be like wandering around New York City asking for John Smith. And yet . . . by serendipity or "Maharaj-ji's grace" as they would call it, when he left a note for Ram Dass at the front desk, saying he had a message from Goenka (who'd told my father if he somehow came across Alpert, to let him know that "he is a man of love and could be a great teacher"), he received a reply with an invitation to Ram Dass's room.

By this point my father had read *Be Here Now* cover to cover countless times, studying it in depth as if it were his personal bible. Incense smoke wafted like perfume throughout the young baba's hotel abode, decorated with photos of an elderly Indian man wrapped in a plaid blanket (common among Maharaj-ji devotees, much the way Lubavitchers display photos of "The Rebbe").

Ram Dass asked my father what else he had planned for his stay in India. "As far as I'm concerned, this is it," my dad told him. "You are the epitome of what I had hoped to experience here." Ram Dass shook his head no, admitting that whatever value my father saw in him was just a reflection of Maharaj-ji; he instructed my dad to go meet the guru four hours away by train in Vrindavan—immediately.

When my father first met Maharaj-ji at his ashram in Vrindavan, he was at first reluctant about the idea of *pranaming* to another human being. "I thought about the protocol of going to a guru, of surrendering yourself, of bowing down, and I wouldn't say it was abhorrent, but it was uncomfortable knowing it's not in our Jewish tradition." And yet, it helped that the guru, well, felt heimish. He had the familiar air and wit of a Jewish *zayde*.

And so, he put aside his concerns and laid his head upon the tucket. Then Maharaj-ji revealed himself through subtle and sensitive psychic details that convinced my father of the guru's unconditional love, soulful presence, and fractalized consciousness, unbound by the confines of his physical body.

"I learned from the guru that it's all one, whether it's called Hinduism, Buddhism, Judaism, or any other ism," my dad told me. "Even though in India, they have all these statues and deities that they appear to be praying to, they see beyond that and know those are just props, and they're praying to one G-d, just like Jews pray to one G-d." *Adonai Echad.*

⁂

As a kid, my exposure to Hinduism came mostly from HinJews—and so it wasn't until I traveled to India for the first time that I got an authentic taste of what the satsang was channeling back home in the States. My dad, his partner, and I tagged along on a trip that his close friend Raghu Markus, executive director of the Love Serve Remember Foundation, was leading, touring us through sites visited by Ram Dass. In the foothills of the Himalayas, we drank chai with local devotees (both now deceased) like Krishna Kumar Sah, better known as K.K., who became Ram Dass's close friend and translator, and American expat RamRani Rosser (once called Yvette), who told us crazy psychedelic tales of her 20s, en route to finding bhakti. We visited the charming Hotel Evelyn in Nainital, boasting views of the lake dotted with boaters and historic *nachas* because Ram Dass and the satsang stayed there in the early '70s.

It wasn't far from Baba's Ashram at Khainchi Dham, nestled high in the mountains, and "clean as a whistle" as my father might say. We had to remove our shoes at the entrance, our bare feet gracing sparkling white marble floors that led us through courtyards featuring statues of the deities beckoning visitors to spend a few moments in prayer, as well as to private rooms sparsely decorated but for one of Maharaj-ji's plaid blankets upon a bed.

I wasn't sure what to feel at the ashram. This was *the* most iconic spot on our trip, the place where so many people met Maharaj-ji and spent most of their time with him (although he also had ashrams in other parts of India). The statues didn't kindle me; not that I expected them to. *Avodah zarah* makes some people highly uncomfortable; for me it carries no spiritual weight. I see them as art, and if it's art that stirs something positive or Divine within someone, all the better. Like my dad (who doesn't spend time with idols, yet decorates his home with them), I've always been firm in my belief in the Jewish concept of one G-d, no matter how many masks or names.

But inside the room with the blanket, however, there was a different energy. My dad's partner burst out in tears (and the snarky, eye-rolling teenager in me wondered if it was performative—like the singing bowl meditations, dance routines, and seminude photos posted on her Instagram stories). I lingered around until she was finished having her moment so I could experience the place on my own. I tried to kneel over and place my forehead on the bed, similar to how one might place their forehead against the kever of a tzadik. It's rare in those moments too that I "know" what to feel. (As I've yet to visit Uman, it is only so far at Kever Rochel in Bethlehem and the kever of Chana and her Seven Sons—*Chana v'Shevat Binya*—inside a cave in Tzfat that have I actually bawled, and it's taken some warm-up.) More often than not, I'm mostly just self-conscious of not having a stronger reaction than I do.

Here, it felt similar. But there was something incredibly peaceful about this room in particular that made me question what my own personal relationship was to Maharaj-ji; I'd never quite had the luxury of exploring that or discovering him on my own.

I guess I'd been born into a life kissed by Maharaj-ji's grace, and as Ram Dass would say, that was no accident—it was my dharma, just as later in life he'd reconciled his own dharma of being born into Judaism and what that meant. But what *did* it mean to me? Who was Maharaj-ji to me anyway? He was my father's guru—and had been grandfathered in as one of the tzadikim in my life too. Maybe to me he was that *zayde* figure, after all.

At the ashram itself my reaction was more empathetic, as I could palpably tune into what my father was feeling. He's a lot of fun and charismatic, but doesn't generally display emotion—and yet, I knew being here moved him, brought him back through time and space, to somewhere deep inside his heart. Sure it was sentimental and nostalgic, but like northern Israel is to me, northern India is the place that most lit up his soul. I was grateful to share that with him. I could relate to that feeling, and to feel it with him was an awesome blessing—because in certain ways, I know our souls are cut from the same cloth.

It's a different kind of closeness than what I share with my mother. To varying degrees of success, she's set out to be my best friend (if only I'd let her), her incessant worry a proxy for love, on call to be there for me at the drop of a hat (even if she takes on more than she can handle and kvetches about it along the way). Whereas my mother's primary role and purpose in life is motherhood, I can't say the same sense of parenthood is true of my father. Vying for closeness and quality time with him, often in competition with his work, partner du jour, and hippie sense of time (or lack thereof), has often led to disappointment. Time with any loved one is precious, but it feels all the more so when there's a 50-year age difference; plus, when he's in a good mood, hanging out with him isn't just fun, it's uplifting and inspiring.

In high school, he took me to visit UC Berkeley; when I started grad school, he flew out with me and my younger sister to install me in New York. We've had our best times in the Bay: trips with my brother and stepsisters to Fisherman's Wharf, one-on-one hikes in Muir Woods, chatting up strangers in Haight-Ashbury, and in recent years, sitting for interviews in Mark McCloud's famous acid blotter art gallery inside his Mission Victorian, where filmmaker Seth Ferranti shot a documentary about LSD.

My dad encourages me to travel. He vibes with everyone at whatever party you invite him to (whether a kirtan, a *farbrengen*, a trance dance, or a "chichi" Hollywood thing), and gets me on a level that my mother can't—because even if she has a free-spirited side, the world to her is a scary place in contrast to the comfortable confines of pet parenthood, ever devoted to her dog and cat. And yet, there's something safe about knowing she's always home, never too distant—emotionally or geographically—to be there for me. My dad, however, gets me from his own inclination toward adventure. My parents truly are each other's foils.

On a hike once at Franklin Canyon with my dad during a visit home from Berkeley, I confronted him about his role and responsibility in all our family *mishigas*. It wasn't an argument, just acknowledgment—for better or worse. It was dusk and smelled like eucalyptus; he was wearing a plaid flannel and jeans, and carrying his walking stick. "You know what, kid, I haven't known what the fuck I'm doing since 1970," he told me. "You're free, just go with the flow."

◂▾▸

To that end, our flow for the rest of our trip didn't exactly match the programmed itinerary Raghu had planned for the *yatra* in northern India, so at different points along the way, we did our own thing. India is like humanity on steroids, someone told me before I went; it's like humanity turned inside out—and what with the colors, sounds, smells, and sensations—I see that all to be true. It's psychedelic in its own right.

In the hills of Jageshwar, we practiced meditation techniques with a young Hindu priest I'd befriended, shutting out the surrounding forest by placing our fingers over our eyes, nostrils, and ears. We smoked ganja with sadhus—often dreadlocked Shiva devotees covered in ash—and went to a Passover seder at Chabad of Delhi, where I also went shopping at Fabindia because Raghu said I needed kurtas or otherwise *tznius* clothing to visit the holy sites.

We observed *Arti* multiple times a day, as ringing bells called in something of a minyan for the group prayer. In a Rajasthani village, I fell in love with a puppy named Ganga Das at the colorful ashram of Baba Sundar Das Ji, young (for a guru) and playful, with long dreads reaching below his exposed belly button and a sizable Western following—but there, I was more interested in talking to the sweet and gentle Baba Ram Krishna Das from a neighboring ashram—very old, skinny and toothless, his eyes deep and piercing with the wisdom of a sage. In Varanasi, we dropped candles (and wishes) into the sacred Ganges River. And in the holy city of Vrindavan, we visited Maharaj-ji's ashram, where my father met his guru for the first time. It was there that a stranger gifted me wooden *mala* beads that I've had ever since; and it was with this *mala* that I'd apply the Na Nach mantra, discovering that the syllables of Na Nach Nachma Nachman MeUman fit perfectly into the 108 beads of the mala, used as a meditation device among Hindus and Buddhists. In later years, I also learned that the gematria of Na Nach (נ נח) is 108. Just as in Judaism, 18—representing chai, or life—is a sacred number, 108 (chai times six) according to Vedic cosmology is also sacred, representing the universe, existence, and creation

During my downtime on this India trip, I journaled, read, offered edits to a rough draft manuscript of my father's memoir, and zipped through an intro book to Kabbalah by Rabbi Dovber Pinson. I shared gleanings from that book with my father, who is always wont to respond enthusiastically (so long as he could follow what I was talking about) whenever I'd share anything remotely spiritual. Anything relating to oneness, presence, or Divine connection usually caught his attention, even with his ADD.

But how much of it did he actually practice or integrate into his daily life? Before every meal, he bows his head in gratitude and blessing—and should he forget to do so (which he never does) he's vowed to fast for seven hours. At 11:11 each night, he spends at least 11 minutes meditating in front of his *puja* table, placed beneath a "Love Everyone" bumper sticker on the wall and adorned with photos of his deceased family and Maharaj-ji; in a drawer inside the puja table, he keeps his *talis* and tefillin, given to him by his ex-father-in-law, my older sister's late grandfather, who survived the Holocaust. My father is a strict vegetarian (not even fish is allowed into the house) and does yoga religiously multiple times a week. In his 80s, he's still doing headstands. But as my friend Lee once so aptly put it, for a guy who's doing all the things and smoking lots of weed on top of it, "Why does he sound like My Cousin Vinny?" My dad's not above cursing (as in, "that fuckin' D.A., man" or "these cops are real motherfuckers"), but yelling isn't allowed in his house (unless he's the one doing it, which is somewhat rare). Then again, as my older sister once joked, "imagine what he'd be like if he didn't meditate."

Regardless, at the core of our relationship is a deep bond and appreciation for who he is and what he's taught me. He thinks I'm fearless because I do psychedelics, when for him a few rocky acid trips and (what was probably a necessary) experience of ego death turned off his calling to explore further; although nowadays, he might get occasionally dosed with psilocybin by his partner, who in any given moment, never mind if it's Tuesday, might be high from mushroom tea.

Really though, aside from weed, at the core of his belief system lies the answer, in the form of practice, to the question: *What more could you need when you're close to G-d?* My dad and I might be a similar type of religious, even if we're practicing different religious expressions—although we both share physical health and belief in one G-d as core values; we're both drawn to experience—to singing, clapping, and movement; and we're both drawn to environments where the locals are much frummer than we are. If my dad, as the "baal teshuva" he is, had gone more for traditional Judaism than for HinJewism, I have an inkling he would've gone Na Nach (and when I fact-checked this statement, he confirmed its truth). He's into bumper stickers anyway. I snapped a picture one Father's Day of my dad on a hike, wearing a faded red T-shirt that said, "I left my heart in Vrindavan." I left mine in Tzfat. Together, we seek and find home in each other.

Chapter 27

OM NAMAH SHIVAYA —A BRACHA OVER THE "SACRED HERB"

At home, "marijuana" was a household term, as in, "Nobody belongs in jail for marijuana"—the famous opening line to my father's radio commercials, which we'd listen for during *"Breakfast with the Beatles"* on Sunday mornings. But in reference to his personal use, he always called it "the sacred herb," and would even say a *bracha*, of sorts, before sparking a joint: *"Om namah Shivaya!"* He calls smoking weed a "religious experience," and evokes the Lord Shiva, whose devotees use cannabis as a sacrament. Also reincarnated as Hanuman (who in turn is believed to be incarnated as Maharaj-ji), Shiva, the blue-skinned Hindu deity, reigns over the power of destruction, which my father reminds me includes destruction of the ego (maybe another reason why he tends toward mind-altering substances with the potential to dampen activity in the default mode network, the seat of the ego inside the brain).

My dad smokes weed exclusively from joints or from his Volcano—what is now considered an old-school vaporizer equipped with an inflatable plastic bag from which you inhale the vapor of heated cannabis flower. I remember when the Volcano first came out, we all thought it was the coolest, most futuristic way to get high. Nowadays it reeks of early aughts cannabis culture.

On one of the various retreats in Maui before Ram Dass "left his body," as they say, my dad asked him for advice about cannabis advocacy. It was after California had legalized weed for adult use, but the new law was, and remains, imperfect. One issue my dad is passionate about is the lack of on-site consumption spaces where people can legally smoke weed indoors, as one would drink alcohol at a bar. The issue here is that it's also illegal to smoke weed outside in public, and many people who rent apartments aren't allowed to smoke there either. "I wanted to express to the Los Angeles City Council and Cannabis Licensing Department that there's a religious experience when it comes to marijuana, and that people have a right to assemble, to come together and enjoy each other's company in a setting where they can use it openly, just like people who use alcohol," my dad explained to me. "I went to Ram Dass to give me words of wisdom, to convey this in a simple way. He told me, 'Tell them that using it is a path to G-d.'"

"When people use the sacred herb, they are less identified with their egos," my dad tells me. Indeed, psychedelics, cannabis, or any other entheogen is known to "open the doors of perception," he says, referring to Aldous Huxley's seminal essay about his experience with mescaline. "You could lose your self-identity, which could be a very stressful experience, but once you let go of the anxiety that you might feel after being in that state, you might come to realize that it's all about love, and that's the truth of our being."

It feels funny to quote my dad in print saying such deep things. As father and daughter, we've been through all sides of this experience and, as much as what he's saying rings true, it's sometimes a lot for me to digest, coming from him. And yet of everything my dad has taught me, the most important and relevant lesson on a daily basis has been to try to understand things as perfect within their imperfections. Does my father always act like it's "all about love"? Of course not. But does his work in the world inspire me to believe that this is nonetheless an irrefutable truth? It does.

"When I became a young criminal defense lawyer, I thought it was a good way to fight authority, by fighting for the rights of the downtrodden or accused," he recounts. "My motivation for participating in marijuana activism as such a big part of my life was that I wanted to relieve suffering, the suffering of those who were arrested and charged, the suffering of those who didn't have access to a good lawyer who believed in the cause, the suffering of the cost to the public of taxes and incarceration, and to return [to] and rekindle the constitutional right to life, liberty, and the pursuit of happiness, which includes the freedom of choice for themselves." Is my dad's ego in his work? Sure. But so is a genuine, authentic commitment to ethics and justice—a love for serving G-d by serving others, as Maharaj-ji had instructed him and others to return to the States and use their talents, like lawyering (in my dad's case) or singing (in Krishna Dass's), as a service.

When my father met Maharaj-ji, he thought that was *it*. He wanted to stay in India and become a devotee. But Maharaj-ji sent him back to America, telling my father he had a "boon"—a skill—and that he had to use it to serve. So my father returned to LA and reopened his law practice.

Not long after, he got a call from Ram Dass, whose good friend Tim Leary had been captured in Kabul, arrested, and returned to his jail cell in the SoCal suburb of Santa Ana—a year and a half after having escaped that prison (he'd been sentenced on a marijuana possession charge), then sought refuge in North Africa, Switzerland, and finally Afghanistan. Leary was facing 10 years for five grams of weed, not to mention any consecutive sentence for the crime of escape.

"I agreed to represent him pro bono because at that time, he had no financial ability, and for me, I thought he was an important icon and represented freedom," my dad says of the LSD mogul. "Maybe in a twisted way, but it was freedom nevertheless." The case garnered a good deal of attention and went all the way to trial. My dad hoped it would illustrate the injustice of marijuana prohibition, and in court he described Leary as a "an eagle beating his wings against the cage," although as *Time* magazine put it, "It took the jury only an hour and a half to turn the defendant into a common jail bird."

My dad took the case for free, in service of what it stood for: Here was a celebrity of the countercultural victimized by a senseless Drug War. The moral of the story was about freedom.

That's always been at the heart of his law practice, and why he inspires me. My father's number one value is a moral one. His contribution to the great cosmic fixing—tikkun olam—lies in fighting the War on Drugs, fighting for the basic human right to alter consciousness.

Chapter 28

THE BAAL SHEM TOV AND NEEM KAROLI BABA: BIRDS OF THE SAME (PSYCHEDELIC) FEATHER

Jewish stoners, at least the neo-Chassidm, love to discuss the possibility that the Baal Shem Tov might have smoked weed.

The Besht famously smoked from a pipe (*lulke*) before he prayed, in order to invoke an aliyat neshama, or ascension of the soul, and travel through Kabbalistic realms of higher reality. Like my dad often does before he hits the "sacred herb," it is said that the Besht even recited a *bracha* over his pipe-smoking. From eating to sleeping, to toking and joking, for the Besht, writes Buxbaum, "Every action and movement was for the service of G-d."

Surely, there was tobacco in the pipe, but stoner speculation might suggest a cocktail of other plants too since the Baal Shem Tov was a master herbalist who picked various grasses and plants to concoct medicinal tinctures. He was known to spend hours in the fields and forests, connecting with nature and thereby with G-d. It's not so far-fetched to assume that his pipe contained the "sacred herb," since cannabis was available within the region. The 13th-century Kabbalistic grimoire (book of magic) Sefer Raziel HaMalakh provides a technique for warding off spirits with wormwood and cannabis, as well as using the latter in certain ointments. And intriguingly, according to the legend and lore depicted in *Cannabis Chassidis*, someone in Brooklyn who apparently was in possession of the Besht's pipe had once tested it and, lo and behold, found cannabis resin.

I'd say, safely, that most of the satsang—Maharaj-ji's Chassidim—smoke weed, or have in the past. But with regard to any entheogen, be it cannabis or LSD, it's only a vehicle to connection, the high itself not a destination.

Yes, I'm calling them Chassidim because the word from which it's derived—*chesed*—means loving-kindness. When I went over this definition with my dad, he cracked up. "Oh my G-d," he exclaimed abashedly, as if he'd accidentally walked backward into traditional Judaism. It's what Ram Dass always talked about all along—well "loving awareness" anyway. Loving awareness is the G-d-consciousness of our souls, underneath our egos, shared by the unified collective. Loving-kindness is the application of that consciousness put into practice. *Chesed* was at the core of Maharaj-ji's teachings.

I always suspected that the satsang were kindred spirits with the Chassidim I met through my psychedelic reporting. And so it was validating when Krishna Das himself made the connection. "When I read *The Light and Fire of the Baal Shem Tov*, it was like reading about Maharaj-ji," KD told me in an interview. "Unbelievable." The Besht was a "great *siddha*," he described, holding all the magic power that any accomplished yogi has, like being in two places at once, or traveling to different dimensions—"paranormal stuff." But at the heart of the overlap between a bodhisattva and a tzadik is that their work is grounded in the mundane world, engaging with common people, through "the joy of merging with G-d, [and with] love as the primary connection."

Joy or *simcha* was a primary mandate in the Chassidish movement. Mystics like the Baal Shem Tov taught that immersion in G-d consciousness granted access to *olam haba* (the world to come) in the here and now. Joy was G-d consciousness, and G-d consciousness was the transcendent, *awes*ome, and infinitely present moment.

In fact, the Torah illustrates that presence was the only way to access HaShem. When G-d asked Moses, "Where are you?" he responded with *Hineni* (I am here). "It's the most 'be here now' story ever. The intersection of where you meet G-d is when you're there now," friend and Torah teacher Nili Salem explained to me, bubbly with excitement. "Every time you meet G-d is when you're present." Family friend Parvati Markus reminded me that, in the Upanishads, this state of enlightened consciousness is called *satchitananda*—being, truth, wisdom, awareness, bliss, joy. And in the discourse of psychedelic science, it's a tenet of the mystical experience.

Substances can get you to this high state of consciousness, like a helicopter can take you to the top of a mountain. But if the helicopter may simply hover, without landing, when it descends you go with it. If you climb up the mountain yourself, however, you don't have to leave. You can stay there up high (at least for a little while), on the ground of the peak itself. Maybe in the latter instance, you've seen the top of the mountain before, from the view of the helicopter, and so as you ascend to the peak, you have an idea of where you're headed. And that memory is invaluable.

As my friend Lee once joked, "Acid's cool, but have you tried Chassidis?" Maharaj-ji was a big Chassid of another well-known tzadik, *Yeshu HaNotzri*—Jesus of Nazareth. KD recounted to me the story of when Ram Dass gave acid to Maharaj-ji. The guru called it good medicine—"yogi medicine" was the term he used—but said that while it "takes you through the doorway, into the room with Christ, you can't stay. The only way to stay is love."

It's hard not to recall what Yitzy Schwartz and many other Chassidish psychonauts have told me—that when they discovered psychedelics, they finally got what the Baal Shem Tov was talking about. But even if he did smoke from a pipe, it was his *dveykus*—closeness to G-d—that got the Besht all fired up, magnetizing those who followed him and his teachings.

In a sense, what's happening now, in the fringy heimish world is a psychedelic Jewish revolution: not one that's reinventing the religion, but rather harkening back to its roots, getting to the *ikar* of original Chassidis, which itself was a means of getting to the *ikar* of the indigenous, earth-based Hebrew tribe and the essence of the shamanic rituals that came from it.

At its core, the Chassidish movement was truer to Judaism, in its original form—as a tribal religion of the Hebrew desert folk—than the academic, Christianized, sterile form that became popular in Europe. Indeed, aboriginal Jewish spirituality has "less to do with religion than it does with direct, uninhibited experience with Creator through Creation," writes Rabbi Gershon Winkler in *Magic of the Ordinary.*

Shalom, the Argentinian medicine man from LA, was the first to introduce me to Winkler's book on shamanism. I was captivated within reading the first chapter, and often *Magic of the Ordinary* plus Heschel's *The Sabbath* are the top two books I suggest to people looking for entry points into psychedelic Judaism. The way that Winkler related Judaism to Indigenous tribal traditions, pointing out that "Judeo-Apache" might be much more apt than "Judeo-Christian," spoke directly to my experience in Jewish medicine ceremonies and reminded me of the way my father would tell me stories about Native Americans when I was a kid, teaching me that the sky, the ground, the trees, the plants were G-d's sanctuary as much as any shul. *Magic of the Ordinary* articulated a type of Judaism that I sensed and experienced, while giving validation to my anti-institutional leanings supporting the idea that Judaism might be less of an "organized," Christianized religion than the mainstream Jewish world makes it seem. After reading it, I never saw Judaism in the same way again.

All of a sudden, rituals like shaking a *lulav* in four directions on the holiday of Sukkot and celebrating the new moon with song and dance at a Kiddush Levanah made better sense to me. If camping in the woods with psychedelic Chassidim over Shabbos helped me connect differently with time and nature, *Magic of the Ordinary* validated my experience as authentically Jewish and human. It's like what one of the sadhus said in a documentary called *Sunseed*—that you'll never find G-d even if you look everywhere, but once you know G-d truly, you see him everywhere. It reminded me of a time doing ayahuasca in Joshua Tree, when I stepped outside to look at the stars and saw G-d in it all, connecting the dots, in the cosmos, in the crappy wooden hand railing I held on to, in our own consciousness, playing the game of learning to be in a body, and be happy in it.

That's the mystery of Judaism: G-d is nowhere to be seen, never to be grasped, and yet he's everywhere, and always accessible—especially in moments of joy, especially when we encounter the spiritual through the somatic. Through traversing different realms of consciousness—from *mocheen d'katnus* (finite mind) toward *mocheen d'gadlus* (infinite mind)—we are able to experience and reconcile this dichotomy. The Divine, according to Jewish shamanic wisdom, "could be experienced only through its physical manifestation," Winkler writes, "not in *spite* of the down home emotional and physical consciousness, but *because* of it." And it's the job of the Jewish shaman to facilitate this, to help lift the veil, or *pargawd*. I thought of those serving medicine in the heimish world, wondering if or how much differently a psychedelic experience was internalized among those familiar with Kabbalah (and the "four worlds" of Creation). And yet, wasn't the idea to arrive at that unified place of oneness? The promise of joy and connection in what lies *beyond*, it turns out, has been at the crossroads of right here, right now. As Tolstoy once put it in one of my favorite quotes, "If you want to be happy, be."

This is the "acid test" for Torah, as Yoseph Needelman put it, by which we mean, the moral of the story of religion, broadly speaking: "Does it set you freer? Or trap you further? . . . Holiness is not without purposes. Its purpose is to liberate: from the mundane, from the compelled, from the illusions of separation, from sadness, bitterness, or frustration. Holiness is for a purpose, and that purpose is to bring deeper and better healing; and health . . . enabling freedom to *be*."

Whereas once, even I thought that traditional Judaism was stifling—guiltily observing my Orthodox neighbors walking to shul every Saturday, the men wearing long coats and the women in long skirts, even on sweltering summer days, wondering what parts of the "rules" like abstaining from driving kept them hooked in—I realize now that the threads of Judaism I connected to most, that I wondered about as a child and found as an adult, led me to some of the freest-feeling moments I'd experienced (singing, dancing, being, celebrating life) and noticing that this celebration looked much the same among the communities I'd spent time in, from the satsang to the psychedelic Chassidim.

PART 4

HOME

"Home is the quality of presence.
It's the quality of being.
Home is always here."

— RAM DASS

Chapter 29

HOME AT THE END OF THE RAINBOW

The moon is shining bright and the stars have been out for almost five hours on a Saturday evening in late October, but we haven't even *bentched* for *shaleshudis* yet—and don't even think to ask about Havdalah before it's "time." It's *Cheshvan*—the month of the fall Rainbow Gathering in Israel—and we just finished *Parshat Lech Lecha*, the one where G-d tells Abraham to leave his father's house, to leave his home, and go on faith to the "land that I will show you." The exact translation for *"lech lecha"* is up for debate. The words mean "go to yourself" or "go for yourself," and however that gets interpreted is at the heart of what the *Parsha* is all about.

Meanwhile, never mind that it technically ended hours ago, we're still in Shabbos. We're *holding by* Judaism's rules, so to speak, because inside that container we have total liberation from the confines of mundane reality.

At this point, we've also been tripping on acid since high noon, when I pulled Reb Nachman's book of parables, *Tales of Ancient Times*, out of my leather backpack at lunchtime around the main circle (where later there would be songs around a campfire), and opened it to page 81, where I'd been keeping a small collection of tabs for moments just like this. It was a motley assortment: some of the lightning bolt paper left over from a Shavuos trip in Mexico a few years ago when we all dosed and hiked up the mountain in

Tepoztlán; a blue gel tab with golden specks that a hippie-chemist friend made; and a tiny ripped piece of white paper that was supposedly Rainbow Family Acid from the last Gathering I was at in Pennsylvania. The four of us each took our choosing, then verbalized our intentions, and made a *l'chaim* before placing the tabs under our tongues. "This might be the only time where I can say *tefilat haderech* on Shabbos," Chaim Leib joked, since halacha prohibits traveling on Shabbos.

On top of it being *Parshat Lech Lecha*, it was also Rachel Imenu's yahrzeit—commemorating the passing of the biblical foremother Rachel, my namesake (after my great-grandmother "Roey," who went by Rose instead of her Yiddish name Rochel once she'd immigrated to New York). In setting my intention, I said something about both *lech lecha*—getting in touch with the core of ourselves, allowing our neshamas to shine through—and that in doing so, may we also tune in to the nurturing ethos of Mama Rochel (as some call her), feeling held by the *Shechina* this Shabbos, and supported by ourselves in a process of re-parenting.

And so after the "Magic Hat," where some focalizers collected donations for the quinoa and cilantro they'd served, we made our way from the dusty open plateau and down to the shaded *maayan*, where we set up a picnic decadent with fruits and nuts, like the delicacies they are when you're living in nature. Besides, even though we'd just had some lunch, we wanted to make Kiddush and *hamotzei*, which would've been a little weird to do communally in a circle of about 100 mostly secular Israelis who'd raise their eyebrows at a crew of Americans doing "Shabbos."

But in truth, Shabbos was not just the vessel for our experience, holding us in its arms, nurturing us with food, wine, and good vibes, but it was literally our "psychedelic sherpa" (a term my friend Jared Epstein came up with), guiding us through the trip. The seder of Shabbos offered physical reference points around which to orient: making the blessings over wine and (gluten-free) bread, the tradition of a leisurely lunch with song, themes in the *Parsha* to explore, *bentching* to close a meal, and an even "higher" third meal before concluding the Sabbath with Havdalah when you can spot at least three stars in the sky (although, halachically you could keep Shabbos till Tuesday, which would be a pretty hardcore hippie move).

Being on acid, at Rainbow, in Shabbos was like being three realms deep into an alternate reality. We were still in Shabbos well after dark, navigating our "third meal" by moonlight. I was so high, I felt like we were "above the stars" like Avraham was in this week's *Parsha*. (In a biblical instance of astral projection, G-d takes Avraham behind his *mazal*, to "look down on the stars," where from this vantage point of being behind time he could read what the stars had fated for him, and see that he and his 90-something-year-old wife, Sara, would finally have children.)

By now, with way more than three stars in the sky, external factors weren't going to distinguish the difference between Shabbos and the new week, whenever we might make Havdalah. Plus, out in nature, it's not like we were going to run to our phones either (sadly, a hallmark of *Motzei* Shabbos for me). Rather, this circum- stance especially forced us to reckon with Shabbos more as a *set*—a state of heart, mind, soul, and ultimate quality of *being*—than a *setting*—a constellation of external factors like the position of the sun in the sky or a meal set with fine wine and fluffy challah. The physical elements are just vehicles anyway, to get us to that state of spiritual elevation. The destination is Shabbos, and it's not a desti- nation anyway, but a realization of a reality that's always there, a few realms deep, to which the portals open on a weekly rotation. On Shabbos, it's said that we get a second soul—one that's more in loving union with G-d on an embodied rather than an intellectual level. *Lech lecha*—go to yourself. I always say, I feel like the truest version of myself on Shabbos. Maybe here, riding the acid, I'd jour- neyed both inside of myself and to myself, arriving at that second soul that I only get to experience on Shabbos.

◈◈◈

I was finishing the first draft of this book when I went to that Israeli Rainbow Gathering, and immediately set to work writing about it when I got back home to the apartment in Tzfat that I'd rented out as something of a writing retreat space for myself. The communal Shabbos acid trip felt like the exemplary "Jewish psychedelic experience" in the context of Rainbow—an experiment in which the ethos of psychedelic idealism is put into practice. As a temporary village built in nature, Rainbow is a sociological construct, replete with its own rules, practices, culture, and even language. Rainbow is so much its own reality that when you're inside it, "Babylon"—the world outside the Gathering—feels so distant and foreign. Much the same way as when you're tripping, the psychedelic zone feels worlds away from the mundane; and when you're in Shabbos, especially in a major city, there can often be a dissonance between your state of being and your external surroundings if most people in the vicinity are not observing Shabbos in some way.

Aaron's sister once told me a story about her young son, who saw an airplane in the sky on a Saturday, and asked his mother, "Why are they flying if it's Shabbat?" "They don't know it's Shabbat," she replied. "Yes, they do," he responded. "They just don't know what Shabbat is."

The point I'm getting at is not that everyone should be *halachically* keeping Shabbat, but that the Shabbos state of being, *bchlal*, however you "observe" it, is a *practice* worth cultivating.

It was easy to refine that state of being living in Tzfat—the literal birthplace of Kabbalat Shabbat—where the energy of Shabbos is palpable in the air and upheld by practically 100 percent of the locals. Physical actions in honor or observance of Shabbat, my friend Zev Padway told me, speaking from a halachic perspective, create the conditions, the vessel to hold you in the psychedelic experience that is Shabbos. I lived right by Zev's vegan, gluten-free cafe in Tzfat's Old City, and knew him before as a legend of the Rainbow Gatherings, a hippie baal teshuva who found religion through his experiences with psychedelics and Rainbow. In much the same way that my father and his friends took on Hindu names, Steve Padway, the former San Francisco gutter punk raised in a secular Jewish family from Ohio, took up Zev—Hebrew for "wolf."

Like meditation or yoga, Shabbos is a practice. It is a practice of being. The ultimate practice of being here now. In fact, even Ram Dass spoke about this: during his 1992 lecture at the American Jewish University (AJU) in Los Angeles, he described Judaism as a mindfulness practice. "Judaism is a way of remaining in the present," he said. "And Shabbos is a great reminder."

I was sitting with my computer, writing this chapter, in the corner of a cozy, candle-lit *kumzitz* in Tzfat, when a local named Yaakov Yitzchak asked me what my book was about. "Judaism, psychedelics, and Ram Dass," I summarized. "You know," he replied, "Ram Dass *mkareved* me." Wait, what?

I first met Yaakov Yitzchak on Rehov Yerushalayim, Tzfat's main drag, late on a Friday night walking home from a Shabbos meal. He had a long white beard and, in his eyes, bore a striking resemblance to my father—who in fact he knew from back when he lived in LA. I'd overheard him chatting to someone on the street and immediately sniffed out the familiarity in the way he spoke, asking him where he was from. "Venice Beach," he told me; I sensed there was at least a 50 percent chance that this old school hippie met my dad, though I wasn't expecting to hear that he'd also been to our house for kirtan, albeit in his former incarnation known as Jeff Richman.

He'd been sitting in the front row of Ram Dass's lecture at AJU—which I was in the middle of writing about at the moment he approached me—when he was inspired to start observing Shabbos. "If Ram Dass was doing it, I knew I had to do it," he said, recalling how Ram Dass tapped him in the center of his chest, as if cementing the decision. One thing led to another, and observing Shabbos catapulted Jeff the Bu-Jew into a baal teshuva, who'd come to Tzfat to study in yeshiva and never left.

In a similar vein to Yaakov Yitzchak's story, Ram Dass himself told me about a time he once visited Jerusalem when two Orthodox boys in black hats ran up to him as he was crossing a square. "Ram Dass, it's you!" They'd done psychedelics, read *Be Here Now*, and got turned back on to Judaism.

It must have felt ironic for a guy who once claimed he was "only Jewish on my parents' side." But for me, hearing the story offered the validation of a full circle, much like when Krishna Das compared Maharaj-ji to the Baal Shem Tov. Psychedelic consciousness occupied the crossroads of the heimish and HinJew worlds that I had always sensed shared more in common at the core than what was apparent at surface level.

But for Ram Dass to admit it was healing—for me, and likely for him—in the way that embracing hurt, rather than dissociating from it, is what liberates you from it. "It was no accident that I was born into a Jewish family, and I finally was able to appreciate its mark on me," Ram Dass wrote about this path back to Judaism, in his memoir. "Only when you honor your karma fully can you begin to be free."

In fact, it was the pain of Jewish trauma that took decades for Ram Dass to even acknowledge, let alone work through, on his path to freedom. "The immensity of the Holocaust in terms of the human condition brought many people so close to the edge of the mystery of 'is there a good G-d?' or 'what is the universe about?'" Ram Dass once said of his visit to Dachau concentration camp. "I realize that part of why I haven't been able to fully acknowledge the incarnational aspect of being Jewish was my fear of the pain, of the horror of the predicament of the Jews."

It didn't help that as a kid, he fell into the stereotypical Jewish plight of self-loathing; being overweight and queer, a young Richard Alpert was the target of bullying and called slurs like "fat dirty Jew." He identified with Judaism in a tribal and cultural sense, but felt little connection to his ancestral origins. To him, Judaism seemed like it was "about power," such as "the power of G-d to unleash plagues" or the power of the Jews "to survive amid oppression." The Jews he grew up with weren't "primarily interested in what happened to Moses up on the mountain—their primary interest is what he brought back," Ram Dass has said. "And the predicament is that ultimately, like the Ten Commandments at first and the way I was taught them . . . you better follow them or else."

But in the decades to come, he would come back around to see Judaism in a new light, as a "love affair between G-d and human." His good friend Reb Zalman is to be credited for getting through to Ram Dass, the Jew. "I remember taking LSD with Zalman, with his *talis* wrapped around us and we were suddenly in the place where Judaism and drugs were as one," Ram Dass once told me, having described Zalman as "the most joyous celebration of Judaism" he'd ever met. "I appreciated how he infused love into the rituals I found so empty as a boy," Ram Dass wrote in his memoir. "Loving G-d is central in Judaism, but I didn't get any of that growing up. Only later did I encounter the mystical, joyous side of Judaism with Zalman. And only when I met Maharaj-ji and opened to my own spiritual heart could I appreciate loving G-d."

◆◆◆

Sometimes, the only way to truly come home is to leave it first: journeying for the sake of return. The process of return itself is the path of healing. As seasoned psychonauts often say, the journey is the medicine.

In Ram Dass's case, he might have stayed dissociated from his Jewish identity, had he not branched out of his Jewish community into psychedelics and then into Hinduism, only to come back around to appreciating Jewish practice through new eyes.

In my case, I needed to leave my childhood home in LA for the homelands of New York and Israel, only to come back around to not only appreciating where I came from, but also integrating the teachings of Ram Dass and Maharaj-ji within the Jewish practices I picked up along the way. And it wasn't until I discovered the Rainbow Gathering that this process of integration began to click—the Gathering a psychedelic experience unto itself (never mind the drugs), weaving together all the threads of what made life meaningful to me. The mission I experienced in Rainbow went beyond psychedelic experience, putting its benefits to use toward tikkun olam.

Years before I went to the Israeli Gathering mentioned above, I attended my first Rainbow in Wisconsin. It felt instantly familiar, and I saw why the standard greeting at Rainbow was "welcome home" (to which you also reply "welcome home"); the culture and ethos of the Gathering reminded me of my own various moments, places, and people of "home."

As a kid, I had met members of the original Rainbow family without even knowing what Rainbow was. For instance, my father's friend Fantuzzi, a Puerto Rican musician from NYC who played at Woodstock, would crash at our house when passing through town, or even come to our Passover seder. All his talk about "peace and love" took on new meaning, as I later saw the Rainbow roots where it was coming from—a temporary society in nature that put in at least a decent effort to uphold those values. Or maybe it just sounded that way when Rainbow family would drop the "loving you" catchphrase when crossing dirt paths down a wooded corridor between camps.

I knew my father had been to a Gathering or two back in the day, and Ram Dass too. In fact, upon stepping into my first Gathering, I came across another bird of the same feather—an old, skinny Jewish man with a walking stick and a sarong, who went by Baba-Ji and escorted me, Aaron, and my dad's partner (who tagged along with us, minus my dad), into the forest. I observed what felt like a conference of tribes, as we passed several camps such as Loven Ovens (they bake bread daily); Krishna Kitchen (they chant Hare Krishna and serve dal); Kiddie Village (where many families camp); Jesus Kitchen (wholesome Christians); Heart Fire Cafe (good food, good people); Serenitea (12-Steppers); and A Camp (A for alcohol, at the edge of the Gathering, since it's otherwise discouraged within Rainbow). A few miles and several hours later, we'd schlepped all our stuff from the car deep into the forest to our destination, Home Shalom.

Having made my first pilgrimage to Rainbow only once I'd moved back to LA, I went there seeking the type of Judaism I missed so much about New York. But really, I was getting to the source of that Judaism, or as close to it as I could. You see, Rainbow has a thick Jewish legacy, rooted in the movements colored by Rebs Zalman Schachter-Shalomi and Shlomo Carlebach that ran parallel to the HinJew movement. The Jewish camp's former incarnations over the decades, like Twelve Tribes and Jerusalem Camp, were led by those like Reb Moshe Geller, who came out of that original psychedelic Jewish movement of the '60s and '70s. (Not to mention, the original map of the Gathering "turned out to be virtually the same as the map of the wandering Hebrew tribes camped in the wilderness," according to Rainbow OG, as in "original Gatherer," Garrick Beck, who verified this fun fact with the folks at 770 Eastern Parkway, the Chabad Lubavitch World Headquarters.)

One of the first iterations of the Jewish camp, Beck told me in an interview I did for a *Tablet* magazine story on Rainbow, was founded by two brothers from Boston, both rabbis, "who had held a psychedelic seder in Eugene, Oregon, [and] sang a lot like Shlomo [Carlebach]." Harkening back to original Chassidish practices and largely inspired by Reb Nachman, "Carlebach sought to 'worship G-d through joy,' and relied on music, dance, and song to enliven the divinity residing in each soul," Michigan State University religious studies professor Morgan Shipley wrote in a paper aptly titled "Psychedelic Judaism in Countercultural America." His strategic outreach took him to the streets of Haight-Ashbury or Berkeley, where he knew he'd find the "holy *hippelach*." When he performed at Berkeley's Peace and Love festival, Shlomo joked that he could tell who all the Jews in the audience were because they were the ones who immediately ran away when a rabbi took to the stage, only to return once they saw that their gentile peers were enjoying his music. "Driven by a sincere belief that the divine penetrates all levels of existence and types of people," Shipley wrote, Carlebach's music spoke to the '60s countercultural ethos of "one love"—which, of course, spoke to the ethos of Rainbow as well, and was central to the philosophy of Reb Zalman.

"The fact of connectedness or 'oneness' that the Sh'ma expresses first became clear" under the influence of LSD, he wrote. Acid helped Zalman realize his vision "not to restore the religion of the shtetl but to renew Judaism," and gave him a perennial view on religion, proving that what he'd experienced in prayer and meditation before as "the oneness and connection with G-d" is ultimately common ground among all spiritual paths. This oneness "was true, but it wasn't just Jewish," he wrote. "It transcended borders. I was sitting in a Hindu ashram with Tim Leary, who was Irish Catholic, and I realized that all forms of religion are masks that the divine wears to communicate with us."

And that's the idea underlying Rainbow: a unified and singular prayer for peace, no matter the concept of G-d one prays to. And yet simultaneously, the Gathering celebrates the diversity of every tribe. As Zalman noted of his first acid trip, "as [Timothy] Leary knew no Yiddish, I found myself in a situation where I could not express myself at the gut level"; as such, familiar cultural contexts may be (for some) a necessary part of any psychedelic experience and integration process—including the psychedelic experience that is Rainbow Gathering.

That's why it was both endearing and perhaps a little repellant for a friend of mine and rabbi to come to Rainbow one year and notice that the Jewish camp I'd invited him to stay at sounded more like Brooklyn than the boonies of a Pennsylvania forest, thanks to all the Yiddish and thick East Coast Jewish accents in the heimish ghetto of the Rainbow, mouthing off to each other in between activities like baking kugel, building a kitchen made of wood, drumming to the beat of a niggun, or brewing mushroom tea. In true form to Reb Zalman's vision, just as Shabbos and a *farbrengen* seamlessly integrate alcohol as a traditional focal point, so too should it be for psychedelics, he once said at an event in early aughts Boulder called "Jews and Drugs."

And so, when I first got into Rainbow, I went seeking a Jewish experience of the flavor that had been so influential during and influenced by the original counterculture. However, just as a psychedelic experience may bring you back to yourself, to the very fibers of your own body, Rainbow for me was a lesson in my own humanity—not just in Jewish experience that felt more authentic than anything I'd experienced before (building a community from scratch in the woods, preparing for Shabbat in a handmade wooden kitchen, singing to the moon) but in human experience. I pooped into a ditch surrounded by the woods. I bathed in a lake. I shared food with strangers, who Rainbow had me consider family.

Rainbow is far from the utopia that some might hope for, and hippie politics can be some of the most contentious out there, but what I nonetheless see in the ethos of the Gathering is a commitment to putting psychedelic consciousness into practical application. It is psychedelic integration embodied; it's not just to have an experience for the sake of itself but to ask yourself, *Now what are you gonna do about it?*

Chapter 30

LSD: LET'S START DAVENING

Davening—prayer, cultivating a relationship with the Divine Source of all inspiration—might be an obvious integration tool once you've had a psychedelic experience. Wondering, *Now what?* Ask G-d.

Ken Kesey encouraged his Merry Pranksters to look further, to walk forward through the door that psychedelics open for you, rather than to simply go round and round in a revolving door of doing acid for the sake of itself. For many Jewish psychonauts of the counterculture, walking through that door looked like walking down the religious path. Grateful Deadheads and psychedelic diehards, the baal teshuva hippie kids of the original Jewish psychedelic renaissance came up with cute little catch phrases like "LSD: Let's Start Davening" or "POT: Put on Tefillin."

The first speaks to our own Divine inspiration, to the neshama. The second speaks to embodied *practice* used in order to tap into, get aligned with, and nourish the neshama—to transcend the physical through material action.

It's said that a tzadik is one whose will is aligned with G-d's. The tzadik has *bituled* themselves so much that their physicality, as Reb Nachman put it, doesn't even create a metaphysical shadow in the way of G-d's light entering into them in a fully embodied experience. Similarly, the word "guru" means "remover of darkness." The path to G-d's light doesn't have to be complex, but rather simply, one that lies just beyond the ego. The Baal Shem Tov especially loved to spend time with peasants and children—whose egos are yet to fully develop—and held that rather than "complex meditations," according to Buxbaum, "simple childlike devotion is key to entering the presence of G-d."

To that end, prayer doesn't necessarily have to be verbal—at least in the broad sense of the term. To me, it's any kind of communication with Source. I've experienced yoga or dance, for instance, to be a prayer with the body.

Once in Goa I met a tattoo artist named Vishal who mistook me for Israeli and offered me a ride on the back of his moped to a beachy trance club called Shiva Valley. On that journey, we stopped on the beach and hiked up a mountain to see the sunrise, where on both accounts we'd been surrounded by feral dogs. I was scared, as if being here was a psychedelic experience unto itself, a leap of faith I'd taken for some reason beyond *reason* that my intuition had nonetheless led me into—perhaps if for no other reason than to develop this piece of Torah about intuition itself, that part of us that tunes into G-d's will and therefore the will of our neshama.

I had to be present enough in myself, in my body, in my gut, in order to intuit the safety of the situation. As Vishal later told me, "You don't know what psychedelic is if you don't know how to be in the moment. Make the moment rich." Even if the moment is rich in adrenaline—as this journey was—the sensation forced me into a presence with my gut, my intuition. And as Vishal told me, "The best way to get in touch with your intuition is to dance."

I interpreted his words through my imagery of the neshama as an inner flame—that piece of the whole, of the greater fire—which, like every flame, therefore has its flicker. When you dance freely and tune into your body, you thus embody the dance of that flicker. Your body, in a way, in its physicality, can make parallel movements to the inner metaphysical fire. On a micro, literal level, this manifests as dance. On a macro, spiritual level, it manifests as the way we dance through life at large. Dance with grace, and you learn to walk the narrow bridge like a skilled tightrope artist who has no fear. The narrow bridge is life, it's our individual *derech*—the path of the soul. We may fumble, or we can tune into our intuition and get aligned with the will of our neshama—which, as our inner piece of Divinity, is ultimately the will of G-d. And thus, the task of moving through life becomes a dance—fun, graceful, and uniquely our own.

Reb Nachman especially encouraged his Chassidim to dance. As Nili once explained it to me, when you lift your feet off the ground you defy the laws of physical and spiritual gravity, overcoming depression, fear, worry, laziness, or whatever else brings you down. "You're planting that energy in your soul when you're dancing," she said. That in and of itself brings joy, and joy is the key ingredient to serving G-d. But the *avodah* in dance, I've learned, comes in when you're not feeling up to it, which is when it's even more important to dance, to prove to yourself that in spite of that weight, because of it, you'll dance anyway. Transform what's heavy and make it light—so light that your feet float from the ground. I saw this Chassidis embodied during the Tu B'Shvat ayahuasca ceremony, observing the men across the room from me, in their white socks and tzitzis, retching over their buckets with nausea, sobbing, writhing, but nonetheless getting up to dance. I've observed time and time again in all kinds of Jewish or indigenous ceremonies (where the style of dance is strikingly similar) that dancing was as much "the medicine" as the music and the brew itself.

The idea is to dance not just in spite of it all and because of it all, transforming the exile of trauma—of fear, dissociation, and heaviness—into the ecstasy of life itself, using our bodies for the reasons G-d gave them to us, to use our limbs to dance through life. To that end, my friend Daniel Kronovet once reminded me of a quote by Victor Frankl: "That which gives light [and makes light—i.e., the opposite of heaviness] must endure burning." One of the first times we went out together, Eilish took me to a bar in Nyack, where we played pool and danced to a funky jazz band. It was there that he described dancing to be like "playing the instrument of the body." But to me, it's like using your body to smile at

G-d. Because like any parent, G-d wants to see his children happy. As such, "holy dancing," according to Chassidis, is said to come from a ruach deep within, whereas dance itself was used to purify the soul and reach new heights.

In other words, when we dance we come into a certain grace. Practice grace in our physical movements, and we metaphysically receive grace. There are countless times I've been graced with the good fortune to dance with my Hula-Hoop: under the stars, in the woods, at the shores, by a campfire, in the glow of neon lights, or simply in a backyard or on a rooftop.

But what is "grace" truly? It was a big theme for the satsang (i.e., "Maharaj-ji's grace") and always made me think of dance, of yoga, of being a kid walking down the hallway with a stack of books on my head to refine my posture. Mostly it's the "flow state" I experience with my Hula-Hoop, such as when I twirl the hoop in my fingertips, gently twisting my wrist to make it flip through the air, before grabbing it within a millisecond, twirling it a few times more with my arm arched above my head before grabbing it back down around my waist, allowing it to settle onto my hips in its spinning rotation, before shimmying my arm beside my torso or grabbing it from behind my tailbone and bringing it back up and then down, extending my right leg to flip it underneath, and starting the choreography all over again, and again, and again. To articulate the body while flowing, we must be *graced* with total present-moment awareness.

For those in the satsang, grace was "the experience of oneness with Maharaj-ji," said Parvati Markus. "There was a time I was sitting in front of him and he was up on the tucket, and I was rubbing his feet, and he kept reaching down and touching my hands. This is in a room of 50 people and he's just talking, doing his thing, and I'm just sitting in front of him, and all of a sudden, I went into a space where I just disappeared. I can't tell you how long it lasted for, but I was gone and merged into whatever that space was. To me, that's grace. It was as if I had swallowed a tab of acid. I didn't have hallucinations, but my ego went. 'I' was gone."

And in that moment of *bitul* and of unity—the primary self becomes the neshama. But to harness that sense of psychedelic grace, once the peak experience is over, it takes the work of embodied integration practice. As Gabrielle Roth, founder of 5Rhythms dance movement project, once put it: "Do you have the discipline to be a free spirit? Can we be free of all that binds and bends us into a shape of consciousness that has nothing to do with who we are from moment to moment, from breath to breath? Dance is the fastest, most direct route to the truth—not some big truth that belongs to everybody, but the get down and personal kind, the what's-happening-in-me-right-now kind of truth." If "prayer is letting go of everything that impedes our inner silence," she continued, "God is the dance and the dance is the way to freedom and freedom is our holy work."

♦♥♦

Psychedelics don't automatically make you a better person. Religion doesn't necessarily make you righteous, either. But the discipline to be free is what psychedelic integration is about; and it's about the discipline of embodied action to foster the conditions that enable us to be free, that hold the space for us to move past ourselves toward spirit. It starts with the discipline of being here now.

Once we've woken up to the present, then it's likely in our state of heightened awareness that we may notice things that are less than flattering about this reality. So what do we do about it?

In Maharaj-ji's words: feed people.

Through direct action, may we actually lose ourselves for the purpose of another. Isn't that the point anyway? Once you get out of your own way, you can be present in the now and do what you were put into a body to do here on earth: serve. That is, serve the Divine by being of service to a cause or a community, a person or a planet, something greater than yourself. And so that's the legacy that I've gleaned from RD's teachings.

It's a responsibility to *be here now*, because when we're present to ourselves, to the world around us, and to the gifts G-d gave us to practice tikkun olam, then it's true we've got work to do. As Rebbe Nachman put it, "Every person needs to say: 'The whole world was created solely for me'; therefore, since the world is created for me at all times I must seek to repair it, I must fulfill its deficiencies and pray for them." In other words, with the present being such a gift, to fully honor and take advantage of it, we must make it a place worth being present to—because, what's the point of being here now if neither the here nor the now are where you want to be?

The general take, from *the* father of Kabbalah, Isaac Luria (a.k.a. Ha'Ari) rests on the Jewish responsibility to be a light unto the nations, and therefore we must search throughout the world for the *nitzotzot*—seeing the good, the light, and the holiness in other people and our surroundings—so that figuratively we may pick them up and put them back together.

Take, for instance, the story of Korach (my bat mitzvah *Parsha*). You see, Korach was fixated on righteousness, learning Torah all day, doing everything religiously to a T, with perfection. He was a Jewish aesthete, devoted to his studies—like a monk. He looked down upon all the other people, but the real tzadikim aren't the ones tucked away, but rather out on the street, feeding the poor, doing spiritual work down here on earth. Real spirituality isn't a masturbatory competition over who can learn the most Torah or be the most holy; perhaps rather it's simply about contributing to the world G-d gave us.

That's why I love the spirit of Rainbow.

◀▼▶

If central to the psychedelic ethos is this idea of "oneness" (as delineated in the "mystical experience"), then at Rainbow, we experienced what that means in practical, embodied terms. As a result of sharing things like food and basic resources to survive, "it teaches you that we're all connected, however mundane it is to say that. Rainbow Gatherings highlight that we all don't just live in our personal void," longtime Rainbow focalizer and activist Tenali Hrenak once told me. "Rainbow Gathering at its best cuts through all that bullshit. Nobody cares what you look like or where you're from; just being a decent human being is what really matters."

Like a trip unto itself, there's this "psychedelic reset that people get into when you take them out of their element," said Shmuel Leaderman, Home Shalom focalizer. Learning to survive in nature breaks people down and puts them in a position to realign, in much the same way psychedelics do.

For Rickshaw, a Quaker who's been going to Rainbow for the past 18 years, "the healing" is what keeps drawing him back. "I look at it as both a spiritual home and also a collection of revolutionary cells," he says. "By escaping Babylon, the question is whether Babylon is in our heads or not." One of the reasons Rainbow is so psychedelic in and of itself is that it takes us out of the dominant, mundane paradigm—much in the same way that psychedelics may dampen the ego, enabling us to break out of old patterns and feel a greater sense of connection to the people, nature, and world around us.

The power to change our reality lies within our minds—an idea similar to the concept so aptly encapsulated in the title of a book by acid evangelist Timothy Leary, *Your Brain Is God*. But to enable that deepening, we need to maintain our *keilim*, which takes a degree of discipline. What are the *keilim* but practices—consistent embodied actions to nourish our souls, strengthen our minds, keep our spirits lively, and maintain the health of our bodies. In short, it's the practice of integration that keeps life psychedelic. And it's a discipline, as Gabrielle Roth would put it, for the sake of being free.

And when we're free, we're home.

◂▾▸

I'm cripplingly indecisive; I often have no sense of my gut feeling. And yes, I still struggle to "be here now." As a teenager, I had doubts about my physical feelings—as if I could intellectually convince myself I wasn't hungry. Because an angsty 16-year-old, wrestling with the dissociative trauma of an eating disorder, had exiled herself from the body, now at almost double that age, I've been working to find my way back home. Baruch Hashem, I got Lyme disease, and I finally had to start listening to my body.

My mother likes to say "your body is a temple." As a kid, I used to roll my eyes at anything she said that was remotely spiritual when, in her thick accent, I couldn't take seriously her signature aphorisms that would spill out from the same mouth that screamed at us when she was overwhelmed or spewed worst-case scenarios after the divorce. In my rebellious way, I'd belittle her words of wisdom by attributing them to the edibles she liked to eat, or marketing language for her yoga teaching business "Om in the Home." But okay, okay, sorry, Mom, you were right, I love you.

Home starts with the body; it is, after all, the seat of the soul here on earth. From there, it extends outward: home is a healthy, relaxed nervous system. Home is the relationship that makes you feel safe; home is family—chosen chevra and satsang, brothers and sisters, your children and your parents; home is the house that feels like you; home is a place where you breathe easy.

And so, eventually, I left LA again, and headed back to New York, and to Israel. I still go back to California often enough. But in seeking home—as one does in the ancient Jewish tradition of wandering in search of home, and in this virtual nomad, post-pandemic day and age—I realized that home itself is a process of discovery, of feeling and of *being*.

As Ram Dass famously said, "We're all just walking each other home." While he might have meant it in terms of walking each other through life, until we leave the body and return to our Creator, I've found it applicable in the psychedelic experience. When you "trip" or "journey," your consciousness visits another realm, and it's a process to come home to mundane, comfortable, grounded reality. I had scribbled down this quote in a notebook once, "Teshuva is the recalibration of consciousness."

Ultimately, when we return home, to ourselves, we're recalibrating our consciousness, over and over again, to the present—the same way creation is a perpetual process of G-d's *ising*.

Home is teshuva. Home is return. Home is coming back to my yoga mat, day in and day out. It's the space inside my Hula-Hoop.

It's the smell of weed, which will always remind me of my dad. It's the sound of KD's "Bernie's Chalisa." It's the heimish familiarity of a warm and cozy Shabbos dinner (bonus points if someone sings "Azamer Bishvochin"). Home is Shabbos, a taste of *olam haba*, the world to come, right here and right now. As Ram Dass said: "Home is the quality of presence. It's the quality of being. Home is always here."

EPILOGUE

I came to Tzfat to complete the first draft manuscript of this book. Over half a year, I'd been writing it in Brooklyn mostly, as well as the Hudson Valley, LA, and other parts of Israel. But there was something about going straight to the source, to the geographical incarnation of psychedelic Judaism that felt essential. And it's here, in a matter of weeks, that I basically rewrote the entire thing.

Like Ken Kesey's acid tests, coming to Tzfat felt almost like a graduation of sorts. I'll explain, but first let me backtrack. You see, there's something to journeying in your day-to-day home that facilitates the integration process and makes the medicine feel relevant to your mundane life. That's why, for instance, I prefer to do ayahuasca in dingy Brooklyn lofts or basements rather than beautiful retreat spaces, because my life most often has taken place in the muck and the magic of the city.

However, when they say "write high, edit sober," I knew that didn't exactly mean getting to work in any of the trippy contexts I've described throughout these pages (unless by "work" we mean reporting and going gonzo). It'd be utterly impractical and so not the vibe to remove myself from the experience of tripping, or sitting in ceremony, to pull out my laptop and focus. So the only way to write from an elevated, yet sober place was to do it from Tzfat.

You see, on a mountaintop, you're both physically high yet grounded with your feet firmly on the earth. It just so happens that here, the earth is filled with the buried bones of tzadikim, the founders of the Kabbalah containing all the mystical secrets of creation itself. I rented a *zimmer* from Rainbow family Zev Padway, in the Old City, just up the hill from the cemetery where people travel from around the world to visit the *kivrei* tzadikim of the Arizal, and countless others. However, less drawn to the *kvarim* of the big name tzadkim, I've found myself taking walks down the hill to a cave on the side of the cemetery, at the kever of Chana v'Shevat Binya. I've shed many joyful tears of heartbreak in there, over the course of the few months finishing this book, doing my hitbodedut, feeling Source as I never have before.

You see, I can't write a book about things like "connecting to G-d," or practicing yoga and doing hitbodedut without, you know, actually having my own practice of connection. There'd be an integrity issue there; I know, because I experienced such an issue while working in the psychedelic start-up space, where having what I considered a "psychedelic life"—one that includes enough work-life balance so as not to activate my nervous system to the point of a Lyme flare-up—came into conflict with the weight of running a "successful" enterprise. If psychedelics are about expanding our consciousness beyond the mainstream paradigm, then why did I feel more and more like a slave under capitalism, as stressed as a banker on Wall Street, but making a fraction of the income? Wasn't the point of starting your own company—especially when it's supposedly rooted in the values of psychedelic wellness, anti-capitalism, and creativity—to establish a new paradigm? As my body broke down, I got more vocal about this seeming paradox at work; things went south and I suffered a very real, professional trauma in the aftermath of it. (I guess you can't write a book that addresses trauma without dealing with your own too.) The *nekuda tova* was that I was practicing hot yoga almost daily, more consistently than I ever had before, because now, I needed it like my life depended on it (and it probably did). Meanwhile, I attempted to focus on writing this book. But only until I escaped to Tzfat was I able to channel flowstate.

Also known as a City of Refuge, Tzfat is the Rainbow to the Babylon of the world beyond its mountaintop. When I say being here is like Ken Kesey's acid test graduation, what I mean is that, if the acid tests measure the "core truth"** of what LSD is all about, then to graduate is to go forward and live that truth. Tzfat feels like living the truth of psychedelic Judaism.

It's got nothing to do with substances (I've been pretty sober since I got here), and more to do with the quality of how easy it is to *be here now*. Never has my body felt so good and my nervous system so regulated. Never have I felt so much presence and so little FOMO (historically, I suffer chronically from FOMO). As Carl Hart told me in an interview for my podcast *Set & Setting* on the Be Here Now Network, "Being present is an altered state."

And being here now, in Tzfat, is like tripping naturally. Just as a psychedelic shows you an alternate reality that feels more real than real, that's Tzfat.

Maybe it's that every third person around here begins their sentences with "Rebbe Nachman says . . ." Maybe it's that time moves differently here, and the rat race is irrelevant. Maybe it's that life here is simple and simultaneously profound. Maybe it's the way kids run around unsupervised in the winding alleyways, or the way the lights twinkle from Rashbi's kever at Mount Meron across the valley. Or maybe it's that every Shabbos meal here is not just a *feast'elle*, as the locals call it, but a vortex enchanted with ecstatic niggunim so high that eyes roll back in a trance and tears stream down smiling cheeks.

I feel like I swallowed the soul of my story in a glass of wine from Kiddush and it's pumping nourishment through my veins. I guess that's what embodiment is about. "Live your yoga," as my mom likes to say. The yoga of my life is this story, flowing through the postures that are these chapters, breathing through it all along the way.

And yet, the story isn't really about drugs or religion. It's about whatever the point of them is. The sustained feeling they engender, and the service they inspire us to do in this world. That's *integration*. Transforming our exile into ecstasy, until we arrive at *olam haba*. Only to realize that it's *davka*, right here, right now.

** I got this quote through a discussion with Yoseph Needelman, who similarly has used "acid test" in this way in his own writing.

GLOSSARY

2C-b: An experimental psychedelic first synthesized by Alexander Shulgin, the "godfather of MDMA," in 1974; gained popularity as a legal analogue to MDMA in the 1980's before being made illegal in 1994; has experienced resurgent popularity in recent years as a more mild and short lived psychedelic than MDMA or LSD, popular as a rave and party drug

2C-i: An experimental psychedelic first synthesized by Alexander Shulgin, the "Godfather of MDMA"

5-MeO-DMT: A strong dissociative psychedelic derived from natural sources, including most commonly the venom of the Sonoran Desert toad; it can also be synthesized in a lab

Acid: (see LSD)

Acid test: the acid tests were parties held by Ken Kesey and the Merry Pranksters, mainly in the San Francisco Bay Area during the 1960; however the term acid test is used in this book in an expanded way to reference measuring a core truth

Adonai Echad: (Hebrew) G-d is one

Aliyah: (Hebrew) to ascend, to rise; also means to immigrate to Israel

Aliyat neshama: (Hebrew) ascension of the soul

Alteland: (Yiddish) old country; literally "old land"

Aneni: (Hebrew) Answer me (usually directed to G-d)

Arti: (Sanskrit) Hindu prayer ritual

Asana: (Sanskrit) posture—i.e., yoga posture

Ashkenazi: adjective to describe Jews of European descent (plural: Ashkenazim)

Ashram: monastic community or religious retreat center, common in Hinduism

Atman: (Sanskrit) the soul, the breath, the self as distinct from the ego

Avodah: (Hebrew) work, worship, service, (often in service of G-d if used in religious context)

Avodah zarah: (Hebrew) idolatry or worship of false gods; literally "strange service"

Ayahuasca: a DMT-containing brew native to South America, made from the chacruna leaf and the yage vine

Azamer Bishvochin: a Friday night Shabbos song, penned by Isaac Luria a.k.a. the Arizal (the father of Kabbalah)

Baal teshuva: (Hebrew) literally "master of return"; refers to once-secular Jews who became more observant (like a born-again Jew)

Baba: (Sanskrit) wise old man, grandfather type

Babylon: the world outside Rainbow Gathering; literally refers to an empire that was antagonistic and oppressive to the Israelites in ancient times

Balagan: (Hebrew) a chaotic, disorganized, or messy situation

Bar Mitzvah: a rite of passage for Jewish 13-year-old boys that signifies becoming a man

Baruch HaShem: (Hebrew) literally "blessed be the name"; colloquially "thank G-d"

Bat Mitzvah: a rite of passage for Jewish 12- or 13-year-old girls that signifies becoming a woman

Bayit: (Hebrew) house

Bchlal: (Hebrew) generally, in general, completely

Beis: (Yiddish) house

Beis HaMikdash: the Holy Temple that was the nucleus and gathering point of Israelite culture in ancient Jerusalem

Bekeshe: (Yiddish) a type of overcoat worn by Chasidish men on Shabbos, holidays, or special events such as a wedding; usually black

Bentch: (Yiddish) to bless; often refers to the blessing said after a meal

Besht: acronym for the Baal Shem Tov, the father of the Chassidish movement

Bhakti: (Sanskrit) devotional worship

Bhandara: (Sanskrit) refers to a feast for a large group of people; in this book it refers to an event at the Neem Karoli Baba Ashram in Taos, during the anniversary of when the guru left his body

Bhang: (Sanskrit) a smoothie or potion containing cannabis; usually distributed on holidays like Shivaratri and Holi

Bicycle Day: April 19, 1943; the official LSD holiday celebrating the first time Albert Hofmann, the chemist who first synthesized LSD, tripped intentionally

Bindi: a red dot worn at the center of the forehead, originally by Hindus, Buddhists, and Sikhs

Bissell: (Yiddish) a little; a bit of

Bitachon: (Hebrew) trust; a sense of positivity based on emunah (faith)

Bitul: (Hebrew) nullification (of self)

Bracha: (Hebrew) a blessing

Breslov: a branch of Chassidism founded by Rabbi Nachman—from Bratslav, Ukraine, and buried in Uman, Ukraine (1772–1810)

Breslover: someone who follows Breslov Chassidis

B'shert: (Yiddish) destiny; meant to be

Bu-Jew: someone who's Jewish but also practices Buddhism

Bubbe: (Yiddish) grandmother

Bukharin: an adjective to describe Jews from central Asia (mainly the Uzbekistan region)

Bureka: a type of pastry popular in Israel (often contains potato, cheese, spinach, meat, or mushroom)

Burner: somebody who goes to Burning Man

Candy flipping: taking MDMA and LSD simultaneously

Cannabinoid: a chemical compound found in cannabis

Carlebach: refers to Rabbi Shlomo Carlebach (1925–1994), who revolutionzied Jewish music and in later years became known as a controversial figure due to allegations of sexual assault; also used as an adjective to describe a type of musical Jewish service or song

Casa: (Spanish) house

CBD: cannabidiol; a type of nonpsychoactive, therapeutic cannabinoid

Chabad: a branch of Chassidism, also known as Chabad-Lubavitch; known specifically for their outreach to secular Jews, such as on college campuses

Chabadnik: a follower of Chabad

Chag: (Hebrew) holiday (plural: chagim)

Chai: (Hindi) tea; (Hebrew) life

Chakra: (Sanskrit) a center of energy in the body

Challah: (Hebrew) bread traditionally eaten on Shabbat

Chanah and her Seven Sons (Chana v'Shevat Binya): heroine in story of Jewish martyrdom during the persecution of the Jews in Syria at the time of Antiochus Ephiphanes; commanded to worship an idol, they refused and were slaughtered

Chanukah: eight-day, wintertime Jewish holiday celebrated by lighting a menorah, eating fried foods, and gifting presents; commemorates the rededication of the Holy Temple, and is signified through themes of miracle

Charedim: "Ultra-Orthodox" Jews, generally characterized by wearing black hats; includes, but not limited to, Chassidim

Charas: (Sanskrit) a type of cannabis concentrate similar to hash

Chassid: (also spelled Hasid); a follower of Chassidis/Chassidish/Hasidic Judaism, a form of Orthodoxy founded by the Baal Shem Tov, a.k.a. Rabbi Israel ben Eliezer (1698–1760), a.k.a. the Besht

Chassidis: (Yiddish) for Hasidism; Chassidut (Hebrew); a branch of Orthodox founded by the Baal Shem Tov

Chayos: (Hebrew) living things; also refers to a category of angels

Chesed: (Hebrew) loving-kindness

Cheshvan: (Hebrew) autumn month on the Hebrew calendar

Chevra: (Hebrew) community of friends; sometimes refers to a specific community, group, or shul

Chiddush: (Yiddish, derived from Hebrew word chidush for "new") novelty; fresh insight

Child's pose: a kneeling position in yoga with knees bent and the forehead on the ground

Chill: a hangout session (i.e., "we're having a chill")

Chiloni: (Hebrew) secular, refers to non-observant Jews, particularly in Israel

Chizzuk: (Hebrew) strength

Cholent: (Hebrew/Yiddish) a traditional Jewish stew usually eaten on Shabbat

Cohenet: literally "priestess"; refers in modern times to women certified or trained as community leaders; can also refer to Cohenet programs of education, training, and certification

Conservadox: blend between Orthodox and Conservative Judaism

Dal: (Sanskrit) Indian lentil dish

D.A.R.E.: Drug Abuse Resistance Education; a now-defunct government Drug War propaganda program in schools

Daven: (Yiddish) to pray

Davka: (Yiddish) deliberately; on purpose

Derech: (Hebrew) path; road

DMT: a powerful (sometimes, naturally occurring) psychedelic that can be smoked on its own or consumed in the form of ayahuasca brew for a longer effect; it has been theorized that DMT is referenced in the Torah and may have been incorporated into prophetic visions

DPA (Drug Policy Alliance): a leading nonprofit organization founded by Ethan Nadelmann, dedicated to fighting the War on Drugs

Drug War (War on Drugs): a governmental campaign founded by President Richard Nixon in 1971, aimed at making drugs illegal

Dveykus: (Yiddish) dveykut (Hebrew); cleaving; clinging to G-d

Echad: (Hebrew) one

Ego death: a temporary shift in the psyche, from a self-centered to completely unbiased perspective; scientifically speaking, it's defined by reduced activity in the brain's default mode network (DMN), the seat of the ego, which could help one reset or rewire thought patterns that are otherwise constrained by the ego; it can manifest as a loss of self-identity, or feelings of oneness with surroundings

Emunah: (Hebrew) faith

Endocannabinoid: a cannabinoid made endogenously by the human body (such as anandamide)

Entheogen: a substance that elicits a spiritual experience

Etrog: (Hebrew) a citron; used in rituals during the Jewish holiday of Sukkot

Farbrengen: (Yiddish) an informal Hasidic gathering where people share words of Torah, sing songs, drink alcohol, and are merry

Feast'elle: Yiddishized diminutive for "feast"

Feral Chassid: a term and inside joke popularized by photojournalist Ahron Moeller to describe Chasidim on camping trips, in the woods, using substances, or otherwise engaging in fringe, offbeat activities

Focalizer: an organizer or instigator of organization or action, used at Rainbow Gatherings to describe hippies who makes things happen within a non-hierarchical system

FOMO: acronym for "fear of missing out"

Frum: (Yiddish) pious; observant of religious law

Galitzia: a region of Europe spanning what's now southeastern Poland through western Ukraine

Galut: (Hebrew) exile

Gan Eden: (Hebrew) Garden of Eden

Ganja: weed; cannabis flower (specifically in Hindu contexts)

Gartel: a belt worn by Chassidim during prayer

G-d: you know who; there is a combination of commandment and tradition Judaism to not fully write or speak names of (and even direct references to) the Most High

Gefilte: shorthand for Gefilte Fish, a traditional frum Shabbos dish served at all meals; literally "filled"

Gematria: (Hebrew) a Kabbalistic method of calculating the numerical value of words, based on the value given to each letter

Goy: (Hebrew, Yiddish) gentile; non-Jew; literally "nation"

Guru: a spiritual teacher in the Hindu tradition

Halacha: (Hebrew) Jewish law, literally "the way"

Hamotzei: (Hebrew) the blessing over bread

Hasbara: (Hebrew) explanation; usually refers to Israeli and Diaspora Jews acting as defenders of the State of Israel in public, educational, political, or media spaces

HaShem: (Hebrew) G-d; literally "the name"

Hanuman: a flying monkey deity in Hinduism, known as a messenger

Hanuman Chalisa: Hindu devotional chant in praise of Hanuman

Har: (Hebrew) mountain or hill, i.e. Har Sinai (Mount Sinai) or Har HaMenuchot (a famous cemetery in Jerusalem)

Hashgacha pratis: (Hebrew) literally "private guidance" or "personal guidance"; usually understood as G-d's personal providence or assistance

Havdalah: prayer ceremony performed after nightfall that marks the end of Shabbat and transition to the week; includes elements like sweet fragrance and fire that activate each of the senses

Heimish: (Yiddish) homey (pronounced hey-mish or hi-mish); also connotes way of life associated with the Yiddish-speaking world (pronounced "hi-mish" in this context)

Hillel: organization for Jewish college students

Hineni: (Hebrew) here I am

HinJew: someone of Jewish background who takes on Hindu practices or customs (e.g., Ram Dass, a.k.a. Richard Alpert)

Hisbodedus: (Yiddish) see Hitbodedut

Hitbodedut: (Hebrew) self-secluded Jewish meditation/prayer/free-form conversation with G-d

Holotropic: oriented or moving toward wholeness; brings a person into a deeper dimension of self and consciousness

Holy Hippelach: (Yinglish) a term of endearment used by Sholomo Carlebach in which he uses the Yiddish plural to refer to the "holy hippies"

Hummus Trail: the most popular spots in India visited by Israelis; in these places there are so many Israelis it's not uncommon to see Hebrew graffiti or cafe menus in Hebrew

Hygge: (Danish) a quality of coziness

Ibogaine: a powerful psychedelic derived from the roots of a West African shrub; used ceremonially among indigenous tribes, and in the West often used to cut opioid addiction

Icaro: South American term for "magic song" used in medicine ceremonies

Ikar: (Hebrew) root

Integration: used in psychedelic contexts to describe the period following a psychedelic experience; often more specifically referring to the process in which one intentionally processes and applies the experience and insights of their psychedelic experience into their life, through personal practice or in individual or group therapeutic settings

Jah: Rastafarian pronunciation of commonly used Hebrew name of G-d

JAP: acronym for Jewish American Princess

Kabbalah: (Hebrew) literally "reception"; school of thought in Jewish mysticism; originated by the masters such as Rabbi Isaac Luria (a.k.a. HaAri, or Arizal; 1534–1572) who lived in Tzfat

Kabbalat Shabbat: (Hebrew) a distinct prayer for welcoming in/receiving the Sabbath on Friday night; developed originally in Tzfat in the 16th and 17th centuries

Kaddish: prayer to honor the deceased

Kanfei rei'ah: (Hebrew) angel wings

Karma: (Sanskrit) a person's fate, determined by their past actions in this lifetime, or in a previous lifetime

Kavanah: (Hebrew) intention

Kedusha: (Hebrew) holiness

Keilim: (Hebrew) vessels (something that holds)

Kep (Keppele): (Yiddish) head; sometimes refers to brain; might also refer to forehead in diminutive keppele

Ketamine: a dissociative psychedelic originally introduced as an anesthetic before also being studied successfully for therapeutic use beginning in the early 2000's, becoming increasingly popular during the current psychedelic renaissance; "K" is also popular as a rave and nightlife drug

Kever: (Hebrew) grave, tomb (plural: kevarim)

Kibitz: (Yiddish) to chat, to shoot the shit

Kiddush: (Hebrew) the blessing over wine

Kiddush Levanah: (Hebrew) Jewish ritual to sanctify the new moon

Kirtan: (Sanskrit) call-and-response-style Indian chanting

Kittel: (Yiddish) white robe that men wear during special occasions like a wedding or on holidays such as Yom Kippur

Kiruv: (Hebrew) outreach; bringing close; bringing secular Jews into the religious fold, often done by Chabad

Kish: (Yiddish) kiss

Kivrei tzadikim: (Hebrew) the graves of *tzadikim* (holy people)

Klezmer: a style of Eastern European Jewish music

Kodesh HaKodeshim: (Hebrew) holy of holies; chamber in the ancient Temple of Jerusalem, where the high priest would hotbox himself on Yom Kippur with incense to atone on behalf of the Jewish people

Kol isha: (Hebrew) voice of a woman; in most frum and chassidish settings it's controversial for men to hear the voice of a woman singing

Ktoret: (Hebrew) incense

Kvetch: (Yiddish) to complain

Kodesh: (Hebrew) holy, sacred

Kotel: (Hebrew) the Western Wall; the only remnant of the Temple of Jerusalem that was destroyed; the holiest site in Judaism

Krekhtz: (Yiddish) sigh/groan

Kripa: (Sanskrit) grace

Kumzitz: (Yiddish) a musical gathering, such as around a campfire or informally in someone's living room; literally "come, sit"

Lech Lecha: (Hebrew) go to yourself, go for yourself; the name of a Torah portion in the book of Genesis

Likutei Moharan: "Collected Works of Our Rebbe"; Rebbe Nachman's magnum opus containing many of his most famous and fundamental lessonss

LSD: classic psychedelic, technically derived from the ergot fungus, but originally synthesized by Swiss chemist Albert Hofmann in 1938

Lubavitch: see Chabad

Lubavitcher Rebbe (Schneerson): leader of Chabad-Lubavitch; almost always refers to Rabbi Menachem Mendel Schneerson (1902–1994); the most recent Rebbe who has not been replaced and is believed by many Chabadniks to be the moshiach (messiah)

Lulav: (Hebrew) a palm branch, which is used along with a cluster of plants, including two boughs of willow and three boughs of myrtle, used ceremonially and sacramentally during holiday of Sukkot

Lulke: (Yiddish) the water pipe the Baal Shem Tov smoked out of

Lungi: (Hindi) a type of sarong; cloth wrapped around the lower half

Maayan: (Hebrew) spring of water

Maharaj-ji: (Sanskrit) a term of endearment referring to Guru Neem Karoli Baba; literally "king"

Mahasamadhi: (Sanskrit) the "great" and "final" samadhi; the act of consciously leaving one's body for the act of death

Mala: (Sanskrit) garland; string of beads used in prayer/meditation

Malach: (Hebrew) messenger, angel

Mamash: (Hebrew) really, very, truly, precisely

MAPS (Multidisciplinary Association for Psychedelic Studies): nonprofit research organization founded by Rick Doblin, currently pursuing MDMA research into PTSD

Matim: (Hebrew) fitting, well suited, appropriate

Mazal: (Hebrew) star, destiny

MD: see MDMA; a shorthand often used in Israel

MDMA: a.k.a. Ecstasy; empathogenic, psychedelic compound popularized by Alexander "Sasha" Shulgin in the 1970s; used in couples therapy, also popular in rave/dance scene, used as a therapeutic treatment for trauma and other conditions

Mechitza: (Hebrew) a partition to separate men and women; often in shuls or at wedding parties, but also in various other environments, like Heimish buses between Brooklyn and Monsey

Medicated: infused with weed

Melave malka: (Hebrew) a jovial gathering with food, music, and Torah talk that happens after Shabbat on Saturday evenings; literally "escorting the queen"

Menorah: (Hebrew) candelabra used on Chanukah, which references the candelabra lit ceremonially/sacramentally in the Mishkan (traveling sanctuary conceived and constructed after Har Sinai) and Beit Hamikdash (the permanent temple in Jerusalem)

Merry Pranksters: the cohort associated with Ken Kesey who lived together communally, spread LSD to the hippies, and traveled around the country in a colorfully painted bus

Mikveh: (Hebrew) bath or living body of water (like a stream, lake, river) in which ritual purifications happen

Mincha: (Hebrew) afternoon prayer (in a series of three prayers for shachris in the morning, mincha in the afternoon, and maariv at night)

Minyan: a quorum of 10 people needed for aspects of Jewish prayer and service/ceremony, restricted to men in frum circles

Mishigas: (Yiddish) craziness

Mishna: (Hebrew) a written collection of Jewish oral teachings that serves as the base for the commentary that makes up the Talmuds

Mishpucha: (Hebrew/Yiddish) family

Mitzvah: (Hebrew) a religious commandment, good deed

Mkarev: (Hebrew) to do kiruv on someone; see kiru

Mocheen d'gadlus: (Hebrew) infinite mind

Mocheen d'katnus: (Hebrew) finite/constricted mind

Modeh Ani: (Hebrew) morning prayer said daily upon waking in which Jews thank G-d for benevolently returning our souls from sleep so that we may experience this day

Molly: see MDMA

Moshav: (Hebrew) an Israeli type of cooperative settlement community, similar to a kibbutz; not to be confused with a settlement in the West Bank, though a Moshav can be located anywhere

Moshav Modiin: the moshav founded in 1964 by Rabbi Shlomo Carlebach; many original members came from or through Reb Shlomo's House of Love and Prayer, in San Francisco (known as the Moshav)

Moshiach: (Hebrew) messiah

Motzei Shabbat: (Hebrew) Saturday evening after Shabbat ends

Muktzeh: (Hebrew) things you can't do/objects you can't touch on Shabbat, if you are shomer Shabbos (i.e. keep Shabbos halachically)

Namaste: (Sanskrit) greeting; the light in me honors the light in you; the divine in me recognizes the divine in you

Na Nach: a stream of transcendent, devotionally joyful, often psychedelic Breslov Chassidim followers of Rebbe Nachman and particularly "the Saba" a.k.a. Rabbi Yisroel ber Odesser; refers to both the the Na Nach way of life and an individual engaging in it, as well as being a universally applicable shorthand mantra or response

Na Nach Nachma Nachman Meuman: the Na Nach mantra of sorts; a Kabbalistic formula based on the letters of Rebbe Nachman's name; apparently Rabbi Yisroel ber Odesser received a mysterious letter, called the Petek, from the spirit of Reb Nachman, signed with Na Nach Nachma Nachman MeUman

Nachas: (Hebrew/Yiddish) pride or satisfaction, often refers to parental or divine satisfaction derived from their progeny

Nachash: (Hebrew) snake

Nag Champa: a type of Indian incense

Nekuda tova: (Hebrew) a good point; often refers to a positivity practice of finding (or simply believing in) the good in everything

Neshama: (Hebrew) soul

Niggun (plural: niggunim): (Hebrew/Yiddish) a tune or melody, often used to describe wordless melodies sung in prayer or kumzitz types of settings

Nitzotzot: divine sparks; according to Kabbalah, when G-d created the world, the "vessels" in which He "contained his infinite light and energy" (through the process of Tzimtzum), were shattered by the "Sin of the Tree of Knowledge" committed by Adam and Eve; the divine sparks of light dissipated throughout the world, often obscured or trapped by klippot; the calling of humanity is to identify and liberate the sparks so that they can reassemble into vessels of infinite light

NORML (National Organization for the Reform of Marijuana Laws): national nonprofit organization advocating for marijuana law reform and legalization; has local chapters in various cities and states

Nu: (Yiddish) go on, well, so?

Olam: (Hebrew) the world; from the root word (*shoresh*) of concealment

Olam haba: (Hebrew) the world to come

OTD: acronym for Off the Derech, referring to people who were once religious and diverged from the path of observant/Orthodox Judaism

Oy veh iz mir: (Yiddish) oy, woe is me

Ozgelatet: (Yiddish) purified, cleansed

Pardes: (Hebrew) orchard; paradise; literally an acronym for the first four letters of the types of Torah interpretation (pshat: literal, remez: reading between the lines, drash: interpretation, sod: the mystical, secret, esoteric meaning)

Pargawd: (Hebrew) veil (of illusion)

Parnassah: (Hebrew) livelihood

Passover: eight-day holiday commemorating the liberation of the Hebrew tribe from slavery in Egypt, most specifically celebrated with a special programmed meal called a "seder"

Pesach: (Hebrew) Passover

Peyos: (Yiddish) sidelocks/side curls worn by Chassidish men

Pirkei Avot: compilation of Jewish ethical teachings

Pranam: (Sanskrit) a gesture of respect or reverence

Psilocybin: the main psychedelic compound in magic mushrooms

Psytrance: psychedelic trance; a genre of music exemplified by bands like Infected Mushroom or Goa Gil

PTSD: post-traumatic stress disorder

Puja: (Sanskrit) worship

Purim: (Hebrew) Jewish holiday commemorating how the Jews were saved from genocide in ancient Persia; celebrated by getting so intoxicated you don't know the difference between good and evil

Rabbeinu: (Hebrew) literally means "our rabbi," often used as shorthand by Chassidim to describe their Rebbe, commonly used by Breslover Chasidim to refer to Rebbe Nachman), or "Moshe Rabbeinu" to refer to Moses

Rainbow Gathering: an iconic hippie gathering that takes place in rotating national forests in the US every summer, peaking with a day of meditation and prayer for peace on the 4th of July; smaller regional gatherings also happen throughout the year and world, such as in Israel, India, Africa, and Europe. The Rainbow Gatherings were initiated in 1972 by recently returned Vietnam Veterans as an alternative to war and consumerism, and no money, corporate structure, or industrial machinery is involved in producing them.

Rapé: a type of South American sacred tobacco snuff

Rashbi: acronym for Rebbe Shimon bar Yochai

Ratzu v'shuv: (Hebrew) running and returning

Rebbe: Chassidish spiritual teacher (like a guru)

Rebbe Nachman: refers to Rabbi Nachman of Breslov beloved Chassidish leader and mystic, author and innovator of groundbreaking Chassidish works and thought

Rebbe Shimon Bar Yochai: one of the most prominent disciples of the martyred Rabbi Akiva and the supposed author of the Zohar, one of the most important works of Jewish mysticism/Kabbalah

Roxies: opioid painkillers

Rosh Chodesh: (Hebrew) beginning of a month on the Jewish calendar

Rosh HaShana: (Hebrew) the Jewish New Year

Ruach: (Hebrew) spirit, breath, wind

Ruach HaKodesh: (Hebrew) holy spirit

Rugelach: (Yiddish) bite-size pastry

Saba: (Hebrew) grandfather; also refers to Breslov Rabbi Yisroel ber Odesser (1888–1994), father of the Na Nach movement

Sabich: a type of Israeli pita sandwich made with eggplant, hard-boiled eggs, and other fixing like hummus, spices, etc.

Sadhu: a religious ascetic or holy person (generally in Hinduism, Buddhism, Jainism)

Sari: women's garment worn in India

Satchitananda: (Sanskrit) being, truth, wisdom, awareness, bliss, joy

Sativa: a cannabis cultivar often associated with a more energetic and creative "head high" (vs. the more mellowing "body high" associated with Indica dominant strains), though the efficacy of the classification is disputed by many in the cannabis community

Satmar: the largest Chassidish sect in America; dominates Williamsburg, Brooklyn; mostly descendants of Holocaust survivors from Hungary

Satsang: (Sanskrit) spiritual discourse or sacred gathering; the community of people surrounding Maharaj-ji and Ram Dass

Seder: (Hebrew) "order"; generally refers to a ritual meal/service during the holidays of Passover and Tu B'Shvat

Sefer: (Hebrew) book of religious literature (plural: Sefarim)

Seminary: religious school; refers in frum culture to schools that young Jewish women attend, usually after high school, often based in Israel

Set and setting: the mental state and the external surroundings going into a psychedelic trip

Seuda: (Hebrew) meal

Seuda shlishit: (Hebrew) third meal, refers to the final meal of Shabbos, held during the afternoon and sometimes extending into the end of Shabbos at nightfall

Shabbos: (Yiddish) Shabbat, the Jewish Sabbath

Shabbos Chazon: (Hebrew) "Shabbat of Vision" refers to the Shabbat before Tisha B'av, which is currently the saddest day of the Jewish calendar but is believed to one day be the most joyful in the Messianic Age

Shakedown: the parking lot scene and open air market at Grateful Dead (now Phish and other jam band) shows; refers to their song "Shakedown Street"

Shalom Aleichem: (Hebrew) "peace to you"; a greeting as well as a traditional song sung on Friday night before the Shabbat meal

Shaleshudis: (Yiddish) third meal; eaten on Shabbat afternoon; Yiddish pronunciation of "Shalosh Seudot"; see Seuda Shlishit

Shaman: refers traditionally to an indigenous person who performs healing through spiritual, ceremonial, ritualistic, and/or plant medicine techniques; in the modern psychedelic lexicon it can refer to a range of psychedelic providers incorporating modalities that typically include some indigenous sources or reference points

Shavasana: (Sanskrit) corpse pose in yoga; lying flat on ground

Shavuos: (Yiddish) see Shavuot

Shavuot: holiday commemorating when Moses received the 10 commandments at Mt. Sinai; many frum Jews stay up learning and meditating for the entire night of Shavuot; literally "weeks," it is the culmination of the seven weeks of counting the Omer that begins on Pesach (Passover)

Shechina: (Hebrew) the imminent presence of G-d, refers also to the divine feminine expression of G-d

Shell: refers in frum culture to a type of long-sleeve shirt, often worn underneath other clothes, by religious women to maintain tznius (modesty) standards

Shidduch: a match, most often used in reference to the purpose of marriage

Shiur: (Hebrew) a lecture on a religious topic

Shiva: (Sanskrit) blue-skinned Hindu deity known to be the god of destruction, yoga, and mind-altering substances, including cannabis as a sacrament

Shkia: (Hebrew) sunset

Shlep: (Yiddish) to drag or pull; can refer to someone dragging something out or taking too long

Sh'ma: (Hebrew) seminal Jewish prayer referring to the oneness of G-d; the prayer starts with the word "sh'ma," meaning "listen"

Shpilkes: (Yiddish) state of anxiety

Shmata: (Yiddish) a rag; informal garment

Shomer Shabbos: observing the *mitzvot* (see *mitzvah*) and laws associated with Shabbat; keeping Shabbat

Shtetl: (Yiddish) Eastern European Jewish village

Shtreimel: (Yiddish) round furry hat worn by Chassidish men on Shabbos and special occasions

Shuckling: (Yiddish) to sway forward and back devotionally in prayer

Shuk: (Hebrew) open-air market

Shul: (Yiddish) synagogue

Shvitz: (Yiddish) to sweat; also refers to a sauna

Siddha: (Sanskrit) a person who's achieved spiritual realization

Siddur: (Hebrew) a Jewish prayer book

Simcha: (Hebrew) joy; a Jewish celebration such as a wedding

Sinai: refers to Mount Sinai (Har Sinai, see Har), where the Ten Commandments were transmitted through Moses; also used in some text and discourse to refer to the collective revelation experienced by the Israelites at Har Sinai which is considered the formative moment of the religion and believed by many to have been a collective psychedelic experience

Spliff: cannabis and tobacco rolled up together into a single smokeable

Stam: (Hebrew) straight up; simply; just because; just like that; for no specific reason; just kidding

Sukkot/Sukkos: (Hebrew/Yiddish) weeklong autumn holiday celebrated at the Beis Hamikdash after the harvest; commemorates how G-d protected the Jewish tribe with the Ananei Hakavod (Clouds of Glory, a manifestation of Shechina) when they exited Egypt; celebrated by erecting temporary dwellings and taking four species of plants to shake in all directions daily in one of the remaining naturally rooted tribal traditions

Tachana Merkazit: (Hebrew) central bus station

Tachless: (Yiddish/Israeli slang) give it to me straight; okay, so practically speaking; essentially

Tadasana: (Sanskrit) mountain pose; standing pose in yoga

Talit (Talis): (Hebrew/Yiddish) fringed garment worn as prayer shawl for men

Tallilot: plural of talit

Talmud: written record of Jewish oral tradition, including commentary on Torah

Tatti: (Yiddish) father

Tchotchke: (Yiddish) a knickknack; small item; trinket

Tefilat HaDerech:

Tehillim: (Hebrew) words of glory or praise; prayers

Teshuva: (Hebrew) return; repentance

THC: the main psychoactive compound in cannabis

Tichel: headscarf covering for Jewish women

Tikkun: (Hebrew) amending; fixing

Tikkun HaKlali: (Hebrew) literally "The General Tikkun/Remedy"; a compilation of 10 chapters of tehilim (psalms) in a particular order curated by Reb Nachman whose regular and situational recital is meant to serve as reparation for sins, as well as providing other spiritual and material benefits

Tikkun Olam: (Hebrew) repair of the world

Torah (big T and little t): the Jewish Bible (Five Books of Moses) is the Big T; any sort of religious teaching (little t)

Trishul: trident belonging to the Hindu deity Shiva

Tu B'Shvat: (Hebrew) the 15th of the Hebrew month of Shvat, a Jewish holiday commemorating the "Rosh Hashana (New Year) of the trees"; often celebrated by eating rare or exotic fruits in a "Tu B'Shvat Seder"

Tubi (Tubi 60): a type of Israeli liquor with somewhat of a cult following

Tucket: a low perch for a guru

Tukhus: (Yiddish) butt, tush

Tzadik (plural: tzadikim): (Hebrew) a spiritual master with a degree of righteousness and enlightenment

Tzimtzum: (Hebrew) contraction; refers in Chassidish teachings to the manner in which G-d created the world, as well as a personal spiritual practice

Tzniut/tznius: (Hebrew/Yiddish) modesty; modest

Tzniusdig: (Yiddish) applied modesty (dressing in a way such as long skirt or long sleeves that shows little skin or form; tznius is often particularly strictly applied to women)

Tzitzit: (Hebrew) knotted ritual fringes worn underneath the clothing by religious men

Uttanasana: (Sanskrit) forward fold, bent pose in yoga in which the legs are straight and the hands are reaching toward the ground

Veda: (Sanskrit) ancient Hindu scriptures

Velt: (Yiddish) world

Wallah: (Hindi) person in charge of or involved with a specific thing (e.g., chai wallah or rickshaw wallah)

Yarmulke: (Yiddish) kippah (Hebrew); religious skullcap for men

Yahrzeit: (Yiddish) anniversary of someone's death

Yatra: (Sanskrit) journey

Yesh: (Hebrew) there is/are, exists

Yeshiva: (Hebrew) a school for Jewish boys or men

Yichud: (Hebrew) seclusion; one-on-one time (comes from the word *yachad*, meaning together)

Yiddishkeit: (Yiddish) Jewishness

Yippie: Youth International Party; radical antiestablishment political group founded in 1968

Yom Kippur: (Hebrew) The Day of Atonement; the most widely observed Jewish high holiday, considered by many to be the holiest day of the year; marked by a full evening and day of devotional prayer, fasting, and other restrictions on physical comforts/pleasures so as to achieve a more angelic state of purity and connection

Zayde: (Yiddish) grandfather

Zimmer: a rental (room, apartment, B&B)

Zis/Ziseh: (Yiddish) sweet

ACKNOWLEDGMENTS

Without the support of a shtetl's worth of loving souls who've supported me along the way, this book would not be here today. But first, thank you to Source for kindling my spirit, for pushing me, for granting me energy and creativity, for giving me life itself—this very life that has become the subject of my first book.

From there, thank you to my family: my father for being among my greatest inspirations, for showing me how to be alive, for teaching me to strive toward what's Divine, and for creating the family that I love so dearly. And to my mother for being there for me at every and any moment, for stepping in as my biggest cheerleader, for reading this book with grace and humor, and showing me what it means to love someone more than you love yourself. To my stepmother for showing me resilience, for teaching me how to be a lady, for taking on the challenging role of stepparent with humility and kindness, and for teaching me what it is to yearn for a better world. To my siblings, I love you all so much. Arielle, you transformed our family and I am so proud of the woman you've become. You are my baby sister, and my teacher. Harrison, Honey, Marlee, without each of you, I wouldn't know what it means to belong to something—even if that something is a clan of loving dysfunction. To Allison for showing me the power of controversy in combination with hard work, and to Juliet and Jaxin for being the best niece and nephew I could ask for. To Stuart for stepping up for me, for our family, time and time again. And to Ama, Jay, Sue, Shannon, Kyle, Uncle Arnold, and Cousin Shelli, thank you for offering a sense of grounding as the only "normal" family I've got.

Of course, those who know me therefore know this book would not be in existence without the brilliant editing, support, thought partnership, creative consulting, and all-around genius of my editor Eden Pearlstein. Thank you for seeing me, for getting inside my head, for chiseling my prose, for seeing the light in the underground and the shadow in the light, for helping me see the poetry of life itself, for teaching me that experience is its own art, especially when you write about it. And to Sally Mason-Swaab and the team at Hay House for taking on a book as weird as this one and giving it a chance, a platform, a voice; for allowing me creative runway, and through publishing this story, solidifying this movement and moment that is the Jewish psychedelic renaissance. Thank you to Aaron Genuth for getting my back in editing the glossary, and to Rami Schwartzer, Meyer Labin, and Daniel Kronovet, for being my beta readers.

And with that, thank you to my colleagues: the team at Ayin Press for taking Jewish publishing further; the team at Lucid News for upholding psychedelic media standards; to Natalie Ginsberg and Zac Kamenetz for your friendship and collaboration in creating the Jewish Psychedelic Summit; to Pinni Baumol for being my psychedelic chevrusa; to Rabbi Harry Rozenberg for interviewing with me time and time again; to Rabbi Doniel Katz, Julie Holland, and Rick Strassman, among many, many others, for your scholarship; and to Zeus Tipado for your fact-checking, open-mindedness and all-around badassery.

This movement is niche no longer, but for those who've been by my side since the beginning of my career—big shout-out to the publicity brilliance of Zoe Wilder and Mike Schnurr—and since the beginning of this book process—my agents Charles Kim and Regina Brooks—I would be nowhere without you. Thank you for seeing my potential.

And then, there's my chevra, all chosen soul family. To Daniella, Tsip, and Nancy for taking me in during my hardest moments, whilst writing this book and beyond. To Rishe and Nili for being among my greatest teachers; to Esther for teaching me to love plants; to Hilary, Melissa, and Lana for going Na Nach with me; to Rivka for being the first to introduce me to the concept of Jewish yoga; to Henny for teaching me the medicine of dance, and to Elana for teaching me that of song; to Angelica for staying at my side with grounded wisdom; to Roxanne for your compassion; to Tamara for being at my side all these years; and to Rachael for witnessing my most formative moments; you are all sisters to me. And to the brothers: to Yoseph for being the OG Jewish psychedelic inspiration, and with Elisheva, coming into the best version of yourself I've seen yet; to Aaron for experiencing so much of this life, this book, by my side; to Hershy for shepherding me into the story, and to Yitzy for processing it with me; to Levi for introducing me to "medicine"; to Daniel for your wisdom, support, and being with me from Berkeley till now and all steps in between; to Meyer, my advice rebbe, I love you and all your heimish chaos; to Matt for your infinite friendship and fart jokes; to Lee and Jared for being wholeheartedly you; to Steve, Zac, Aydin, and the Rainbows for teaching me about family; to Meir for teaching me the art of recognizing my nervous system (and for the Prius); to Rabbi Dan and David for grounding me in the "medicine" space; to Kian for grounding me in where I come from; to Dan for being my gay fairy; and to Zev for giving me my home of all homes in Tzfat— and to the chevra of Tzfat (you know who you are, thank you for inspiring me, for playing your music, for teaching me about Na Nach, for welcoming me in with open arms). There are so many other friends who have been unendingly supportive and helped me see the world through kaleidoscopic eyes; to list everyone I risk accidentally leaving someone out, but I want to say, I see you and I love you.

Yet, without my father's satsang, I wouldn't know what it is to have a chevra. So thank you to the satsang: Parvati, thank you for reading and rereading this book and lending your love and insights (to me and my dad); Mohan, thank you for being my uncle and taking me in at the 11th hour to finish final copy edits on the book here in Rockland; Raghu, thank you for seeing me, for bringing me into the Be Here Now Network; Annapurna, thank you for being an aunt and for validating Yiddishkeit in the HinJew velt; Rhoney for teaching me the power of women behind the psychedelic revolution, and Seth for showcasing it; and KD, thank you for your all your wisdom and for creating the soundtrack to my childhood.

Moment by moment, the love surrounding me has taught me what home feels like, what family truly is and can become. This book may be done, but life is still always beginning. Eilish, thanks for trying it out with me. Wherever it goes, thank you for your love.

Of course, none of us would be who we are without one of my greatest teachers, friends, and trolls—in body and beyond: Ram Dass, Richard Alpert, Reuben ben Chaim Yosef. This book is really for you. To the Baal Shem Tov and Maharaj-ji, your love infuses us all. And to Reb Nachman, thank you for being my rebbe.

ABOUT THE AUTHOR

Madison in Tzfat (2023)
Photo *credit:* David Morgan

Madison Rachel Margolin is a journalist covering psychedelics, cannabis, spirituality, and Jewish life. Co-founder of *DoubleBlind* Magazine, she has written for publications like *Rolling Stone*, *Playboy,* and *VICE*, among several other outlets, and works as a contributing editor to both *Ayin Press* and *Lucid News*. Also a co-founder of the Jewish Psychedelic Summit and host of the Be Here Now Network's *Set & Setting* podcast, Madison has traveled everywhere from pot farms in the Emerald Triangle to the shores of the Ganges River, and all over Israel/Palestine, exploring the role of plant medicine in religion, mental health, and conflict resolution. With almost a decade's worth of experience covering psychedelics, cannabis, and religion/spirituality, Madison's work has been featured in *The New York Times*, *Forbes*, KCRW, and other outlets. She offers classes, workshops, and consulting on the topic(s) of Judaism and psychedelics. Learn more at her website, madisonmargolin.com or by following her at @madisonmargolin on Instagram. In her "off" time, you can catch her doing yoga, dancing, spinning her hula hoop, or if it's Shabbos, practicing what it means to "be here now."

Madison (age 16) with her mother and brother with Ram Dass in Maui

Madison (around age 2 or 3) with Timothy Leary and her father, Bruce Margolin

CONNECT WITH
HAY HOUSE
ONLINE

🌐 hayhouse.co.uk   f @hayhouse

📷 @hayhouseuk   🐦 @hayhouseuk

▶ @hayhouseuk   ♪ @hayhouseuk

Find out all about our latest books & card decks • Be the first to know about exclusive discounts • Interact with our authors in live broadcasts • Celebrate the cycle of the seasons with us • Watch free videos from your favourite authors • Connect with like-minded souls

'The gateways to wisdom and knowledge are always open.'

Louise Hay